Reading Development and the Teaching of Reading

Reading Development and the Teaching of Reading

A PSYCHOLOGICAL PERSPECTIVE

Edited by
Jane Oakhill and Roger Beard

BLACKWELL
Publishers

Copyright © Blackwell Publishers 1999

First published 1999

2 4 6 8 10 9 7 5 3 1

Blackwell Publishers Ltd
108 Cowley Road
Oxford OX4 1JF
UK

Blackwell Publishers Inc.
350 Main Street
Malden, Massachusetts 02148
USA

British Library Cataloguing in Publication Data

A CIP catalogue record for this book is available from the British Library.

Library of Congress Cataloging in Publication Data

Reading development and the teaching of reading: a psychological
  perspective / [edited by] Jane Oakhill and Roger Beard.
      p.   cm.
    Includes bibliographical references and index.
    ISBN 0–631–20681–7 (hbk.: alk. paper). – ISBN 0–631–20682–5
  (pbk. : alk. paper)
    1. Reading.   2. Reading, Psychology of.   I. Oakhill, Jane.
  II. Beard, Roger.
  LB1050.2.R424 1999
  428'.4 – dc21   99–10517
                                                                 CIP

Typeset in 10½ on 13 pt Sabon
by Best-set Typesetter Ltd, Hong Kong
Printed in Great Britain by MPG Books Ltd,
Victoria Square, Bodmin, Cornwall.

This book is printed on acid-free paper

Contents

List of Figures   vii

List of Tables   viii

Preface   ix

Acknowledgements   xvii

List of Contributors   xviii

1   The New Literacy: *Caveat Emptor*   1
    PHILIP B. GOUGH

2   How Research Might Inform the Debate about Early
    Reading Acquisition   12
    KEITH E. STANOVICH AND PAULA J. STANOVICH

3   Cognitive Research and the Misconceptions of Reading
    Education   42
    CHARLES A. PERFETTI

4   Constructing Meaning: The Role of Decoding   59
    PHILIP B. GOUGH AND SEBASTIAN WREN

5   Phases of Development in Learning to Read Words   79
    LINNEA C. EHRI

6   Learning to Read Words Turns Listeners into Readers:
    How Children Accomplish this Transition   109
    MORAG STUART, JACKIE MASTERSON AND
    MAUREEN DIXON

7 Dyslexia: Core Difficulties, Variability and Causes   131
   CARSTEN ELBRO

8 Meaninglessness, Productivity and Reading:
   Some Observations about the Relation between the
   Alphabet and Speech   157
   BRIAN BYRNE AND ALVIN M. LIBERMAN

9 Phonological Development and Reading by Analogy:
   Epilinguistic and Metalinguistic Issues   174
   USHA GOSWAMI

10 The Messenger may be Wrong, but the Message
    may be Right   201
    CONNIE JUEL

11 Afterword: The Science and Politics of Beginning
    Reading Practices   213
    MARILYN JAGER ADAMS

Subject Index   228
Author Index   231

Figures

4.1 Reprint of the first page of Ken Goodman's *Phonics Phacts* (Goodman, 1993, p. 1); numbers indicate the total number of miscues made by 101 subjects on each word in the passage   61

4.2 Number of miscues per word in the first page of Ken Goodman's *Phonics Phacts*   63

4.3 Number of miscues made by each of 101 students reading the first page of Goodman's *Phonics Phacts*   64

4.4 Passage used by Gollasch in a study of error identification   68

4.5 Comparison of reading times on each line of text between subjects reading the 'Gollasch' version and those reading the 'clean' version of the text   69

5.1 Connections formed between graphemes and phonemes during the full alphabetic phase   93

Tables

4.1 Summary of the nature of the miscues made by 101
students reading aloud the first page of Goodman's
Phonics Phacts   62

4.2 The proportions of correct identifications in each of
the cue conditions   66

4.3 Number and proportion of readers who reported each
error in the Gollasch text   69

4.4 A comparison of the reading times on each line of text   70

5.1 Characteristics and capabilities of pupils at various
phases of word reading development   99

6.1 Means and standard deviations for scores in each
experimental condition, by reading quotient group   115

6.2 Means and standard deviations of scores on all
experimental tests, by reading quotient group   117

6.3 Means and standard deviations for scores of each
alternative choice, by three groups of children differing
in phoneme segmentation ability   125

7.1 Observed reading abilities at the beginning of grade 2
as a function of predicted group membership based
on language measures at the beginning of kindergarten   141

7.2 True prediction in a younger group of children using
the regression equation from the older group (table 7.1)   143

9.1 Levels of phonological development   178

Preface

There has been increasing emphasis in recent years on the idea that reading should not be viewed as an isolated skill, or set of skills, but that it is necessarily related to the purposes it fulfils in particular social and cultural contexts. Whilst such considerations are important, other aspects of reading and its development are often ignored. We have brought together this collection partly as a counterweight to recent sociological and anthropological views of literacy (a collection of which can be found in Street, 1993). Whilst acknowledging the undoubted contribution of language, and motivational and cultural factors, to the acquisition of literacy, we should not forget the contribution of scientific experimental research to our understanding of reading and its development. In this book, our general aim is to provide an overview of an alternative perspective on literacy and its acquisition, to which we adhere. We aim to show that psychological research into the nature of the reading process and its development cannot be ignored if we want to better understand children's reading and how to teach it.

The book starts with a chapter by Philip Gough, in which he makes a distinction between two meanings of literacy which seem to have been conflated in recent writings: the ability to read and write, on the one hand, and the broader concept of being educated, on the other. Like Gough, the contributors to this book are concerned with how children learn to read, and how best to teach them. They might also be interested in the broader implications of literacy, but this is not the focus of their research. Like Gough, we agree that the concept of literacy cannot be stretched to include such wide assertions as: 'reading now takes on a broader meaning and includes social inter-actions' (Street, 1993) or 'We came to the conclusion that this talk is "reading"' (Maybin and Moss, 1993). Our perspective is that teaching literacy is primarily about teaching the skills of reading and writing. Once learned, these skills can be applied and extended in a wealth of ways which might come within the remit of the broader definition of literacy.

Street (1984) argues we should talk of literacies as pluralistic, rather than literacy as a monolithic concept. However, there are several difficulties in proceeding with such a pluralistic assumption. Linguistically, it treats a 'non-count noun' as a 'count noun' (Quirk et al., 1985). Consequently, such a change brings with it the ques-tion, if there is more than one literacy, of how many literacies there are. Street appears to equate different literacies with different cul-tures. Yet, if we accept this argument, we shall end up, as Gough points out, with as many 'literacies' as we can define cultures. Furthermore, this assumption raises another question: of what the defining boundaries are between one literacy and another. We agree, of course, that literacy can be adapted to different cultural purposes, but we would argue that all 'literacies' are, indeed, based on a common set of what Street rather disparagingly refers to as 'narrowly conceived psychological skills' – broadly, the skills that enable people to decipher the writing system or systems that they need to use.

The chapters by Keith and Paula Stanovich and Charles Perfetti both address, in different ways, some of the major disagreements that have arisen in recent decades about how skilled reading should best be characterized, and how reading should be taught. Stanovich and Stanovich argue that beyond the core points of agreement about instructional practices in early reading, there are crucial points of disagreement. However, they go on to suggest that most of these disagreements are resolvable empirically and, indeed, that there is a reasonable scientific consensus on many of the critical issues. For example, the use of context to aid word recognition is not more characteristic of good readers than it is of poor readers; developing phonological sensitivity is critical for early success in reading acqui-sition; and instructional programmes that emphasize spelling-to-sound decoding skills result in better reading outcomes than those that do not, because alphabetic coding is the critical subprocess that supports fluent reading (in alphabetic scripts). Keith and Paula Stanovich argue convincingly that these conclusions (all of which are well supported by empirical research) will necessitate a change in the underlying theoretical model of reading held by most 'whole-language' advocates. They suggest that 'whole-language' advocates might still retain most of their broad socio-educational goals (e.g. teacher empowerment), but should jettison the unwarranted adherence to a processing model of reading that is outdated and not congruent with the latest research evidence.

Charles Perfetti's chapter makes some overlapping points, and again suggests how well-established and important findings from research can inform reading instruction. He considers four specific contributions from research in cognitive psychology, and draws out the main implications from each of them. First, skilled readers, though flexible in their comprehension, pay close attention to the words on a page – they read most words, rather than skip them. Second, skilled readers are not dependent on contextual cues to help with word recognition (Stanovich and Stanovich make a very similar point, but in a different way). Third, contrary to popular misconceptions, even skilled readers make use of phonology (the sounds of the words) when they read. The connections between graphemes and phonemes are activated during reading for meaning (though this activation may not be necessary for word identification). Interestingly, Perfetti cites some of his own data showing that retrieval of phonological word forms occurs even when reading Chinese, which is usually (though slightly erroneously) thought of as a logographic system, in which the basic units (logographs) correspond to morphemes. Fourth, Perfetti, like Stanovich and Stanovich, points out that in order to learn to read, the child must learn to decipher the code – the particular way in which writing encodes speech in his or her own language. Children do need to learn to get 'meaning from print': but, to do that, they need to know how to decipher the print so that they can use their already well-developed language understanding skills to get the meaning. In relation to this point, Perfetti also considers the way in which phonological awareness and reading acquisition develop in tandem, and the important implication: that phonological training should not take place in isolation, but that such training should be linked in with word reading (a point taken up by Connie Juel in her contribution). Philip Gough and Sebastian Wren, in their chapter, take up the point that even in skilled adult reading, the process is solidly 'bottom up' (that is, driven by the print on the page) rather than 'top down' (driven by contextual cues to the meaning of the text). In one of their experiments they convincingly demonstrate that, even in the case of adult readers, it is hugely more efficient to decode the words than to attempt to hypothesize what they might be.

In her chapter, Linnea Ehri outlines her four-stage model of reading development together with the research that supports it. Once more, there is emphasis on the alphabetic stages of learning to read, and the crucial importance of a developing understanding of spelling-to-sound relations in the movement through these stages. Like Perfetti, Ehri argues for the importance of phonology, even in skilled word recognition. Morag Stuart, Jackie Masterson and Maureen Dixon demonstrate clearly that early phonological awareness, together with knowledge of single letter–sound correspondences, contributes to children's ability to exploit the alphabetic principle. They present some of their own data to demonstrate that children who are reading well by the age of six are those who have developed phonological recoding processes. By contrast, children of the same age who are falling behind in reading tend to have a strong reliance on learned sight vocabulary. Stuart et al.'s work has clear implications for the initial stages of teaching reading, and they discuss these at the end of their chapter.

Carsten Elbro's chapter highlights central aspects of recent insights into dyslexia. He discusses the core problem in reading and spelling, and considers some types of variability of dyslexia, possible proximal and underlying causes, and early prevention. Elbro concludes that there is now considerable evidence that the majority of poor readers have difficulties with the acquisition of the alphabetic nature of written language. They fail to acquire the fundamental correspondences between letters and sounds, and between letter patterns and sound patterns, and it is these deficits that prevent dyslexics from learning to read at a normal rate. Fortunately, as Elbro points out, the consequences of these encoding problems may be to some extent overcome by early intervention: programmes that combine initial reading instruction with a well-structured programme designed to enhance segmental awareness have been shown to be successful.

Byrne and Liberman begin their chapter by outlining three important conclusions from research which have been alluded to, more or less directly, in many of the preceding chapters: that phonological awareness is poorly developed in pre-literate children; that phonological awareness is one of the best predictors of success in learning to read; and that training designed to increase phonological awareness will also increase the likelihood that a beginning reader will make good progress. In their chapter, however, they argue that there are crucial aspects of the nature of the speech code that need to be understood before the above conclusions can be properly understood. In particular, they challenge the conventional view that the fundamental elements of speech are sounds, and defend instead their alternative view that the fundamental units of speech are 'articulatory gestures'. Their explication of this point, and the repercussions of their view for an understanding of the relation between speech and print, is essential reading for those who want to fully understand exactly what it is that the child has to learn, why that learning might be difficult and, in particular, why learning to read cannot be like learning to speak, as some whole-language theorists have argued.

Usha Goswami considers how units larger than single graphemes can be used in helping children to learn to read. Goswami's chapter gives an overview of the role of phonological development and orthographic analogies in children's early reading development. She points to the evidence showing that children can more readily conceptualize the onsets and rimes of words ('str-ing', 'f-ish') than the individual phonemes, and suggests how this ability might be capitalized on to teach children spelling patterns. Goswami stresses that this approach should be integrated within more traditional methods of teaching children about letter–sound mappings, rather than being regarded as a replacement for such methods. She also counters some recent criticisms of the onset–rime approach to teaching reading.

Connie Juel's chapter shows how we do not need to abandon the more soundly based aspects of the 'whole-language' approach in order to accommodate the views of the other contributors to this volume on the importance of phonological skills in learning to read.

Her work illustrates how, rather, instruction of the sort that is rec-ommended (either explicitly or implicitly) by other contributors can be used in conjunction with 'real books'. However, Juel also presents evidence suggesting that beginning readers will benefit from some direct instruction in the code, as well as from experience of reading texts with controlled vocabularies.

The final chapter, by Marilyn Adams, like the first one, by Philip Gough, is a defence of science. Adams emphasizes the vital impor-tance of science, and in this context, the importance of a scientific approach to studying reading, reading development and reading problems.

Together, the chapters in this book will provide an important con-tribution to debates about the significance of what are sometimes called 'The New Literacy Studies' (Street, 1993; Willinsky, 1990), especially to how these studies are defined and what they may assume. The use of the word 'new' raises central questions of definition, as Philip Gough's chapter in this volume indicates. One of the most insightful studies of the way definitions are used in educa-tion has come from Israel Scheffler (1960). Scheffler distinguishes between three types of definition, 'stipulative', 'descriptive' and 'pre-scriptive'. Experimental research by psychologists adopts 'stipulative' (or 'operationalized') definitions, in order to facilitate the necessarily 'controlled and circumscribed' studies to which Stuart et al. refer in their chapter. Ethnographic and other sociological studies tend to adopt or seek to establish 'descriptive' (or 'essentialist') definitions, advancing particular constructs to enable them to discuss different 'literacies'. Thus the 'New Literacy Studies' can be said to be devel-oping new philosophical lines of enquiry, rather than seeking to replace 'old' notions of literacy in the ways some writers have implied.

It follows that the sociological and psychological perspectives on literacy may need to be reconciled or even integrated in some way, according to the conceptual or methodological needs of different investigations. A key implication of the present volume is that the New Literacy theorists may need to consider carefully the stipulative definitions of literacy which they are assuming (although under-standably not concentrating upon). The need for such care is appar-ent in the light of what may be called the 'new (or at least recent) reading studies' (including what has already been called 'the new phonics'). These studies (e.g. Adams, 1991; Beard and Oakhill, 1994;

Stanovich and Stanovich, this volume) suggest that the recent orthodoxies in the teaching of literacy in both the UK and USA have in
some ways been misinformed.

At the heart of these orthodoxies lie radical assumptions about the
nature of the reading process, about the role of phonological skills
in learning to read, and about the efficacy of teaching approaches
which rely upon different types of text, including environmental
print. Recent reading studies have indicated the misleading nature of
some of these radical assumptions: that reading is not some kind of
guessing game (Gough and Wren, this volume; Juel, this volume), that
phonological skills are important in learning to read (Adams, 1990;
as well as several other authors in this volume), and that over-reliance
on any kind of text (including environmental print) is unlikely to be
effective unless underpinned by attention to the links between the
orthography and the phonology of English (Ehri, 1992).

Going beyond the scope of this volume and, indeed, the New
Literacy Studies, there are further papers 'waiting to be written'
which examine the ideological influences on how misplaced orthodoxies become so widely accepted. Similarly, it is revealing to ask why
the problematic aspects of such orthodoxies take so long to receive
appropriate critical scrutiny (see Beard, 1993, ch. 1).

We hope that the present volume will be seen not just as a counterweight to recent sociological perspectives on literacy, but also as
an extension of their spirit of innovation and dissemination. There
are other kinds of 'newness' in psychological reading research, as
well. If 'reading' has 'changed' (Street, 1993) in relation to how it
can be viewed in its social contexts, so too has our understanding of
the ways in which the processing of print is accomplished by the
human mind.

Jane Oakhill
Roger Beard

References

Adams, M. J. (1990) *Beginning to Read*. Cambridge, MA: MIT Press.

Adams, M. J. (1991) Why not phonics and whole language? In W. Ellis (ed.),
All Language and the Creation of Literacy. Baltimore, MD: Orton
Dyslexia Society.

Beard, R. (ed.) (1993) *Teaching Literacy: Balancing Perspectives*. London: Hodder and Stoughton.

Beard, R., and Oakhill, J. (1994) *Reading by Apprenticeship?* Slough: National Foundation for Educational Research.

Ehri, L. (1992) Reconceptualizing the development of sight word reading and its relationship to recoding. In P. Gough, L. Ehri and R. Treiman (eds), *Reading Acquisition*, Hillsdale, NJ: Lawrence Erlbaum, pp. 107–43.

Maybin, J., and Moss, G. (1993) Talk about texts: Reading as a social event. *Journal of Research in Reading*, 16, 138–47.

Quirk, R., Greenbaum, S., Leech, G., and Svartvik, J. (1985) *A Comprehensive Grammar of the English Language*. Harlow: Longman.

Scheffler, I. (1960) *The Language of Education*. Illinois: Charles C. Thomas.

Street, B. V. (1984) *Literacy in Theory and Practice*. Cambridge: Cambridge University Press.

Street, B. V. (1993) The New Literacy Studies. *Journal of Research in Reading*, 16 (2), 81–97.

Willinsky, J. (1990) *The New Literacy*. London: Routledge.

Acknowledgements

The origins of this book were in a special issue of the *Journal of Research in Reading*, 18 (a United Kingdom Reading Association journal), published in 1995. Denis Vincent, editor of the *Journal of Research in Reading*, provided invaluable assistance in the preparation of this book.

List of Contributors

Marilyn Jager Adams, Harvard University Visiting Scholar, BBN Technologies, Cambridge, Massachusetts, USA.

Roger Beard, Reader in Literacy Education, School of Education, University of Leeds, Leeds, UK.

Brian Byrne, Professor of Psychology, School of Psychology, University of New England, Armidale, New South Wales, Australia.

Maureen Dixon, Lecturer in Psychology, School of Social Sciences, University of Greenwich, London, UK.

Linnea C. Ehri, Distinguished Professor of Educational Psychology, Graduate School of the City University of New York, New York, USA.

Carsten Elbro, Professor of Applied Linguistics, Department of General and Applied Linguistics, University of Copenhagen, Copenhagen, Denmark.

Philip B. Gough, Barbara Pierce Bush Regents Professor, Department of Psychology, University of Texas, Austin, Texas, USA.

Usha Goswami, Professor of Cognitive Developmental Psychology, Behavioural Sciences Unit, Institute of Child Health, University College, London, UK.

Connie Juel, Thomas G. Jewell Professor of Education, McGuffy Reading Center, Curry School of Education, University of Virginia, Charlottesville, Virginia, USA.

Alvin M. Liberman, Professor Emeritus, University of Connecticut, Haskins Laboratories, New Haven, Connecticut, USA.

Jackie Masterson, Senior Lecturer in Psychology, Department of Psychology, University of Essex, Colchester, UK.

Jane Oakhill, Reader in Experimental Psychology, Laboratory of Experimental Psychology, University of Sussex, Brighton, UK.

Charles A. Perfetti, Professor of Psychology and Linguistics and Senior Scientist, Learning Research and Development Center, University of Pittsburgh, Pittsburgh, Pennsylvania, USA.

Keith E. Stanovich, Professor of Human Development and Applied Psychology, Department of Human Development and Applied Psychology, Ontario Institute for Studies in Education, University of Toronto, Toronto, Ontario, Canada.

Paula J. Stanovich, Associate Professor of Curriculum, Teaching and Learning, Department of Curriculum, Teaching and Learning, Ontario Institute for Studies in Education, University of Toronto, Toronto, Ontario, Canada.

Morag Stuart, Senior Lecturer in Psychology, Department of Psychology and Special Needs, Institute of Education, London, UK.

Sebastian Wren, Department of Psychology, University of Texas, Austin, Texas, USA.

Chapter One

The New Literacy: *Caveat Emptor*

PHILIP B. GOUGH

In a recent issue of the *Journal the Research in Reading,* Brian Street and his colleagues have offered us a New Literacy (see Street, 1993). What is a reading educator to make of the New Literacy? I would hope that the teacher would take it for what it is, a novel way of looking at literacy that engendered some provocative ideas. I would hope that the teacher would not take it as a replacement for the old literacy, what Street calls 'the autonomous model' of literacy, for as I see it, some of the New Literacy's central ideas are highly questionable.

Literacy and Literacy

Some of my concern about Street's proposal may arise from terminology. Since the Romans first used the term, literacy has had two distinct meanings: the ability to read and write on the one hand, and being educated on the other. Let us call these literacy$_1$ and literacy$_2$. The broader meaning (literacy$_2$) would seem to subsume the narrower (literacy$_1$), but that is far from certain.

For example, in recent years, the term literacy has been stretched considerably, especially as it has been linked with adjectives to form compounds like computer literacy, historical literacy, musical literacy,

First published in *Journal of Research in Reading*, 18 (1995), pp. 79–86.

workplace literacy, and even literacy literacy (Kintgen, 1988). One might assume that these new literacies would include the ability to read and write about their subject matters, but that is not necessarily the case. A recent book entitled *Jewish Literacy* (Telushkin, 1991) is subtitled 'The most important things to know about the Jewish religion, its people, and history' without mention of reading or writing. Visual literacy, as defined by Vallance (1995), does not involve the ability to read and write at all; it is simply 'being able to appreciate and participate in the cultural conversation that is recorded in images'. Or, to take still another example, a book entitled *Political Literacy* (Gale, 1994) is advertised to 'explode the myth that justice is delivered in the measured, seemingly disinterested, written decisions of America's highest courts'. It is not clear what this has to do with the ability to read and write, or why it should even have literacy in the title. (Wouldn't a more descriptive title have been something like 'Justice without Justice' or 'Unjust Justice' or 'Justice Not'? The answer is, of course, that the author is calling for 'changes in the way the public is educated about the justice system'; he would change our educational system with respect to literacy$_2$.) Thus literacy in the broader sense has all but lost its relationship to literacy in the narrow; literacy$_2$ is closer to *competence*, or *knowledge*, than to literacy$_1$.

Our concern as educators may well be with both kinds of literacy. But our first concern as *reading* educators should be with the narrow, with literacy$_1$. Since Street's paper appeared in this journal, I would assumed that it is a new perspective on literacy$_1$ which he and his colleagues are offering us. So from this point on, I shall take literacy to refer to literacy$_1$, the ability to read and write.

There is a second terminological distinction which I think it is important to draw. Sommers (1994) drew this distinction with respect to history: 'There are, as most people are aware, two meanings to the word *history*. On the one hand, history refers to a series of events that actually happened. On the other hand, there is History, an *account* of what happened.'

It seems to me that this is a very sensible distinction. Samuel Noah Kramer (1981) once wrote a fascinating account of the first writing and its consequences; he gave it the provocative title *History Begins at Sumer*. Did history begin in 3200 BC? Clearly not. People had lived and loved and fought and died for millennia before 3200 BC.

But since they had no writing to record those events, there had been no History.

I think it would be sensible for us to adopt this same distinction with respect to literacy. There is literacy, the ability which enables many people to read and write, and there is Literacy, our account of their reading and writing.

There are, of course, many ways of looking at literacy, many Literacies. We can look at it as educators or as historians, as anthropologists or psychologists or sociologists, as feminists or Marxists. We undoubtedly benefit from looking at literacy from these different perspectives. Looking at literacy in a different way almost certainly offers us new information, and even new ways of thinking about literacy. The anthropological perspective on literacy, as presented by the likes of Goody (1977, 1987), Heath (1983), Scribner and Cole (1981), and the authors of the 'New Literacy' issue of the *Journal of Research in Reading*, has provided a novel perspective, much new data, and a number of provocative ideas about literacy and its uses in social contexts.

What is this new perspective? Street contrasts it with what he calls the autonomous model of literacy; he would have us reject this in favour of a New Literacy, a Literacy based on an anthropological or ethnographic approach. According to this model, there is not a single literacy 'with a capital L and a single Y'. Literacy is instead socially defined, and there are (presumably) as many literacies as there are social groups to define them. Literacy is not an objective reality, a skill which we can assess. Instead it is a political matter, part of a contest over resources. In the end, there is not a universal skill called literacy, for literacy can only be culturally defined.

I confess to subscribing to the autonomous model, 'a literacy narrowly conceived as individual, psychological skills'. I believe that literacy (literacy$_1$) is a single thing. I believe that learning to read and write *does* contribute to social progress, to personal improvement and mobility, perhaps to better health, almost certainly to cognitive development (see Stanovich and Stanovich, in this volume). While I may not believe that texts can be 'wrenched out of their cultural contexts', I do believe that texts have independent meanings. I further believe that readers can be 'separated from the society that gives meaning to their uses of literacy', and that their cognitive skills, importantly including their ability to read and write, can be assessed, and thus 'abstracted from social persons and cultural locations'.

My disagreements with Brian Street are many. But I think they can be reduced to three, three arguments regarding literacy which I would dispute. One is that Street and his collaborators consider literacy social; I do not. A second is that they see literacy as political; I would not have it so. The third is that they define literacy as relative; I take this to be an empirical question, to be settled by research, not by fiat. Let us consider each in turn.

Is literacy social?

Street and his ethnographic colleagues would have us think of literacy as social. Introducing a recent collection entitled *The Ethnography of Reading,* Boyarin (1993) says that 'most of the essays share the task of dissolving the stereotype of the isolated reader, showing that not only is all reading socially embedded, but indeed a great deal of reading is done in social groups'.

What can this mean? Let us grant that Literacy is 'socially embedded'. Congresses, parliaments, and school boards discuss it; the meaning and import of literacy is surely a matter to be socially negotiated. But I would argue that the act of reading, that is, literacy itself, is one of the least social of human activities.

When I think of social activities, I think of conversations, of football games, of parliamentary debates. Reading may be involved in these activities. We converse about what we have read, we read the programme or the score at the game, a speaker may even read a statement to the House. But to call these 'literacy activities' is like calling an aspirin bottle 'Discourse-bound' (Gee, 1990, has done just this); they are social activities because they directly involve other people, and they only incidentally involve reading.

Ordinary reading, in contrast, strikes me as one of the most private, unsocial things which people do. We often do it alone, and if we do it in the presence of others (as in libraries or aircraft), we interact with others only at the cost – the interruption – of our reading. I think that reading is most naturally construed as an act which is primarily *not* social, and it distorts our ordinary language to call it so.

Street argues that it is a mistake to think that 'readers can be separated from the society that gives meaning to their uses of literacy'. My response is to say, why not? When I watch a Wimbledon tennis match, I separate those players from the society which gives meaning to their uses of their racquets; I am interested in the players and their game, not that society. Why can't I do the same with readers?

Is literacy political?

Street would have us recognize that there is a political dimension to literacy. As he puts it, it is part of the struggle over resources in our society.

Street is certainly right that literacy (and Literacy) can be politicized. Literacy is and always has been an intensely ideological and political issue. As Monaghan (1991) points out, literacy campaigns have been driven by the religious importance of reading the Bible. But in the Cuban (1961) and Nicaraguan (1980) revolutions, political motivations were woven into literacy teaching materials, just as religious ones had been used earlier; the first lesson in the Nicaraguan reader was entitled *La Revolución* (containing all five vowels of Spanish). In the US, phonics instruction has been adopted by the political right; many of the advocates of whole language are far to the political left (e.g., Edelsky, 1992, 1994; Shannon, 1988, 1990).

But the fact that politicians make use of literacy should not make the study or the teaching of literacy political. We whose central interest is literacy, not politics, should stay clear of the latter in our work. There are certainly students of literacy who would have us use literacy instruction to change society in directions they favour. Paolo Freire, for example, vigorously promotes this in this writings (e.g., Freire and Macedo, 1987). But I maintain that they are wrong: we should not do this.

The New Literacy is decidedly political. One of its advocates has maintained that our 'mainstream' approach is 'but part of an educational arsenal which works against the interests and achievements of students from particular cultures and sub-cultures'. They would probably argue that we who uphold the autonomous model are equally political, if only implicitly. For example, Willinsky (1994) refers to print as 'the public broadcasting system of Protestantism, capitalism, and the middle class'. So teaching someone to read that print might be viewed as inculcating those values.

I question this. Protestantism, capitalism, and the middle class are not the only things represented in print; so are Catholicism, communism, and the upper and lower classes. I have no idea how Jane Oakhill or Peter Bryant or Usha Goswami vote in British elections (nor, as a reading researcher, do I care). As I see it, we 'autonomists' are seeking the best way to teach children to read without regard to how those children might subsequently vote.

The autonomous view of literacy (at least my version of it) holds that while literacy may be adopted by politicians, we should do our best to keep politics out of literacy research and (especially) literacy instruction. One of the basic principles in much of the English-speaking world is the separation of church and state. At least in America, most would not question the wisdom of this principle. For similar reasons, I would argue for the separation of politics and education. Politically, we citizens disagree in many ways, about abortion, about nuclear disarmament, about welfare. But whatever our differences, we all want our children to learn to read and write. We want them to be able to read textbooks and novels and poems and letters and magazines and newspapers and even our arguments about our political disagreements. But, in a democracy, I hope that most of us want others, including our children, to make up their own minds about these matters. Some of us might like our children (and those of others) inculcated with our own views. But what if their teacher holds views with which we disagree? Do we really want our children's political views shaped by the views of their teachers? I have always believed that, as a professor, I should teach my subject matter as best I can; I have no business using the privileged status of my position to influence my students' views on political questions. I hold the same view regarding the reading teacher.

Many of the New Literacists are on the left. But so are many autonomists. Like Street and company, they are filled with compassion about the disadvantaged; they abhor the mistreatment of minorities. But they recognize that one of the best things they can do for every human being is to give them literacy. They would not try to achieve their political ends through the minds of innocent children.

Is literacy relative?

Street's perspective is that of an anthropologist. One of the guiding ideas of anthropology is cultural relativism. Applied to literacy, this yields the view that literacy means different things to different people. This is almost certainly true; people have different Literacies. But does this mean that there are different kinds of literacy?

Many of us were educated to believe in cultural relativism. In the words of Robin Fox (1989, p. 24), it was part of 'the whole secular ideology' of our time. Anthropologists taught us that human behaviour was fundamentally shaped by the culture in which we were nurtured: 'what we ascribe to human nature is no more than a reaction to the restraints put upon us by our civilization' (Boas, 1928).

In recent years, cultural relativism has been seriously challenged. In his book *Human Universals* Brown (1991) shows us that six classic examples of cultural determinism have been undermined by later research.

One is the matter of colour terms. The colour spectrum is continuous; it could be divided in almost any way. Anthropologists used to tell us that colour naming was arbitrary. But two of them (Berlin and Kay, 1969) assembled lists of colour terms from speakers of 98 different languages. They found that the focal point of the basic colours was the same across languages. Moreover, while languages vary in the number of basic colour terms they have, the order in which those terms enter the language is far from arbitrary, but instead seems to be universal.

A second example is Margaret Mead's study of Samoan adolescence, *Coming of Age in Samoa*. Mead reported that adolescence was not a stressful period for Samoans, mainly because of their casual sexual code. But Freeman (1983) has shown that Mead was seriously (even intentionally) misinformed, that Samoans have much the same attitude toward adolescent sex as us (and find adolescence just as difficult).

Still a third example is the matter of facial expressions, long thought (LaBarre, 1947; Birdwhistell, 1970) to be culturally determined. But research by Izard (1971) and Ekman (1972) has shown that raters of facial expressions drawn from a great variety of cultures were substantially in agreement on which emotions were indicated by various facial expressions.

I will not belabour Brown's point; the interested reader is referred to his fascinating book. But he concludes that these cases 'raise anew the need to look more carefully at human universals and at extremist conceptions of cultural relativity'.

In the present context, this raises the question of whether literacy is, in fact, relative. There are persuasive reasons, even from the autonomous perspective, to think that it might be. But to us it is an empirical question, one to be settled by research, not by theoretical (or political) argument.

Within the autonomous camp, a popular view of comprehension goes something like this: A text contains many gaps; the reader must fill in those gaps, using background knowledge and inference. From this it follows that the result – the gist, or theme, structure – is a product of the text *and* the reader. Since no two readers are provided with exactly the same background knowledge, or draw the same inferences, if follows that the same text will yield different meanings for each reader.

There is some truth to this idea. But the same could be said of every experience, from seeing the sun rise to listening to Beethoven's Ninth Symphony. We each interpret everything personally, individually. But life is possible only to the extent that our perception is veridical, that we perceive the world as it is. And communal life, social life, is tolerable only to the extent that our communications are truthful. What these observations suggest is that there is a communality to meaning, that while we each may assign an individual reading to any text, that text must convey a common meaning to each of us.

Common sense says that we depend upon this assumption every day of our lives. We look at the front page to see what Bill Clinton or Tony Blair said yesterday, and we expect it to reliably report what they said. We read the sports page to see if Arsenal won, and if it says they did, we believe it. We read our biology textbook to learn about frogs, and we expect it to tell us the truth about frogs.

From this perspective, the view that texts have no independent meaning seems like errant, if not pernicious, nonsense. Still, the idea that what we extract from a text, or how we might interpret its meaning, might be relative, that it might be related to what we know or believe about that subject and that text, seems much more reasonable. Readers bring different values and different amounts of background knowledge to any text; readers of *The Times*, the

Telegraph, and the *Guardian* know that those newspapers put different slants on the news. How much readers might extract from a text, what inferences they might draw from it, and of course how they might value that text, could very well be a relative matter.

But as I see it, this is an empirical question. Is the reader who is good at reading one text (or kind of text) good at reading another, and the poor reader always poor? Or is someone who is literate in one context illiterate in another?

A recent dissertation at the University of Texas addressed this question. Cynthia Peterson (1993) examined the literacy of 135 naval reservists in two domains, baseball and computers. Peterson measured the reservists' reading comprehension, listening comprehension, and decoding ability in each domain; she also measured the extent of their background knowledge about both subjects. What she found was that the correlation between the reservists' comprehension across the two domains, whether listening or reading, was quite modest. It appears that literacy, as a skill, is not constant, but is relative to subject-matter domain, and it depends upon the extent of the reader's background knowledge in that subject. But the correlation in decoding ability across the two (baseball and computers) was very high, and virtually independent of the readers background knowledge. Peterson's study led her to conclude that literacy consists of two skills. One, comprehension, could be considered relative; it certainly varies with subject matter. The other, decoding, cannot be considered relative; it can be applied equally well in any domain.

Some Conclusions

As I see it, reading is no more social than anything else we do, and less social than most of those things; it is simply wrong to think of it primarily as social. As I see it, while literacy is certainly a political matter, we who work with it should stay out of those politics, at least in our work; to politicize reading instruction can only promote a totalitarian society. As I see it, while literacy is in part (the comprehension part) a relative matter, the other part (the ability to decode) is not.

This final conclusion has some implications for assessment. If comprehension is relative to background knowledge, then background knowledge must be taken into account in assessing someone's literacy. (In the US, the states of Illinois and Michigan attempt to do just this). But if decoding is not relative, then we can validly assess it in complete ignorance of the reader's background knowledge or culture, and we should do so.

Assessment is not popular among educators, in part, I suspect, because they are egalitarians. They do not like to rank individuals. But I contend that there are individual differences in literacy: some can read well, others not so well, still others cannot read at all. Despite Street's protestations, there are illiterates in our society, and in our society, they are seriously handicapped. We autonomists would 'devalorize' no one; we would teach everyone to read.

References

Berlin, B., and Kay, P. (1969) *Basic Color Terms: Their Universality and Evolution*. Berkeley, CA: University of California Press.

Birdwhistell, R. L. (1970) *Kinesics and Context: Essays on Body Motion Communication*. Philadelphia: University of Pennsylvania Press.

Boas, F. (1928) Foreword. In M. Mead, *Coming of Age in Samoa*, New York: Morrow.

Boyarin, J. (ed.) (1993) *The Ethnography of Reading*. Berkeley, CA: University of California Press.

Brown, D. E. (1991) *Human Universals*. Philadelphia: Temple University Press.

Edelsky, C. (1992) A talk with Carole Edelsky about politics and literacy. *Language Arts*, 69, 324–9.

Edelsky, C. (1994) Education for democracy. *Language Arts*, 71, 252–63.

Ekman, P. (1972) Universal and cultural differences in facial expressions of emotions. In J. K. Cole (ed.), *Nebraska Symposium on Motivation, 1971*, Lincoln: University of Nebraska Press, pp. 207–83.

Fox, R. (1989) *The Search for Society*. New Brunswick: Rutgers University Press.

Freeman, D. (1983) *Margaret Mead and Samoa: The Making and Unmaking of an Anthropological Myth*. Cambridge, MA: Harvard University Press.

Freire, P., and Macedo, D. (1987) *Literacy: Reading the Word and the World*. South Hadley, MA: Bergin & Harvey.

Gale, F. G (1994) *Political Literacy*. Albany, NY: State University of New York Press.

Gee, J. P. (1990) *Sociolinguistics and Literacy: Ideology in Discourses*. Philadelphia: Falmer Press.

Goody, J. (1977) *The Domestication of the Savage Mind*. Cambridge, England: Cambridge University Press.

Goody, J. (1987) *The Interface between the Written and the Oral*. Cambridge, England: Cambridge University Press.

Heath, S. B. (1983) *Ways with Words: Language, Life, and Work in Communities and Classrooms*. New York: Cambridge University Press.

Izard, C. E. (1971) *The Face of Emotion*. New York: Appleton-Century-Crofts.

Kintgen, E. R. (1988) Literacy literacy. *Visible Language, 22* (2), 149–68.

Kramer, S. N. (1981) *History Begins at Sumer*. Philadelphia, PA: University of Pennsylvania.

LaBarre, W. (1947) The cultural basis of emotions and gestures. *Journal of Personality, 16,* 49–68.

Mead, M. (1928) *Coming of Age in Samoa*. New York: Morrow.

Monaghan, E. J. (1991) Literacy in eighteenth-century New England: Some historical reflections on issues of gender. In M. Conrad (ed.), *Making Adjustments: Changes and Continuity in Planter Nova Scotia, 1769–1800,* New York: Aacademic Press, pp. 12–44.

Peterson, C. L. (1993) Background knowledge and the decomposition of literacy in skilled adult readers. Unpublished doctoral dissertation, University of Texas at Austin.

Scribner, S., and Cole, M. (1981) *The Psychology of Literacy*. Cambridge, MA: Harvard University Press.

Shannon, P. (1988) *Broken Promises: Reading Instruction in 20th Century America*. Granby, MA: Bergin & Garvey.

Shannon, P. (1990) *The Struggle to Continue: Progressive Reading Instruction in the United States*. Portsmouth, NH: Heinemann.

Sommers, C. H. (1994) *Who Stole Feminism?* New York: Simon & Schuster.

Street, B. V. (1993) The New Literacy studies. Guest editorial, *Journal of Research in Reading, 16* (2), 81–97.

Telushkin, J. (1991) *Jewish Literacy: The Most Important Things to Know about the Jewish Religion, its People, and History*. New York: Morrow.

Vallance, E. (1995) The public curriculum of orderly images. *Educational Researcher, 24* (2), 4–13.

Willinsky, J. (1994) *Empire of Words: The Reign of the OED*. Princeton, NJ: Princeton University Press.

Chapter Two

How Research Might Inform the Debate about Early Reading Acquisition

KEITH E. STANOVICH AND PAULA J. STANOVICH

The so-called 'reading wars' that have characterized education in most English-speaking countries have seen their latest incarnation in the whole-language versus phonics-emphasis controversy of the last ten years (e.g., Beard and Oakhill, 1994; Chall, 1992; Goodman, 1992; Groff, 1989; Liberman and Liberman, 1990; Mather, 1992; McKenna, Robinson and Miller, 1990; McKenna, Stahl and Reinking, 1994; Mosenthal, 1989; Perfetti, 1991; Pressley and Rankin, 1994; Weaver, 1989). These disputes have generated acrimony, sapped the field's energies, and most important of all, have confused and demoralized educators. As one scholar said to the senior author: 'The longstanding either/or, black white of reading may spark lively debate on an intellectual level; but when we consider the more pragmatic aspects of our field, that is, teaching reading to children or adults, dualism becomes dangerous. We stand to hurt innocent bystanders!' (Stanovich, 1990a, p. 221).

In this chapter we attempt to outline a strategy for resolving the disputes between the whole-language and phonics camps in reading instruction. The strategy has five steps: (1) First look for points of agreement between opposing positions. (2) When doing so, invoke a 'spirit of charity' whereby all sides are encouraged to stretch their

Preparation of the manuscript was supported by grant no. 0GP0001607 from the Natural Sciences and Engineering Research Council of Canada to Keith E. Stanovich.

principles to the maximum to accommodate components of the other position. (3) Step back and take a look at what might be a larger degree of agreement than anyone supposed. Use the convergence to foster trust and a willingness to let the remaining disputes be settled by empirical evidence. (4) Next, isolate the crucial differences. Try to make these few in number but clearly defined so that they are amenable to scientific test. (5) Agree to let the evidence adjudicate the critical testable predictions that differ between the two camps.

We will argue here that such a strategy can contribute to some degree of rapprochement between the factions of the reading wars. Perhaps more importantly it will clarify the state of the evidence for educational practitioners who have had to endure the overheated rhetoric that has become common in reading publications (see McKenna et al., 1994).

It is, in fact, not difficult to find points of agreement between the two camps. Indeed, some figures who have been central in the controversies have themselves emphasized the points of convergence and agreement. For example, Jeanne Chall, author of the seminal *Learning to Read: The Great Debate* (1967; 1983), has repeatedly pointed out that many of the recommendations and practices that are commonly associated with whole language have appeared repeatedly in her writings. She reminds us that 'Teaching only phonics – and in isolation – was not a recommendation of the Great Debate in 1967 or 1983' (1989, p. 525). Chall is at pains to remind her readers that, in common with many whole-language advocates, she 'also recommended that library books, rather than workbooks, be used by children not working with the teacher and that writing be incorporated into the teaching of reading' (p. 525) and she reminds us that 'The history of reading instruction teaches us that literature, writing, and thinking are not exclusive properties of any one approach to beginning reading' (p. 531).

Chall thus points to some issues on which the viewpoints of the two camps display considerable convergence. Chall (1989) also has no compunctions about admitting that 'Some teachers may inadvertently overdo the teaching of phonics, leaving little time for the reading of stories and other connected texts' (p. 531). Clearly there is plenty of scope for the 'principle of charity' to operate here. Corresponding to Chall's statement that 'some teachers may inadvertently overdo the teaching of phonics' we simply need the companion admission that 'some children in whole language classrooms do not pick up the alphabetic principle through simple immersion in print and writing activities, and such children need explicit instruction in spelling–sound correspondences' – a concession having the not inconsiderable advantage of being consistent with voluminous research evidence (e.g., Adams, 1990; Adams and Bruck, 1993; Anderson, Hiebert, Scott and Wilkinson, 1985; Byrne, 1992; Castle, Riach and Nicholson, 1994; Felton, 1993; Iversen and Tunmer, 1993; Share, 1995; Share and Stanovich, 1995; Vellutino, 1991).

Is the whole-language movement prepared to make such an admission? Some readings of the whole-language literature would seem to answer this question in the negative (McKenna et al., 1994; Perfetti, 1991; Pressley and Rankin, 1994; Vellutino, 1991). Indeed, Adams (1991) argues that the central tenets of the whole language movement are: '(1) teacher empowerment, (2) child-centered instruction, (3) integration of reading and writing, (4) a disavowal of the value of teaching or learning phonics, and (5) subscription to the view that children are naturally pre-disposed toward written language acquisition' (p. 41). Educators working from a variety of different perspectives might well endorse points nos 1 to 3. Clearly the key points of difference are issues no. 4 and no. 5.

If Adams (1991) is correct that no. 4 and no. 5 are the critical points of difference, then these define the falsifiable hypotheses that separate the two camps. These two points of difference suggest that it might be wise to examine the cognitive processing models under-lying the tenets of the two camps as the possible source of the conflict. This is very fortunate because it is precisely in the domain of cogni-tive processing models of reading in which we have a good deal of empirical evidence, much of it having been generated in the last 10–15 years (and thus much of it little known to practitioners). In the following sections, we review the aspects of this evidence that have the most straightforward practical implications for instructional practice and for adjudicating the disputes that are the cause of the reading wars (more comprehensive reviews are contained in Adams, 1990; Adams and Bruck, 1993; Share, 1995; and Share and Stanovich, 1995).

The Role of Context in Word Recognition

Contemporary whole-language practice rests on the information processing assumptions of what have been termed top-down models of reading. Advocates of such models have consistently argued that skilled readers rely less on graphic cues than do less-skilled readers. Smith's (1971; 1973; 1975) well-known hypothesis is that, being sensitive to the redundancy afforded by sentences, good readers develop hypotheses about upcoming words and are then able to confirm the identity of a particular word by sampling only a few features in the visual array. Good readers should process words faster because their use of redundancy lightens that load on their word decoding mechanisms.

Whole-language advocates have carried over into the present debates an important assumption from the earlier top-down models: that guessing words based on the previous context of the passage is an efficacious way of reading and of learning to read. This claim – that contextual effects are more implicated in the performance of better readers – has often been made by proponents of top-down models:

> Skill in reading involves not greater precision, but more accurate first guesses based on better sampling techniques, greater control over language structure, broadened experiences and increased conceptual development.   (Goodman, 1976, p. 504)

> Guessing in the way I have described it is not just a preferred strategy for beginners and fluent readers alike; it is the most efficient manner in which to read and learn to read.   (Smith, 1979, p. 67)

> The more difficulty a reader has with reading, the more he relies on the visual information; this statement applies to both the fluent reader and the beginner. In each case, the cause of the difficulty is inability to make full use of syntactic and semantic redundancy, of nonvisual sources of information.   (Smith, 1971, p. 221)

These claims still serve as foundational assumptions about reading acquisition in the whole-language literature. In fact, an emphasis on the role of contextual guessing actually represents a classic case of mistaken analogy in science and has been recognized as such for over a decade.

Briefly, the history of the issue is this. Models of reading acquisition and individual differences in reading ability were dominated for a considerable time by top-down conceptualizations (e.g., Smith, 1971) that were considerably influenced by analysis-by-synthesis models of speech perception, and interactive models of recognition that were derived by analogy to artificial intelligence work in speech perception (e.g., Rumelhart, 1977). The problem here is that the analogy to written language is not apt. The ambiguity in decontextualized speech is well known. For example, excised words from normal conversation are often not recognized out of context. This does not hold for written language, obviously. A fluent reader can identify written words with near perfect accuracy out of context. In short, the physical stimulus alone completely specifies the lexical representation in writing, whereas this is not always true in speech. The greater diagnosticity of the external stimulus in reading, as opposed to listening, puts a greater premium on an input system that can deliver a complete representation of the stimulus to higher-level cognitive systems.

Another problem concerns the assumptions that have been made about the properties of contextual information. It is often incorrectly assumed that predicting upcoming words in sentences is a relatively easy and highly accurate activity. Actually, many different empirical studies have indicated that naturalistic text is not that predictable. Alford (1980) found that for a set of moderately long expository passages of text, subjects needed an average of more than four guesses to correctly anticipate upcoming words in the passage (the method of scoring actually makes this a considerable underestimate). Across a variety of subject populations and texts, a reader's probability of predicting the next word in a passage is usually between 0.20 and 0.35 (Aborn, Rubenstein and Sterling, 1959; Gough, 1983; Miller and Coleman, 1967; Perfetti, Goldman and Hogaboam, 1979; Rubenstein and Aborn, 1958). Indeed, as Gough (1983) has shown, this figure is highest for function words, and is often quite low for the very words in the passage that carry the most information content.

A large amount of much more direct empirical evidence exists of the issue of context use. This research has consistently indicated that the word recognition of better readers is *not* characterized by more reliance on contextual information. Before reviewing this research evidence, however, it is imperative to highlight the issue of levels of processing, because failure to emphasize this principle has confused the literature on the effects of context for so long. For example, there *is* considerable evidence that better readers are better able to use contextual information to facilitate their *comprehension* processes (Baker and Brown, 1984; Stanovich and Cunningham, 1991). However, research in recent years has shown that hypotheses about context use in comprehension were inappropriately generalized to the *word-recognition* level.

When research on context use at the word-recognition level is examined, it shows that studies employing a wide variety of paradigms have failed to find that good readers rely more on context for word recognition than poorer readers. Many discrete-trial reaction-time studies of context effects have been conducted to investigate this question. Most of these studies have used priming paradigms where a context (sometimes a word, sometimes a sentence, and sometimes several sentences or paragraphs) precedes a target word to which the subject must make a naming or lexical decision response. Although this paradigm does not completely isolate the word-recognition level of processing (Seidenberg, Waters, Sanders and Langer, 1984; West and Stanovich, 1982; 1986), it does so more than most other methodologies that have been used. The finding has consistently been that not only do the poorer readers in these studies use context, but they often show somewhat larger contextual effects than do the better readers (Becker, 1985; Ben-Dror, Pollatsek and Scarpati, 1991; Briggs, Austin and Underwood, 1984; Bruck, 1988; 1990; Perfetti, 1985; Pring and Snowling, 1986; Schvaneveldt, Ackerman and Semlear, 1977; Schwantes, 1985; 1991; Simpson and Foster, 1986; Simpson, Lorsbach and Whitehouse, 1983; Stanovich, 1980; 1986; Stanovich, Nathan, West and Vala-Rossi, 1985; Stanovich, West and Feeman, 1981; West and Stanovich, 1978; West et al., 1983).

Because the reaction-time paradigms that more specifically isolate the pre-lexical from the post-lexical level (processes before and after word recognition has taken place) of processing (Seidenberg, Waters, Sanders and Langer, 1984; West and Stanovich, 1982; 1986) have generally not been applied to children at the earliest stages of reading acquisition, researchers have relied largely on analyses of oral reading errors to make inferences about the use of context by these children. This is problematic because, as has often been pointed out (e.g., Kibby, 1979; Leu, 1982; Wixson, 1979), an oral reading error can occur for a variety of reasons. Many oral reading errors reflect comprehension processes as well as word recognition processes. This is certainly the case for self-corrections, for example, which clearly implicate comprehension processes occurring well after lexical access. Creating indices of contextual processing based on measures such as self-corrections seriously confounds levels of processing.

Nevertheless, analyses of initial substitution errors (first errors – before self-correction – in which one phoneme is substituted for another) have been used to throw light on the issue of the facilitation of word recognition by context, and it is likely that these errors do partially implicate processes operating at the word-recognition level. Fortunately, the results of oral reading error studies largely converge with those of reaction-time studies. When skilled and less-skilled readers are reading materials of comparable difficulty (an important control, see Stanovich, 1986) the reliance on contextual information relative to graphic information is just as great – in many cases greater – for the less-skilled readers (Allington and Fleming, 1978; Biemiller, 1970; 1979; Harding, 1984; Juel, 1980; Lesgold, Resnick and Hammond, 1985; Leu, DeGroff and Simons, 1986; Nicholson and Hill, 1985; Nicholson, Lillas and Rzoska, 1988; Perfetti and Roth, 1981; Richardson, DiBenedetto and Adler, 1982; Simons and Leu, 1987; Whaley and Kibby, 1981). The results from studies of text disruption effects, timed text reading, and a variety of other paradigms also display a similar pattern (Allington and Strange, 1977; Biemiller, 1977–8; Ehrlich, 1981; Lovett, 1986; Nicholson, 1991; Schwartz and Stanovich, 1981; Stanovich, Cunningham and Feeman, 1984; Strange, 1979).

Thus, the results from many different paradigms indicate that the effects of background knowledge and contextual information attenuate as the efficiency of word recognition processes increases. Efficient word recognition has the properties of autonomous, or modular, processing as defined in recent work in cognitive science (e.g., Fodor, 1983; Forster, 1979; Humphreys, 1985; Norris, 1990; Perfetti and McCutchen, 1987; Stanovich 1990b) – the properties of speed, low capacity usage, and obligatory execution, free from interference by other ongoing operations. The key to the rapid acquisition of reading skill is the development of word recognition mechanisms that have these properties.

The consistent trend in the literature indicating that contextual effects on word recognition decrease as reading skill increases has led several theorists to conceptualize the logic of contextual facilitation on word recognition as compensatory in nature (Durgunoglu, 1988; Perfetti, 1985; Perfetti and Roth, 1981; Stanovich, 1980; 1986; 1991). It is hypothesized that the information processing system is arranged in such a way that when the bottom-up stimulus analysis processes that result in word recognition are deficient, the system compensates by relying more heavily on other knowledge sources (e.g., contextual information). Thus, the key point that top-down theorists got wrong, and the key error that has been perpetuated by the inheritors of the top-down view – the whole-language movement – is the assumption that contextual dependency is always associated with good reading. In fact, the word recognition skills of the good reader are so rapid, automatic, and efficient that the skilled reader need not rely on contextual information. In fact, it is poor readers who guess from context – out of necessity because their decoding skills are so weak.

In summary, contextual information is simply no substitute for the ability to decode the words on the page. But here we encounter another point of difference between camps in the reading wars. Phonics advocates stress that the acquisition of decoding ability requires the child to acquire some special processing skills and that some children need to be explicitly taught these skills. Whole-language advocates emphasize that decoding skills can be acquired naturally through immersion in a print-rich environment. Again, fortunately, there is ample evidence with which to adjudicate this controversy.

How 'Natural' is the Process of Reading Acquisition?

The disagreement about the necessity of teaching decoding skills follows from the background assumptions of the two camps concerning whether reading acquisition should be characterized as an 'unnatural' task (Gough and Hillinger, 1980) or as a 'natural' task (Goodman, 1986) for young children. Typical of the latter view is the statement from Goodman's (1986) popular book for parents and teachers, *What's Whole in Whole Language?*

> Why do people create and learn written language? They need it! How do they learn it? The same way they learn oral language, by using it in authentic literacy events that meet their needs. Often children have trouble learning written language in school. It's not because it's harder than learning oral language, or learned differently. It's because we've made it hard by trying to make it easy. Frank Smith wrote an article called '12 Easy Ways to Make Learning to Read Hard.' Every way was designed to make the task easy by breaking it up in small bits. But by isolating print from its functional use, by teaching skills out of context and focusing on written language as an end in itself, we made the task harder, impossible for some children.   (p. 24)

The way that this passage equates written language learning with oral language learning illustrates a recurring theme in the whole-language literature: that learning to read is just like learning to speak. However, as many cognitive psychologists have pointed out (see Adams, 1990; Adams and Bruck, 1993; Liberman, 1992; Liberman and Liberman, 1990; Perfetti, 1991), the use of the speech/reading analogy ignores the obvious facts that all communities of human beings have developed spoken languages but only a minority of these exist in written form, that speech is almost as old as the human species but that written language is a recent cultural invention of only the last three or four thousand years, and that virtually all children in normal environments develop speech easily, whereas most children require explicit tuition to learn to read and substantial numbers of children have difficulty even after intensive efforts on the part of teachers and parents. The argument of Liberman and Liberman (1990) is typical of current scientific thinking on the oral/written language distinction:

> Reflecting biological roots that run deep, speech employs a single, universal strategy for constructing utterances. All languages form all words by combining and permuting a few dozen consonants and vowels, meaningless segments that we will sometimes refer to, loosely, as phonemes. On the other hand, scripts, being artifacts, choose variably from a menu of strategies. Some, like the one we use, represent

the phonemes. Others represent the more numerous syllables. Still others, like the Chinese, take the considerably more numerous mor- phemes as their irreducible units. . . . Surely it is plain that speech is biologically primary in a way that reading and writing are not. Accord- ingly, we suppose that learning to speak is, by the very nature of the underlying process, much like learning to walk or to perceive visual depth and distance, while learning to read and write is more like learn- ing to do arithmetic or to play checkers.   (p. 55)

Research has consistently supported the view that reading is not acquired naturally, in the same way as speech. In a seminal paper, Gough and Hillinger (1980) asserted that, in actuality, we should con- sider learning to read to be an 'unnatural act'. This characterization followed from their two-stage model of the earliest stages of reading acquisition. Gough and Hillinger (1980) posited that the first stage was one of paired-associate learning utilizing minimal cues. That is, children initially begin to associate spoken words with particularly salient cues in the visual array. However, the paired-associate proce- dure based on distinctive visual cues is not generative; that is, it is of no help in recognizing unfamiliar words (see Jorm and Share, 1983; Share, 1995).

Normal progress in reading dictates that the child make the tran- sition to the next stage of acquisition, which requires some degree of visual and speech analysis. Unlike the first stage, where the child acquires words naturally and often spontaneously, the fully analytic stage (what Gough and Hillinger term the cipher stage) is not natural and almost always requires intervention by an outsider (teacher, parent, sibling) who gives cues to support analytic processing and/or presents words in ways that foster such processing (Adams, 1990; Share, 1995).

Subsequent research has tended to support Gough and Hillinger's (1980) conceptualization (see Gough, Juel and Griffith, 1992). Byrne (1992) has presented evidence indicating that fully analytic pro- cessing of words is not the natural processing set of pre-literate four-year-old children. He demonstrated that learning to discriminate FAT from BAT did not enable the children to discriminate FUN from BUN with greater than chance accuracy. The children's per- formance illustrates what would be expected from a child who had not passed beyond Gough and Hillinger's (1980) paired-associate stage.

Young pre-literate children often spontaneously learn to name words on television, advertisements, cereal boxes, and billboards. This particular phenomenon has frequently spawned characterizations of reading diametrically opposed to that of Gough and Hillinger (1980) – characterizations that view learning to read as a 'natural' act, directly analogous to learning spoken language. However, the results of a study by Masonheimer, Drum, and Ehri (1984) have indicated that this type of word learning is like that of Gough and Hillinger's paired-associate stage rather than the later, more analytic processing that is so predictive of success in early reading.

Gough (1993; Gough and Juel, 1991) had a group of five-year-olds learn sets of words written on flashcards to a criterion of two successive correct trials. One of the flashcards was deliberately marred by a thumbprint on the corner. During the test phase, when the children were shown the thumbprinted word on a clean card, less than half could identity the word. Almost all of them, however, produced the word when shown a thumbprinted card with no word on it. As an additional test, children were shown a thumbprinted card containing a word other than the one which accompanied it during training. Almost all children named the word that accompanied the thumbprint during training, rather than the word that was presently one the card.

The results of Gough (1993) converge nicely with those of Byrne (1992) and Masonheimer et al. (1984) and are consistent with the idea that learning spelling-to-sound correspondences is an 'unnatural' act for young children. Results from an important classroom study also support this conclusion. Seymour and Elder (1986) studied a class of new entrants into a Scottish primary school where the emphasis was on the development of a 'sight vocabulary' via whole-word methods, and no phonics training occurred during the first two terms. An examination of their subsequently developed word recognition skills indicated that they were not generative: the children could not recognize unfamiliar words that they had not been taught. Unlike the case of children who have developed some spelling-to-sound decoding skills, the error responses of these children were drawn only from the set of words that they had been taught (see also Gough et al., 1992).

Researchers are largely agreed on which information processing abilities are the most important predictors of how fast children will move out of the 'natural' paired-associate stage and into the 'unnatural' stage where alphabetic coding skills are used. In the last ten years, phonological processes have been under intense scrutiny (Berent and Perfetti, 1995; Goswami and Bryant, 1990; Rack, Hulme and Snowling, 1993; Rack, Hulme, Snowling and Wightman, 1994; Siegel and Ryan, 1988; Snowling, 1987; Stanovich, 1986; 1992; Stanovich and Siegel, 1994; Torgesen, Wagner and Rashotte, 1994). The theoretical reason for this attention has been the recognition that to enable the powerful self-teaching mechanism inherent in an alphabetic orthography (Gough and Hillinger, 1980; Jorm and Share, 1983; Share, 1995), the child must learn the general principle that spelling corresponds to sound and then must learn sufficient exemplars of spelling-to-sound correspondences to support efficient decoding.

In order to utilize the alphabetic principle, the child must adopt an analytic attitude toward both written words and the spoken words they represent; that is, the child must discover and exploit the fact that the mapping takes place at the level of letters and phonemes. Segmenting visual words into letter units is well within the perceptual capabilities of every nonimpaired school-age child. However, the development of the tendency to exhaustively process all of the visual detail in words (particularly the sequence of interior letters) may be difficult for some children (Frith, 1985; Stanovich, 1992; Stanovich and West, 1989). Nevertheless, an even greater source of individual differences resides in the sounds to which the letters map. Segmenting speech at the level of phonemes is notoriously difficult for young children (Bruce, 1964; Calfee, Chapman and Venezky, 1972; Goswami and Bryant, 1990; Lewkowitz, 1980; Liberman, Shankweiler, Fischer, and Carter, 1974; Williams, 1984), and the ability to do so is strongly correlated with the ease of initial reading acquisition. Note, however, that this does not mean that we must necessarily wait for phonological segmentation ability to emerge fully before introducing words and the alphabetic principle. To the contary, there is much evidence indicating that the more sophisticated types of segmentation skills are themselves developed by instruction in word decoding (Ehri, 1989; Goswami and Bryant, 1990). The point is that phonological segmentation and alphabetic coding skill are in a tightly intertwined reciprocal relationship in the early stages of reading acquisition and that these skills are mutually facilitative.

The emphasis on analytic language skills in recent research highlights another point of contention between different camps in the reading wars: Do children best acquire reading skill in a holistic manner or through direct instruction that emphasizes analytic attention to language components (e.g., phonemes, words, etc.)?

Analytic versus Holistic Approaches to Reading Acquisition

We have argued that successful reading acquisition seems to require the development of an analytic processing stance towards words that is probably not the 'natural' processing set adopted by most children and that some children have extreme difficulty in adopting an analytic processing set. The latter group of children will, as a result, have considerable difficulty building up knowledge of subword spelling–sound correspondences – and such knowledge appears to be almost a necessary prerequisite of fluent reading (Adams, 1990; Adams and Bruck, 1993; Gough et al., 1992; Jorm and Share, 1983; Share, 1995; Snowling, 1980; Stanovich, 1982; 1986; 1992; Vellutino, 1991; Vellutino and Scanlon, 1987).

What makes the analytic processing set difficult for some children? To induce subword spelling–sound correspondences, children must become sensitive to the subword units both in the written word and in the representation of the spoken word. Research indicates that some children have problems dealing with subword units of speech representations. This deficit in segmental language skills is sometimes termed a lack of phonological awareness or phonological sensitivity (e.g., Ball, 1993; Bentin, 1992; Bowey, Cain and Ryan, 1992; Bradley and Bryant, 1978; 1985; Bruck, 1990; 1992; Bruck and Treiman, 1990; Bryant, Maclean, Bradley and Crossland, 1990; Goswami and Bryant, 1990; Snowling, 1987; Stahl and Murray, 1994; Stanovich, 1982; 1986; 1992; Stanovich, Cunningham and Cramer, 1984; Vellutino and Scanlon, 1987; Wagner and Torgesen, 1987; Wagner, Torgesen, Laughon, Simmons and Rashotte, 1993; Wagner, Torgesen and Rashotte, 1994).

Becoming aware of the segmental structure of language appears to be a prerequisite to rapid reading acquisition in an alphabetic orthography. Lack of phonological sensitivity inhibits the learning of the alphabetic coding patterns that underlie fluent word recognition (Bryant et al., 1990; Goswami and Bryant, 1990; Stanovich, Cunningham and Cramer, 1984; Tunmer and Hoover, 1992; Tunmer and Nesdale, 1985). Alphabetic coding is the most critical subprocess that supports fluent reading and that is deficient in cases of reading disability (Bruck, 1990; 1992; Rack, Snowling and Olson, 1992; Siegel and Ryan, 1988; Snowling, 1980; Stanovich and Siegel, 1994).

Thus, it is not surprising that researchers have moved to earlier developmental levels to demonstrate the efficacy of training in phonological processing skills. They have demonstrated that training kindergarten and preschool children in phonological sensitivity skills can lead to faster rates of reading and spelling acquisition (Ball, 1993; Ball and Blachman, 1991; Blachman, 1989; Blachman, Ball, Black and Tangel, 1994; Bradley and Bryant, 1983; 1985; Byrne and Fielding-Barnsley, 1991; 1993; Cunningham, 1990; Hatcher, Hulme and Ellis, 1994; Lie, 1991; Lundberg, Frost and Peterson, 1988; Torgesen, Morgan and Davis, 1992; Treiman and Baron, 1983; Williams, 1980; Wise, 1991). Because these training programmes invariably involved the segmentation of words, this research evidence flies in the face of the frequent admonitions not to fractionate language, on the part of whole-language advocates:

> Careful observation is helping us to understand better what makes language easy or hard to learn. Many school traditions seem to have actually hindered language development. In our zeal to make it easy, we've made it hard. How? Primarily by breaking whole (natural) language up into bite-size, but abstract little pieces. It seemed so logical to think that little children could best learn simple little things. We took apart the language and turned it into words, syllables, and isolated sounds. Unfortunately, we also postponed its natural purpose – the communication of meaning – and turned it into a set of abstractions, unrelated to the needs and experiences of the children we sought to help. (Goodman, 1986, p. 7)

A large data base now contradicts this position. Liberman and Liberman (1990) argue that, from a linguistic perspective, this is not surprising:

Communication among nonhuman animals is different in a critically important way, for, so far as anyone has been able to determine, the natural animal systems have no phonology (nor do they have syntax, for that matter), and, as a consequence, their message-carrying potential is severely limited. Lacking the phonological structures that make lexical generativity possible, nonhuman animals can convey in their natural communication only as many word-meanings as there are distinctively different signals they can make and perceive, and that is, at most, a few dozen. . . . Thus, in contrast to language, which is lexically open because word meanings are conveyed by arranging and rearranging meaningless signal elements, the nonhuman systems attach meaning directly to each element and are, as a consequence, tightly and irremediably closed. We see, then, that language would pay a terrible price if it were not phonologically based. Perhaps it would be of some comfort to the Whole Language people that in such a non-phonological world there would be no 'bite-size abstract little pieces' for teachers to break a word into. . . . Each word would be conveyed by an unanalyzable signal, so meaning would be conveyed directly, just at Whole Language seems to think it should be. Unfortunately, there would not be many words.   (pp. 56–7)

The admonition to 'not break up' language is not very helpful to teachers faced with children who are struggling in reading. In contrast, the growing knowledge of the role of phonological processing in reading holds out great hope for educational applications. First, phonological sensitivity can be assessed very early in development, prior to school entrance (Blachman, 1989; Maclean, Bryant and Bradley, 1987). Secondly, the research cited above indicates that phonological sensitivity can be increased through appropriate preschool experiences, and that such training results in a significant increase in word recognition and spelling skills. This training is even more effective when combined with practice in recognizing letter–sound correspondences (see Hatcher et al., 1994). All of this research converges with the findings from instructional-comparison studies of slightly older children indication that a code emphasis is more efficacious in early reading instruction than holistic programmes that de-emphasize phonological analysis and letter–sound training – particularly for poor readers (Adams, 1990; Adams and Bruck, 1993; Brown and Felton, 1990; Chall, 1983; 1989; Evans and Carr, 1985; Felton, 1993; Foorman, Francis, Novy and Liberman,

1991; Iversen and Tunmer, 1993; Perfetti, 1985; 1991; Stanovich, 1986; Tunmer and Nesdale, 1985; Vellutino, 1991; Williams, 1980; Wise, 1991).

Critiques of the Research Consensus

Despite the existence of voluminous evidence for the conclusions that we have summarized above, these still exist whole-language advocates who dispute this evidence (e.g., Goodman, 1992; Grundin, 1994). Their critiques revolve around two basic criticisms, one of which is more general and philosophical and the other more empirical.

The first, more general criticism, is that the researchers who have generated the evidence on how context works in word recognition and on the importance of decoding skills conceive of reading as synonymous with word recognition. For example, Grundin (1994) states that such researchers assume that 'word recognition – or rather word pronunciation – amounts to reading' (p. 9) and that such researchers argue that 'all we have to do is decide how to teach word reading' (p. 9). Contrary to these assertions, the investigators who have conducted the studies on the importance of phonological sensitivity and decoding have *not* assumed that 'reading amounts to word recognition' and do not assert that we do not need to worry about reading development once decoding skills are established. It is, in fact, impossible to track down any such assertions in the writings of the investigators who are being criticized. Such criticisms are often hurled – without any specific attribution – at researchers whose findings support the practice of phonics instruction. Typically, the passages from Grundin's (1994) article given above were accompanied by no citations – no quotes from actual researchers who had stated such things. In the absence of any evidence that a researcher actually has made such a statement, such charges should be taken for what they appear to be – strawmen assertions designed to trigger negative associations in the mind of the reader.

Nevertheless, these assertions are repeated with such frequency that we must risk belabouring the obvious in order to reiterate an important point – that to emphasize the importance of word recognition in the reading process is not to deny that the ultimate purpose of reading is comprehension. Adequate word recognition skill is a necessary but not sufficient condition for good reading comprehension. Although it is possible for a person to have adequate word recognition skill yet still display poor reading comprehension, the converse virtually never occurs. For example, it has never been empirically demonstrated that some instructional innovation could result in good reading comprehension without simultaneously leading to the development of at least adequate word recognition ability. Because word recognition skill will be a byproduct of any successful approach to developing reading ability – whether or not the approach specifically targets word recognition – lack of skill at recognizing words is almost always a reasonable predictor of difficulties in developing reading comprehension ability. This is the reason why many researchers have focused on word recognition as a critical component of the reading process – not because they view word recognition and reading as one and the same thing.

Related to the 'word recognition is not reading' objection is the more legitimate rejoinder that the bulk of the studies demonstrating positive effects for training in phonological sensitivity and decoding skills have used word recognition as the criterion variable. One might raise the legitimate question of whether the positive effects of these training programmes generalize to reading comprehension or text reading. This second, more empirically based objection is one that must be taken more seriously. Fortunately, there is some evidence which does address this issue if generalizability. Although it is true that most of the studies demonstrating positive effects for training in phonological sensitivity and decoding skills have focused on word recognition as the criterion variable, there are several studies that have used reading comprehension or text reading as the criterion variable (e.g., Bradley and Bryant, 1985; Brown and Felton, 1990; Cunningham, 1990; Evans and Carr, 1985; Hatcher, Hulme and Ellis, 1994; Iversen and Tunmer, 1993; Juel, 1994; Lie, 1991; Olofsson, 1993; Pflaum, Walberg, Karegianes and Rasher, 1980; Tunmer and Nesdale, 1985). These studies provide converging evidence by indicating that children given training in phonological sensitivity and/or alphabetic coding show superior outcomes on measures of comprehension and text reading as well as word recognition. Based on the results of these studies, there currently is every reason to believe that the positive effects of teaching decoding skills will generalize to reading comprehension performance.

Summing Up the Evidence

We have suggested that there are more points of convergence between phonics and whole-language advocates than is typically emphasized in most writings in this contentious field. All sides can agree on a variety of educational practices: on the importance of good literature for children, on the importance of early writing experiences for teaching children how language works, and many other practices (Cunningham, 1992; Griffith and Olson, 1992; Spiegel, 1992; Trachtenburg, 1990; Yopp, 1992). Disagreements between the camps are selectively focused around the necessity of explicit analytic instruction in word decoding in the early years of schooling. The current differences between the camps are all traceable to differing underlying assumptions about the process of reading that were present in the debates about top-down versus bottom-up models of reading that began over twenty years ago (Goodman, 1967; 1968; Gough, 1972; LaBerge and Samuels, 1974; Samuels and Kamil, 1984; Smith, 1971; Stanovich, 1980). Two decades of empirical research have largely resolved these debates in favour of the bottom-up models. A greater use of context cues to aid word recognition is not a characteristic of good readers, developing phonological sensitivity is critical for early success in reading acquisition, and instructional programmes that emphasize spelling–sound decoding skills result in better reading outcomes because alphabetic coding is the critical subprocess that supports fluent reading.

The way now seems clear for whole-language advocates to reconstitute their position in a scientifically respectable way. They could retain most of their broad socio-educational goals (teacher empowerment, equal opportunity for all learners, engaged learning, etc.), but jettison the unwarranted adherence to a processing model of reading that is outdated and not congruent with the latest research evidence. Indeed, such a move might raise the status of the whole-language movement by showing that it is responsive to scientific evidence and rational argument. Ironically, such an evolution of foundational assumptions might enable whole-language advocates to marshal wider support for their broader socio-educational goals. Certain natural allies (e.g., phonics advocates who share progressive socio-political goals) are currently estranged from the whole-language movement because of the latter's adherence to an outdated model of the reading process that is not consistent with existing empirical evidence.

References

Aborn, M., Rubenstein, H., and Sterling, T. D. (1959) Sources of contextual constraint upon words in sentences. *Journal of Experimental Psychology, 57*, 171–80.

Adams, M. J. (1990) *Beginning to Read: Thinking and Learning about Print.* Cambridge, MA: MIT Press.

Adams, M. J. (1991) Why not phonics and whole language? In W. Ellis (ed.), *All Language and the Creation of Literacy*, Baltimore, MD: Orton Dyslexia Society, pp. 40–52.

Adams, M. J., and Bruck, M. (1993) Word recognition: The interface of educational policies and scientific research. *Reading and Writing: An Interdisciplinary Journal, 5*, 113–39.

Alford, J. (1980, May) *Predicting Predictability: Identification of Sources of Contextual Constraint on Words in Text.* Paper presented at the meeting of the Midwestern Psychological Association, St Louis.

Allington, R. L., and Fleming, J. T. (1978) The misreading of high-frequency words. *Journal of Special Education, 12*, 417–21.

Allington, R. L., and Strange, M. (1977) Effects of grapheme substitutions in connected text upon reading behaviors. *Visible Language, 11*, 285–97.

Anderson, R. C., Hiebert, E. H., Scott, J., and Wilkinson, I. (1985) *Becoming a Nation of Readers.* Washington, DC: National Institute of Education.

Baker, L., and Brown, A. L. (1984) Metacognitive skills and reading. In P. D. Pearson (ed.), *Handbook of Reading Research*, New York: Longman, pp. 353–94.

Ball, E. (1993) Phonological awareness: What's important and to whom? *Reading and Writing: An Interdisciplinary Journal, 5*, 141–59.

Ball, E. W., and Blachman, B. A. (1991) Does phoneme segmentation training in kindergarten make a difference in early word recognition and developmental spelling? *Reading Research Quarterly, 26*, 49–66.

Beard, R., and Oakhill, J. (1994) *Reading by Apprenticeship?* London: NFER.

Becker, C. A. (1985) What do we really know about semantic context effects during reading? In D. Besner, T. Waller, and G. MacKinnon (eds), *Reading Research: Advances in Theory and Practice*, New York: Academic Press, vol. 5, pp. 125–66.

Ben-Dror, I., Pollatsek, A., and Scarpati, S. (1991) Word identification in isolation and in context by college dyslexic students. *Brain and Language*, 40, 471–90.

Bentin, S. (1992) Phonological awareness, reading, and reading acquisition. In R. Frost and L. Katz (eds), *Orthography, Phonology, Morphology, and Meaning*, Amsterdam: North-Holland, pp. 193–210.

Berent, I., and Perfetti, C. A. (1995) A rose is a REEZ: The two-cycles model of phonology assembly in reading English. *Psychological Review*, 102, 146–84.

Biemiller, A. (1970) The development of the use of graphic and contextual information as children learn to read. *Reading Research Quarterly*, 6, 75–96.

Biemiller, A. (1977–8) Relationships between oral reading rates for letters, words, and simple text in the development of reading achievement. *Reading Research Quarterly*, 13, 223–53.

Biemiller, A. (1979) Changes in the use of graphic and contextual information as functions of passage difficulty and reading achievement level. *Journal of Reading Behavior*, 11, 307–19.

Blachman, B. A. (1989) Phonological awareness and word recognition: Assessment and intervention. In A. G. Kamhi and H. W. Catts (eds), *Reading Disabilities*, Austin: PRO-ED, pp. 133–58.

Blachman, B. A., Ball, E. W., Black, R. S., and Tangel, D. M. (1994) Kindergarten teachers develop phoneme awareness in low-income, inner-city classrooms. *Reading and Writing: An Interdisciplinary Journal*, 6, 1–18.

Bowey, J. A., Cain, M. T., and Ryan, S. M. (1992) A reading-level design study of phonological skills underlying fourth-grade children's word reading difficulties. *Child Development*, 63, 999–1011.

Bradley, L., and Bryant, P. E. (1978) Difficulties in auditory organization as a possible cause of reading backwardness. *Nature*, 271, 746–7.

Bradley, L., and Bryant, P. E. (1983) Categorizing sounds and learning to read – a causal connection. *Nature*, 301, 419–21.

Bradley, L., and Bryant, P. E. (1985) *Rhyme and Reason in Reading and Spelling*. Ann Arbor: University of Michigan Press.

Briggs, P., Austin, S., and Underwood, G. (1984) The effects of sentence context in good and poor readers: A test of Stanovich's interactive–compensatory model. *Reading Research Quarterly*, 20, 54–61.

Brown, I. S., and Felton, R. H. (1990) Effects of instruction on beginning reading skills in children at risk for reading disability. *Reading and Writing: An Interdisciplinary Journal*, 2, 223–41.

Bruce, D. (1964) The analysis of word sounds by young children. *British Journal of Educational Psychology*, 34, 158–70.

Bruck, M. (1988) The word-recognition and spelling of dyslexic children. *Reading Research Quarterly*, 23, 51–69.

Bruck, M. (1990) Word-recognition skills of adults with childhood diagnoses of dyslexia. *Developmental Psychology*, 26, 439–54.

Bruck, M. (1992) Persistence of dyslexics' phonological awareness deficits. *Developmental Psychology*, 28, 874–86.

Bruck, M., and Treiman, R. (1990) Phonological awareness and spelling in normal children and dyslexics: The case of initial consonant clusters. *Journal of Experimental Child Psychology*, 50, 156–78.

Bryant, P. E., Maclean, M., Bradley, L., and Crossland, J. (1990) Rhyme and alliteration, phoneme detection, and learning to read. *Developmental Psychology*, 26, 429–38.

Byrne, B. (1992) Studies in the acquisition procedure for reading: Rationale, hypotheses, and data. In P. B. Gough, L. C. Ehri, and R. Treiman (eds), *Reading Acquisition*, Hillsdale, NJ: Erlbaum, pp. 1–34.

Byrne, B., and Fielding-Barnsley, R. (1991) Evaluation of a program to teach phonemic awareness to young children. *Journal of Educational Psychology*, 83, 451–5.

Byrne, B., and Fielding-Barnsley, R. (1993) Evaluation of a program to teach phonemic awareness to young children: A 1-year follow-up. *Journal of Educational Psychology*, 85, 104–11.

Calfee, R. C., Chapman, R., and Venezky, R. (1972) How a child needs to think to learn to read. In L. Gregg (ed.), *Cognition in Learning and Memory*, New York: John Wiley, pp. 139–82.

Castle, J. M., Riach, J., and Nicholson, T. (1994) Getting off to a better start in reading and spelling: The effects of phonemic awareness instruction within a whole language program. *Journal of Educational Psychology*, 86, 350–9.

Chall, J. S. (1967) *Learning to Read: The Great Debate*. New York: McGraw-Hill.

Chall, J. S. (1983) *Learning to Read: The Great Debate* (updated edition). New York: McGraw-Hill.

Chall, J. S. (1989) Learning to read: The great debate 20 years later. *Phi Delta Kappa*, 70(7), 521–38.

Chall, J. S. (1992) The new reading debates: Evidence from science, art, and ideology. *Teachers College Record*, 94, 315–28.

Cunningham, A. E. (1990) Explicit versus implicit instruction in phonemic awareness. *Journal of Experimental Child Psychology*, 50, 429–44.

Cunningham, P. M. (1992) What kind of phonics instruction will we have? In C. Kinzer and O. Leu (eds), *Literacy Research, Theory and Practice: 41st NRC Yearbook*, Chicago, IL: NRC.

Durgunoglu, A. Y. (1988) Repetition, semantic priming, and stimulus quality: Implications for the interactive–compensatory model. *Journal of Experimental Psychology: Learning, Memory, and Cognition, 14*, 590–603.

Ehri, L. C. (1989) The development of spelling knowledge and its role in reading acquisition and reading disability. *Journal of Learning Disabilities, 22*, 356–65.

Ehrlich, S. (1981) Children's word recognition in prose context. *Visible Language, 15*, 219–44.

Evans, M. A., and Carr, T. H. (1985) Cognitive abilities, conditions of learning, and the early development of reading skill. *Reading Research Quarterly, 20*, 327–50.

Felton, R. H. (1993) Effects of instruction on the decoding skills of children with phonological-processing problems. *Journal of Learning Disabilities, 26*, 583–89.

Fodor, J. (1983) *Modularity of Mind*. Cambridge: MIT Press.

Foorman, B. R., Francis, D. J., Novy, D. M., and Liberman, D. (1991) How letter–sound instruction mediates progress in first-grade reading and spelling. *Journal of Educational Psychology, 83*, 456–69.

Forster, K. I. (1979) Levels of processing and the structure of the language processor. In: W. E. Cooper and E. Walker (eds), *Sentence Processing: Psycholinguistic Studies presented to Merrill Garrett*, Hillsdale, NJ: Erlbaum Associates, pp. 27–85.

Frith, U. (1985) Beneath the surface of developmental dyslexia. In K. Patterson, J. Marshall, and M. Coltheart (eds), *Surface Dyslexia*, London: Erlbaum, pp. 301–30.

Goodman, K. S. (1967) Reading: A psycholinguistic guessing game. *Journal of the Reading Specialist, 6*, 126–35.

Goodman, K. S. (1968) The psycholinguistic nature of the reading process. In K. S. Goodman (ed.), *The Psycholinguistic Nature of the Reading Process*, Detroit, MI: Wayne State University Press, pp. 13–26.

Goodman, K. S. (1976) Reading: A psycholinguistic guessing game. In H. Singer and R. B. Ruddell (eds), *Theoretical Models and Processes of Reading*, Newark, DE: International Reading Association, pp. 497–508.

Goodman, K. (1986) *What's Whole in Whole Language?* Portsmouth, NH: Heinemann.

Goodman, K. S. (1992) I didn't found Whole Language. *The Reading Teacher, 46*, 188–99.

Goswami, U., and Bryant, P. (1990) *Phonological Skills and Learning to Read*. Hove, England: Lawrence Erlbaum.

Gough, P. B. (1972) One second of reading. In J. Kavanagh and I. Mattingly (eds), *Language by Ear and Eye*, Cambridge, MA: MIT Press, pp. 331–58.

Gough, P. B. (1983) Context, form, and interaction. In K. Rayner (ed.), *Eye Movements in Reading*, New York: Academic Press, pp. 203–11.

Gough, P. B. (1993) The beginning of decoding. *Reading and Writing: An Interdisciplinary Journal*, 5, 181–92.

Gough, P. B., and Hillinger, M. L. (1980) Learning to read: An unnatural act. *Bulletin of the Orton Society*, 30, 171–6.

Gough, P. B., and Juel, C. (1991) The first stages of word recognition. In L. Rieben and C. Perfetti (eds), *Learning to Read: Basic Research and its implications*, Hillsdale, NJ: Lawrence Erlbaum Associates, pp. 47–56.

Gough, P. B., Juel, C., and Griffith, P. (1992) Reading, spelling, and the orthographic cipher. In P. B. Gough, L. C. Ehri, and R. Treiman (eds), *Reading Acquisition*, Hillsdale, NJ: Erlbaum, pp. 35–48.

Griffith, P. L., and Olson, M. W. (1992) Phonemic awareness helps beginning readers break the code. *The Reading Teacher*, 45, 516–23.

Groff, P. (1989) An attack on basal readers for the wrong reasons. In C. Weaver and P. Groff, *Two Reactions to the Report Card on Basal Readers*, Bloomington, IN: ERIC Clearinghouse on Reading and Communication Skills, pp. 8–13, 23–30, 38–44.

Grundin, H. (1994) Who's romancing reality? A response to Keith Stanovich. *The Reading Teacher*, 48, 8–10.

Harding, L. M. (1984) Reading errors and style in children with a specific reading disability. *Journal of Research in Reading*, 7, 103–12.

Hatcher, P., Hulme, C., and Ellis, A. W. (1994) Ameliorating early reading failure by integrating the teaching of reading and phonological skills: The phonological linkage hypothesis. *Child Development*, 65, 41–57.

Humphreys, G. W. (1985) Attention, automaticity, and autonomy in visual word processing. In D. Besner, T. Waller, and G. MacKinnon (eds), *Reading Research: Advances in Theory and Practice*, New York: Academic Press, vol. 5, pp. 253–309.

Iversen, S., and Tunmer, W. E. (1993) Phonological processing skills and the Reading Recovery Program. *Journal of Educational Psychology*, 85, 112–26.

Jorm, A., and Share, D. (1983) Phonological recoding and reading acquisition. *Applied Psycholinguistics*, 4, 103–47.

Juel, C. (1980) Comparison of word identification strategies with varying context, word type, and reader skill. *Reading Research Quarterly*, 15, 358–76.

Juel, C. (1994) *Learning to Read and Write in One Elementary School*. New York: Springer-Verlag.

Kibby, M. W. (1979) Passage readability affects the oral reading strategies of disabled readers. *The Reading Teacher, 32,* 390–6.

LaBerge, D., and Samuels, S. (1974) Toward a theory of automatic information processing in reading. *Cognitive Psychology, 6,* 293–323.

Lesgold, A., Resnick, L., and Hammond, K. (1985) Learning to read: A longitudinal study of word skill development in two curricula. In G. MacKinnon and T. Waller (eds), *Reading Research: Advances in Theory and Practice,* London: Academic Press, vol. 4, pp. 107–38.

Leu, D. (1982) Oral reading error analysis: a critical review of research and application. *Reading Research Quarterly, 17,* 420–37.

Leu, D. J., DeGroff, L., and Simons, H. D. (1986) Predictable texts and interactive–compensatory hypotheses: Evaluating individual differences in reading ability, context use, and comprehension. *Journal of Educational Psychology, 78,* 347–52.

Lewkowitz, N. (1980) Phonemic awareness training: What to teach and how to teach it. *Journal of Educational Psychology, 72,* 686–700.

Liberman, A. M. (1992) The relation of speech to reading and writing. In R. Frost and L. Katz (eds), *Orthography, Phonology, Morphology, and Meaning,* Amsterdam: North-Holland, pp. 167–78.

Liberman, I. Y., and Liberman, A. M. (1990) Whole language vs code emphasis: Underlying assumptions and their implications for reading instruction. *Annals of Dyslexia, 40,* 51–77.

Liberman, I. Y., Shankweiler, D., Fischer, F., and Carter, B. (1974) Explicit syllable and phoneme segmentation in the young child. *Journal of Experimental Child Psychology, 18,* 201–12.

Lie, A. (1991) Effects of a training program for stimulating skills in word analysis in first-grade children. *Reading Research Quarterly, 26,* 234–50.

Lovett, M. W. (1986) Sentential structure and the perceptual spans of two samples of disabled readers. *Journal of Psycholinguistic Research, 15,* 153–75.

Lundberg, I., Frost, J., and Peterson, O. (1988) Effects of an extensive program for stimulating phonological awareness in preschool children. *Reading Research Quarterly, 23,* 263–84.

Maclean, M., Bryant, P., and Bradley, L. (1987) Rhymes, nursery rhymes, and reading in early childhood. *Merrill-Palmer Quarterly, 33,* 255–81.

Masonheimer, P. E., Drum, P. A., and Ehri, L. C. (1984) Does environmental print identification lead children into word reading? *Journal of Reading Behavior, 16,* 257–71.

Mather, N. (1992) Whole language reading instruction for students with learning disabilities: Caught in the cross fire. *Learning Disabilities Research and Practice, 7,* 87–95.

McKenna, M., Robinson, R., and Miller, J. (1990) Whole language: A research agenda for the nineties. *Educational Researcher, 19* (8), 3–6.

McKenna, M., Stahl, S., and Reinking, D. (1994) A critical commentary on research, politics, and whole language. *Journal of Reading Behavior, 26,* 1–22.

Miller, G. R., and Coleman, E. B. (1967) A set of thirty-six prose passages calibrated for complexity. *Journal of Verbal Learning and Verbal Behavior, 6,* 851–4.

Mosenthal, P. B. (1989) The whole language approach: Teachers between a rock and a hard place. *The Reading Teacher, 42* (8), 628–9.

Nicholson, T. (1991) Do children read words better in context or in lists? A classic study revisited. *Journal of Educational Psychology, 83,* 444–50.

Nicholson, T., and Hill, D. (1985) Good readers don't guess – Taking another look at the issue of whether children read words better in context or in isolation. *Reading Psychology, 6,* 181–98.

Nicholson, T., Lillas, C., and Rzoska, M. (1988) Have we been misled by miscues? *The Reading Teacher, 42* (1), 6–10.

Nicholson, T. (1986) Reading is not a guessing game – The great debate revisited. *Reading Psychology, 7,* 197–210.

Norris, D. (1990) Connectionism: A case for modularity. In D. Balota, G. Flores d'Arcais, and K. Rayner (eds), *Comprehension Processes in Reading*, Hillsdale, NJ: Erlbaum Associates, pp. 331–43.

Olofsson, A. (1993) The relevance of phonological awareness in learning to read: Scandinavian longitudinal and quasi-experimental studies. In R. M. Joshi and C. K. Leong (eds), *Reading Disabilities: Diagnosis and Component Processes*, Dordrecht, Netherlands: Kluwer Academic, pp. 185–98.

Perfetti, C. A. (1985) *Reading Ability.* New York: Oxford University Press.

Perfetti, C. A. (1991) The psychology, pedagogy, and politics of reading. *Psychological Science, 2,* 70–6.

Perfetti, C. A., Goldman, S., and Hogaboam, T. (1979) Reading skill and the identification of words in discourse context. *Memory and Cognition, 7,* 273–82.

Perfetti, C. A., and McCutchen, D. (1987) Schooled language competence: Linguistic abilities in reading and writing. In S. Rosenberg (ed.), *Advances in Applied Psycholinguistics*, Cambridge: Cambridge University Press, vol. 2, pp. 105–41.

Perfetti, C. A., and Roth, S. (1981) Some of the interactive processes in reading and their role in reading skill. In A. Lesgold and C. Perfetti (eds), *Interactive Processes in Reading*, Hillsdale, NJ: Erlbaum Associates, pp. 269–97.

Pflaum, S., Walberg, H. J., Karegianes, M., and Rasher, S. (1980) Reading instruction: A quantitative analysis. *Educational Researcher*, 9, 12–18.

Pressley, M., and Rankin, J. (1994) More about whole language methods of reading instruction for students at risk for early reading failure. *Learning Disabilities Research and Practice*, 9, 157–68.

Pring, L., and Snowling, M. (1986) Developmental changes in word recognition: An information-processing account. *Quarterly Journal of Experimental Psychology*, 38A, 395–418.

Rack, J. P., Hulme, C., and Snowling, M. J. (1993) Learning to read: A theoretical synthesis. In H. Reese (ed.), *Advances in Child Development and Behavior*, San Diego, CA: Academic Press, pp. 99–132.

Rack, J., Hulme, C., Snowling, M., and Wightman, J. (1994) The role of phonology in young children learning to read words: The direct mapping hypothesis. *Journal of Experimental Child Psychology*, 57, 42–71.

Rack, J. P., Snowling, M. J., and Olson, R. K. (1992) The nonword reading deficit in developmental dyslexia: A review. *Reading Research Quarterly*, 27, 28–53.

Richardson, E., DiBenedetto, B., and Adler, A. (1982) Use of the decoding skills test to study differences between good and poor readers. In K. Gadow and I. Bialer (eds), *Advances in Learning and Behavioral Disabilities*, Greenwich, CT: JAI Press, vol. 1, pp. 25–74.

Rubenstein, H., and Aborn, M. (1958) Learning, prediction, and readability. *Journal of Applied Psychology*, 42, 28–32.

Rumelhart, D. E. (1977) Toward an interactive model of reading. In S. Dornic (ed.), *Attention and Performance*, New York: Academic Press, vol. 6, pp. 573–603.

Samuels, S. J., and Kamil, M. L. (1984) Models of the reading process. In P. D. Pearson (ed.), *Handbook of Reading Research*, New York: Longman, pp. 185–224.

Schvaneveldt, R., Ackerman, B., and Semlear, T. (1977) The effect of semantic context on children's word recognition. *Child Development*, 48, 612–16.

Schwantes, F. M. (1985) Expectancy, integration, and interactional processes: Age differences in the nature of words affected by sentence context. *Journal of Experimental Child Psychology*, 39, 212–29.

Schwantes, F. M. (1991) Children's use of semantic and syntactic information for word recognition and determination of sentence meaningfulness. *Journal of Reading Behavior*, 23, 335–50.

Schwartz, R. M., and Stanovich, K. E. (1981) Flexibility in the use of graphic and contextual information by good and poor readers. *Journal of Reading Behavior*, 13, 263–9.

Seidenberg, M. S., Waters, G. S., Barnes, M. A., and Tanenhaus, M. K. (1984) When does irregular spelling or pronunciation influence word recognition? *Journal of Verbal Learning and Verbal Behavior*, 23, 383–404.

Seidenberg, M. S., Waters, G. S., Sanders, M., and Langer, P. (1984) Pre- and post-lexical loci of contextual effects on word recognition. *Memory and Cognition*, 12, 315–28.

Seymour, P. H. K., and Elder, L. (1986) Beginning reading without phonology. *Cognitive Neuropsychology*, 3, 1–36.

Share, D. L. (1995) Phonological recoding and self-teaching: Sine qua non of reading acquistion. *Cognition*, 55, 151–218.

Share, D. L., and Stanovich, K. E. (1995) Cognitive processes in early reading development: Accommodating individual differences into a model of acquisition. *Issues in Education: Contributions from Educational Psychology*, 1, 1–56.

Siegel, L. S., and Ryan, E. B. (1988) Development of grammatical-sensitivity, phonological, and short-term memory skills in normally achieving and learning disabled children. *Developmental Psychology*, 24, 28–37.

Simons, H. D., and Leu, D. J. (1987) The use of contextual and graphic information in word recognition by second-, fourth-, and sixth-grade readers. *Journal of Reading Behavior*, 19, 33–47.

Simpson, G. B., and Foster, M. R. (1986) Lexical ambiguity and children's word recognition. *Developmental Psychology*, 22, 147–54.

Simpson, G. B., Lorsbach, T., and Whitehouse, D. (1983) Encoding and contextual components of word recognition in good and poor readers. *Journal of Experimental Child Psychology*, 35, 161–71.

Smith, F. (1971) *Understanding Reading*. New York: Holt, Rinehart and Winston.

Smith, F. (1973) *Psycholinguistics and Reading*. New York Holt, Rinehart and Winston.

Smith, F. (1975) The role of prediction in reading. *Elementary English*, 52, 305–11.

Smith, F. (1979) *Reading without Nonsense*. New York: Teachers College Press.

Snowling, M. (1980) The development of grapheme–phoneme correspondence in normal and dyslexic readers. *Journal of Experimental Child Psychology*, 29, 294–305.

Snowling, M. (1987) *Dyslexia*. Oxford: Basil Blackwell.

Spiegel, D. L. (1992) Blending whole language and systematic direct instruction. *The Reading Teacher*, 46 (1), 38–44.

Stahl, S. A., and Murray, B. (1994) Defining phonological awareness and its relationship to early reading. *Journal of Educational Psychology*, 86, 221–34.

Stanovich, K. E. (1980) Toward an interactive–compensatory model of individual differences in the development of reading fluency. *Reading Research Quarterly*, *16*, 32–71.

Stanovich, K. E. (1982) Individual differences in the cognitive processes of reading, I: Word decoding. *Journal of Learning Disabilities*, *15*, 485–93.

Stanovich, K. E. (1986) Matthew effects in reading: Some consequences of individual differences in the acquisition of literacy. *Reading Research Quarterly*, *21*, 360–407.

Stanovich, K. E. (1990a) A call for an end to the paradigm wars in reading research. *Journal of Reading Behavior*, *22*, 221–31.

Stanovich, K. E. (1990b) Concepts in developmental theories of reading skill: Cognitive resources, automaticity, and modularity. *Developmental Review*, *10*, 72–100.

Stanovich, K. E. (1991) Word recognition: Changing perspectives. In R. Barr, M. L. Kamil, P. Mosenthal, and P. D. Pearson (eds), *Handbook of Reading Research*, New York: Longman, vol. 2, pp. 418–52.

Stanovich, K. E. (1992) Speculations on the causes and consequences of individual differences in early reading acquisition. In P. Gough, L. Ehri, and R. Treiman (eds), *Reading Acquisition*, Hillsdale, NJ: Erlbaum Associates, pp. 307–42.

Stanovich, K. E., and Cunningham, A. E. (1991) Reading as constrained reasoning. In S. Sternberg and P. Frensch (eds), *Complex Problem Solving: Principles and Mechanisms*, Hillsdale, NJ: Erlbaum, pp. 3–60.

Stanovich, K. E., Cunningham, A. E., and Cramer, B. (1984), Assessing phonological awareness in kindergarten children: Issues of task comparability. *Journal of Experimental Child Psychology*, *38*, 175–90.

Stanovich, K. E., Cunningham, A. E., and Feeman, D. (1984) Relation between early reading acquisition and word decoding with and without context: A longitudinal study of first-grade children. *Journal of Educational Psychology*, *76*, 668–77.

Stanovich, K. E., Nathan, R., West, R. F., and Vala-Rossi, M. (1985) Children's word recognition in context: Spreading activation, expectancy, and modularity. *Child Development*, *56*, 1418–28.

Stanovich, K. E., and Siegel, L. S. (1994) The phonotypic performance profile of reading-disabled children: A regression-based test of the phonological-core variable-difference model. *Journal of Educational Psychology*, *86*, 24–53.

Stanovich, K. E., and West, R. F. (1989) Exposure to print and orthographic processing. *Reading Research Quarterly*, *24*, 402–33.

Stanovich, K. E., West, R. F., and Feeman, D. J. (1981) A longitudinal study of sentence context effects in second-grade children: Tests of an interactive–compensatory model. *Journal of Experimental Child Psychology, 32,* 185–99.

Strange, M. (1979) The effect of orthographic anomalies upon reading behavior. *Journal of Reading Behavior, 11,* 153–61.

Torgesen, J. K., Morgan, S., and Davis, C. (1992) Effects of two types of phonological awareness training on word learning in kindergarten children. *Journal of Educational Psychology, 84,* 364–70.

Torgesen, J. K., Wagner, R. K., and Rashotte, C. A. (1994) Longitudinal studies of phonological processing and reading. *Journal of Learning Disabilities, 27,* 276–86.

Trachtenburg, P. (1990) Using children's literature to enhance phonics instruction. *The Reading Teacher, 43,* 648–54.

Treiman, R., and Baron, J. (1983) Phonemic-analysis training helps children benefit from spelling–sound rules. *Memory and Cognition, 11,* 382–9.

Tunmer, W. E., and Hoover, W. (1992) Cognitive and linguistic factors in learning to read. In P. B. Gough, L. C. Ehri, and R. Treiman (eds), *Reading Acquisition,* Hillsdale, NJ: Erlbaum, pp. 175–214.

Tunmer, W. E., and Nesdale, A. R. (1985) Phonemic segmentation skill and beginning reading. *Journal of Educational Psychology, 77,* 417–27.

Vellutino, F. R. (1991) Introduction to three studies on reading acquisition: Convergent findings on theoretical foundations of code-oriented versus whole-language approaches to reading instruction. *Journal of Educational Psychology, 83,* 437–43.

Vellutino, F., and Scanlon, D. (1987) Phonological coding, phonological awareness, and reading ability: Evidence from a longitudinal and experimental study. *Merrill-Palmer Quarterly, 33,* 321–63.

Wagner, R. K., and Torgesen, J. K. (1987) The nature of phonological processing and its causal role in the acquisition of reading skills. *Psychological Bulletin, 101,* 192–212.

Wagner, R. K., Torgesen, J. K., Laughon, P., Simmons, K., and Rashotte, C. A. (1993) Development of young readers' phonological processing abilities. *Journal of Educational Psychology, 85,* 83–103.

Wagner, R. K., Torgesen, J. K., and Rashotte, C. A. (1994) Development of reading-related phonological processing abilities: New evidence of bidirectional causality from a latent variable longitudinal study. *Developmental Psychology, 30,* 73–87.

Weaver, C. (1989) The basalization of America: A cause for concern. In C. Weaver and P. Groff, *Two Reactions to the Report Card on Basal Readers,* Bloomington, IN: ERIC Clearinghouse on Reading and Communication Skills, pp. 7, 14–22, 33–7.

West, R. F., and Stanovich, K. E. (1978) Automatic contextual facilitation in readers of three ages. *Child Development, 49,* 717–27.

West, R. F., and Stanovich, K. E. (1982) Sources of inhibition in experiments on the effect of sentence context on word recognition. *Journal of Experimental Psychology: Learning, Memory, and Cognition, 8,* 385–99.

West, R. F., and Stanovich, K. E. (1986) Robust effects of syntactic structure on visual word processing. *Memory and Cognition, 14,* 104–12.

West, R. F., Stanovich, K. E., Feeman, D., and Cunningham, A. (1983) The effect of sentence context on word recognition in second- and sixth-grade children. *Reading Research Quarterly, 19,* 6–15.

Whaley, J., and Kibby, M. (1981) The relative importance of reliance on intraword characteristics and interword constraints for beginning reading achievement. *Journal of Educational Research, 74,* 315–20.

Williams, J. (1980) Teaching decoding with an emphasis on phoneme analysis and phoneme blending. *Journal of Educational Psychology, 72,* 1–15.

Williams, J. (1984) Phonemic analysis and how it relates to reading. *Journal of Learning Disabilities, 17,* 240–5.

Wise, B. W. (1991) What reading disabled children need: What is known and how to talk about it. *Learning and Individual Differences, 3,* 307–21.

Wixson, K. L. (1979) Miscue analysis: A critical review. *Journal of Reading Behavior, 11,* 163–75.

Yopp, H. K. (1992) Developing phonemic awareness in young children. *The Reading Teacher, 45,* 696–703.

Chapter Three

Cognitive Research and the Misconceptions of Reading Education

CHARLES A. PERFETTI

The connection between research and practice is not a simple one of the first producing and the second consuming, especially in education.[1] There are obstacles to the use of good research in any field, and in reading education the obstacles are compounded. For one thing, research on reading abounds, promiscuously popping up in disciplines of all sorts and in publications of widely varying quality. That makes it difficult to distinguish what is both valid and useful from what is sterile, spurious, or both. Second, the problems of practice are more complex than the conclusions that come from research. When there is an incongruence between simple conclusions and complex realities, one may despair that the research is irrelevant.[2]

Nevertheless, there has been enough quality research to inform reading education on some basic issues. It is important, whatever the

---

This chapter is a revised version of an article titled 'Cognitive Research Can Inform Reading Education', published in a special issue of the *Journal of Research in Reading*, 18 (1995), pp. 106–15, 'Experimental research into literacy and its development', edited by J. Oakhill, R. Beard, and D. Vincent. The differences between the chapter and the original article are minor.

[1]   See Glaser (1976, 1982) for an insightful analysis of how research and practice connect in education.

[2]   The problem, more often, however, is that there is an additional layer of analysis that must be done to implement recommendations from simple conclusions into practice. It is never quite clear who is to do this work

additional complexities, to try to assess what has been clearly demonstrated by sound research. I focus exclusively here on sound research on a particular problem: research about the cognitive processes that underlie skilled reading and learning how to read. This is a narrow scope and must be (and has been) supplemented by good research on relevant social, cultural, and instructional aspects of the problem.

There are four clear contributions of cognitive research that deserve special attention. This attention is deserved for two reasons. First, in each case the evidence has accumulated in a reliable fashion. The conclusions do not rest on a single study or two, but on solid results from converging research. Second, in each case the results speak clearly to issues of reading instruction. Indeed, in each case they imply that certain reading goals should be privileged over others. Finally, these four solid results span a range of school levels from skilled reading through middle-grade to beginning reading. What is especially interesting is that not only are they based on good evidence, they contradict false beliefs that are widely held. They are as follows: (1) Contrary to the belief that context allows readers to just sample a small number of the words in a text, skilled readers read most words rather than skip them. (2) Contrary to the belief that poor reading arises from a failure to use context, less skilled readers rely heavily on context. (3) Contrary to a belief that the sounds of words (their phonology) are irrelevant once children learn to read, skilled readers use phonology in reading. (4) Contrary to the view that learning to read is only or mainly about 'meaning making', children learn to read successfully by learning how their writing system works. These facts, as explained in the remainder of this chapter, expose misconceptions that can be obstacles to effective reading instruction.

The Use of Context in Reading

There is a pervasive belief that, in reading, context is critical: context that provides the background of what is being read and that con-

---

in education. It is neither the job of teachers nor researchers. But the failure to get it done is no doubt one of the greatest obstacles to research-stimulated improvements in education.

siders the goals of the reader. This belief is based on common sense and it is supported by evidence. Thus, the evidence indeed shows that skilled readers adjust their reading goals, make inferences, use context, and monitor their comprehension during reading (see Yuill and Oakhill, 1991). These higher-order abilities and strategies are very important to skilled comprehension. But it is necessary to consider carefully the scope of their application. They apply generally to an interactive reading process that rests on a high level of skill in identifying words; they do not apply effectively as substitutes for this skill. For example, the importance of context in reading needs to be understood in light of at least two additional facts. First, skilled readers actually identify words, rather than using context, to skip them. Second, less skilled readers use context in identifying words, and, in fact, appear to be forced into high dependence on context by weak word-level skills. Both of these important facts overturn misconceptions about reading.

Skilled readers identify words when they read

The incorrect idea that skilled reading involves a strategy of sparse sampling of words coupled with a heavy use of context can be put to rest by clear evidence to the contrary. The evidence comes from studies that monitor what readers' eyes do when they read. From such studies have come the following picture: First, the eyes gain information useful for reading only when they are at rest, fixated on a specific small region of the text. When the eyes move, as they do in rapid saccades after each fixation, there is no information gained. Thus, the experience of reading is one that is smooth and free of interruptions; but the actual mechanics of reading involves alternations of stops (fixations) and movements, with only the fixations providing useful information.

Most important is the fact that readers' eyes fixate on most words on the page when they are reading for most purposes, from over 50 per cent to nearly 80 per cent depending on the reading purpose and the type of word. So-called content words – nouns, adjectives, verbs – are read more often than so-called function words – forms of *to be*, articles, prepositions. However, some of this difference appears to be due to differences in the length of these different classes of words. The reader's ability to direct his or her eyes to a certain word is quite limited (Rayner and Pollatsek, 1989). And reading for gist can get by with fewer eye fixations than reading in order to answer questions (Just and Carpenter, 1987). But the general picture is clear: Readers fixate on most of the content words on the page and their ability to answer comprehension questions is generally limited to text locations that they have actually fixated (Just, Carpenter and Masson, 1982).

There is no mystery about why readers sample texts densely. It is a simple matter of retinal sensitivity. The eyes can make out the letters of a word only within a degree or two of central visual angle. The effect of this is to allow a window of reading that is confined to only 4–6 spaces to the right of the eye's fixation (Rayner and Pollatsek, 1989). That's enough to read a word, and sometimes the first couple of letters of the immediately following word. But it demonstrates the limits of peripheral vision in the actual reading of words. Thus, readers must read lots of words in order to read effectively. The use of context is important, and one finds shorter fixation times on words that are more predictable (Ehrlich and Rayner, 1981). But this context effect does not extend to skipping words.

Less skilled readers use context

The use of context, to repeat the obvious, is important in reading. Both the context provided by the text itself and that provided by the reader's knowledge help the reader interpret words and sentences. Without the use of context, the reader would not be able to figure out the relevant meaning aspects of words – because most words have multiple general senses rather than specific meanings – nor to draw appropriate inferences – because such inferences depend on implicit information provided by other parts of the text or the reader's knowledge.

The importance of context has been widely appreciated. Less widely appreciated, but well established by research, are two equally important facts about context use. (1) Skilled readers do not use context much to identify words; they use context to interpret words and sentences. (2) Less skilled readers, by contrast, use context to identify words. These facts came to light in research some years ago by Stanovich and West (1981) and by Perfetti, Goldman, and Hogaboam (1979). The basic result in these studies was that differences between skilled and less skilled readers in the speed of word identification were large when words were presented in isolation, but were reduced when words were presented in context. Fuller theoretical accounts of these results are in Stanovich (1980; 1981) and Perfetti and Roth (1981).

These findings appeared counterintuitive to people who had become accustomed to thinking of context use as a characteristic of skilled readers and 'word calling' (word reading devoid of meaning) as characteristic of poor readers. Actually, the results are very sensible and easily understood: Skilled readers identify words too quickly on the basis of lexical processes for context to have much effect. Less skilled readers are slower in identifying words, because they lack basic word identification skill; thus they are able to benefit from the additional boost of context. Indeed, when the basic word identification speed of skilled readers is slowed down, context facilitates identification (Perfetti and Roth, 1981). The hallmark of skilled reading is fast *context-free* word identification combined with a rich *context-dependent* text understanding.

In summary, there are two misconceptions about reading that arise from an undifferentiated acceptance of the importance of context. As with most misconceptions, these arise from observation that has some element of truth in it: Context, broadly conceived as the implicit information external to a printed word, is very important in effective reading – reading with comprehension. But the use of context is a complex of component language and cognitive processes, not a simple skill that a reader either has or does not have. As research seeks to understand the different specific components of context, the fact is that identifying words is a central part of reading that is not evaded by the use of context.

Skilled Readers Use Phonology

How skilled readers identify words is another question that has been answered by research, and again the research answer overturns some misconceptions. It is common to assume that reading, for a skilled reader, involves a visually based print-to-meaning process. The facts emerging from an intense 20-year period of word identification research are otherwise. Despite differing conclusions on the details of word identification, the research points to an important role for phonology. The differences concern whether phonology 'mediates' all written word identification: When phonology is observed is it 'pre-lexical' – in which case it may actually mediate the access to a word's meaning – or is it 'post-lexical' – in which case it may result from identification? This question has received slightly differing answers from well conceived research. However, a penetrating analysis by Van Orden, Pennington, and Stone (1990) makes a good case in favour of a natural mediating role for phonology in word identification. Empirical results from Lukatela and Turvey (1990) and Perfetti, Bell, and Delaney (1988), among many others, also have helped make the case that phonology plays a role in skilled readers' identification of words.

There is also much research consistent with an alternative view on this question, that phonology mediates word identification only for low frequency words with regular spelling patterns (Paap and Noel, 1991; Seidenberg, Waters, Barnes and Tanenhaus, 1984). This alter-native conclusion conforms with Dual Route Theory (Coltheart, 1978), which assumes that word identification takes place along the faster of two mechanisms, one that involves the conversion of letters to phonemes prior to word identification and one that 'looks up' the word on the basis of its spelling.

Given these different conclusions concerning the details of word identification, it is important to get clear on the consensus that exists. On all accounts, the connections between written units – letters and strings of letters – and speech units (phonemes) are activated during word identification. The only question is how often this activation actually produces word identification. The consensus ranges from quite often (low frequency words) to very often (virtually all words). (See Berent and Perfetti, 1995, for a model based on separate cycles of consonant and vowel phonology that reconciles these differences.) Thus, regardless of the details that bring about word identification, all accounts are consistent with the possibility that phonological information is activated *as part of word reading*. That is, even when phonology does not 'mediate' identification, the phonological form of the word is retrieved as a part of the identification process. As Perfetti and Zhang (1995) have put it, phonology, like meaning, is a *constituent* of identification. Especially interesting in this respect is recent evidence that this retrieval of phonological word forms may be universal across writing systems (Perfetti, Zhang and Berent, 1992; Perfetti and Zhang, 1995).

Support for this universality hypothesis is evidence on reading Chinese, which is usually (although not entirely accurately), believed to be a writing system based on a logographic principle; i.e., basic units in the writing system correspond to word meanings rather than to speech units. In fact it has been common to assume that reading Chinese is strictly a process of print-to-meaning, with no role for phonology. The research, however, reveals a different picture. In a series of studies using different word processing tasks, Perfetti and Zhang (1995) have found that the phonological forms of written Chinese words are activated even when the subject is required to do only semantic processing. What Perfetti and Zhang called the *word identification reflex*, the retrieval of a phonological word form as part of word identification, occurs in Chinese as well as English.

Finally, it is important to note that the research consensus on the role of phonology in skilled reading extends to comprehension. Although much of the research has used methods that focus on the reading of single words, research requiring the reading of texts also provides evidence for phonological processes (see Perfetti, Zhang and Berent, 1992). As the phonological forms of words are activated, the evidence suggests, they become part of what the reader uses to remember and comprehend the text. Given phonology's importance in supporting comprehension, it would be especially convenient that this phonology is activated automatically as part of ordinary word reading, just as the research suggests.

Thus far, I have reviewed evidence that points to basic characteristics of skilled reading. Skill in reading involves reading words rather than skipping them; it involves context-free word reading skill; and it involves phonology. Context is used for higher-level processes of meaning interpretation rather than for word identification. The final section addresses how this skill comes about. What is it that must be learned by a child in order to become a skilled reader?

Successful Readers Learn how their Writing System Works

The central fact for learning to read is that a child must learn a writing system, specifically how the writing system encodes his or her language (see Perfetti and Zhang, 1996). Learning to read is often defined in other terms, such as learning to 'get meaning from print'. This meaning-getting idea is not wrong, but it is incomplete. It highlights the *goal* of learning to read – to get meaning – while ignoring *what*, exactly, is to be learned. Whatever else learning to read is, it is a kind of learning. Children do not need to learn that language has meaning; they do not have to learn how to use context to figure out meanings. They are well practised in these things in the uses they have made of language before they come to school. What they need to learn is what is new for them as they encounter reading: the print forms that carry the meaning of the language they already know. Thus, the new thing to be learned is the writing system. How does the child's writing system work?

Writing systems differ just as languages do. However, while the child seems to know implicitly (and biologically) the principles of language design prior to acquiring spoken language (Pinker, 1984), there appears to be no parallel case to make for writing systems. As products of human invention, they vary in how they work. A child learning to read English, Italian, Hungarian, and Korean learns an alphabetic writing system, in which graphic units associate with phonemes; to learn to read Japanese Kana is to learn a syllabary system, in which graphic units correspond to syllables; to learn to read Arabic, Hebrew, and Persian (Farsi) is to learn a modified alphabetic system in which consonants are more reliably represented than are vowels. Finally, the case that most contrasts with English and other alphabetic orthographies is Chinese, which is usually said to be a logographic system; i.e., one in which the basic principle is morphological: The writing system provides units that correspond to meanings (morphemes) rather than to phonemes or syllables. This standard story of Chinese is misleading, however, because there is actually a considerable amount of syllable-based phonology in the writing system (DeFrancis, 1989).

Whether the child will learn an alphabetic or logographic system, or no system at all, is a matter of cultural and national traditions. It is interesting that even the mere possibility of writing systems may not be part of the natural language endowment. The design of (spoken) languages may be universal, the design of writing systems appears not to be. Nevertheless, there is an important fact about writing systems that is easy to overlook, especially when Chinese is treated as if it were strictly a meaning-based system. All writing systems, even Chinese, make some reference to speech. As DeFrancis (1989) has argued, no full writing system has ever evolved to be based only on a mapping of written units to meanings. The implications of this fact are important: Writing systems have developed to represent speech. The only differences among them are (1) which units of speech are represented in the basic units of the writing system (phonemes or syllables), and (2) to what extent a meaning-based principle exists to compete with the speech-based principle. This second difference amounts to the question of how reliably speech units are represented by units of the writing system.

The alphabetic principle

Reading in an alphabetic orthography requires the child to learn the alphabetic principle one way or another. But the alphabetic principle is difficult, as indicated by the lateness and uniqueness of its discovery by the Phoenicians and Greeks. Its discovery (or invention) lagged far behind the writing systems that provided symbols merely for objects and meanings (Gelb, 1952). It should not be surprising then, as Gleitman and Rozin (1977) noted, that learners might have some trouble in 'replicating' this discovery.

Phonological awareness

An obstacle for learners of the alphabetic principle is that young children are likely to have only dim awareness of the phonological structure of their language. Because phonemes, especially stop consonants, are abstractions over highly variable acoustic events, they are not readily accessible as discrete speech segments. The child learning to read an alphabetic writing system needs to discover the alphabetic principle, but may lack at least half of what is needed. Letters must be associated with phonemes, but the child may not have an adequate representation of phonemes.[3]

[3]   The child also may have no advance knowledge about how a writing system might map phonological or even acoustic properties of the language. Rozin, Bressman and Taft (1974), for example, found that many preschool children could not perform their *mow–motorcycle* test, which asked children which of two printed words corresponded to each of two spoken words, 'mow' and 'motorcycle'. Successful performance on

This assumption that children have inadequate explicit representations of phonemes (phonemic 'awareness') has been well established. Earlier studies by Liberman, Shankweiler, Fischer, and Carter (1974) that found failure among 4- and 5-year-old children in a tapping task – tap once with a stick for each sound in a short word – were followed by a number of studies that confirmed the general inability of many pre-literate children to demonstrate awareness of phonemes in various tasks. More important, studies began to show a relationship between phonemic awareness and learning to read (Fox and Routh, 1976; Lundberg, Olofsson and Wall, 1980; Stanovich, Cunningham and Cramer, 1984; Tunmer, Herriman and Nesdale, 1988). The literature demonstrating the details of this relationship has become substantial (see Rieben and Perfetti, 1991, and Brady and Shankweiler, 1991, for collections of research).

The question raised by the correlation between phonemic awareness and learning to read is whether the first is a necessary cause of the second. The evidence of training studies (Bradley and Bryant, 1983; Treiman and Baron, 1983; Vellutino and Scanlon, 1991) gives some support to the causality conclusion, as do longitudinal studies using cross-lag correlations (Mann, 1991; Perfetti, Beck, Bell and Hughes, 1987). At least some phonological knowledge functionally mediates learning how to read in an alphabetic writing system.

Nevertheless, it seems clear that literacy itself is necessary for the development of a full-blown phonemic awareness. Studies of adult illiterates (Morais, Cary, Alegria, and Bertelson, 1979; Morais, Bertelson, Cary, and Alegria, 1986) found that adults who had not learned to read were very weak in tasks requiring analysis of phonemic structure, although they did much better at syllable-level and rhyming tasks. Such results suggest the limited level of phonological awareness that can be developed outside of literacy contexts. Indeed, although there are many opportunities for oral language use to promote rhyming and syllabic ability, there is little outside of literacy contexts that can serve to draw attention to the existence of phonemes.

---

this task requires not awareness of phonemes, but merely the idea that acoustic length might correspond to visual length or number of letters. Lundberg and Torneus (1978) reported in Sweden, where reading instruction does not begin until 8, even 6-year-old children performed inconsistently on the *mow–motorcycle* test.

The consensus from the research is that the relationship between phonemic awareness and learning to read is not one-directional but reciprocal. Perfetti et al. (1987) found that, prior to instruction, a simple ability to synthesize phonemes into syllables predicted progress in first-grade reading, whereas an ability to delete the initial or final phonemes from syllables did not; instead, the deletion performance, a more analytic ability, was initially predicted by progress in learning to read, and, as it developed with literacy gains, in turn, predicted further progress in reading. Such results strongly suggest that for the more analytic phonemic abilities there is a dynamic and reciprocal relationship, in which phonemic ability is first promoted through literacy acquisition and which then enables further gains in literacy.

It is important to be clear about the implications of the research on phonemic awareness. The fact that literacy affects phonemic awareness as well as vice versa does not negate the functional role of knowledge of phonemes in learning to read. It rather reflects the invisibility of phonemic structures, i.e. the fact that specific phonemes are not a salient part of the perceptual experience of hearing words. Moreover, this lack of visibility can be compounded in the reading situation, which requires the child to coordinate temporally represented phonemes with spatially represented print. Good literacy instruction makes phonemes more visible while it promotes their mapping to printed symbols. The research on the role of phonological awareness in reading has two general implications for reading instruction. First it implies that some forms of phonological awareness instruction can be part of an effective pre-reading programme. In the United States, the National Research Council Report *Preventing Reading Difficulties in Young Children* (National Research Council, 1998) recommends such instruction, for example, simple syllable and phoneme blending activities, as part of American kindergarten classes. Second, the fact that reading and more sophisticated (analytic) phonemic awareness develop in tandem implies that phonological awareness instruction can be effectively linked to initial literacy instruction in the first grade.

Effective learning

There is more to learning to read than gaining phonological awareness. It may be modest progress to replace a misconception, e.g., whole language, with an exaggeration, even one based on a solid research-based principle such as phonological awareness. It is not, in my view, phonological awareness itself, but learning how the writing system works that deserves the focus of beginning reading instruction. Phonological awareness is part of that learning to the extent that all writing systems depend on speech. Awareness of phonemes is part of that learning for alphabetic systems. The function of this awareness, however, is to support the learning of the orthographic-to-speech mappings that underpin the writing system. To learn to read, the child must acquire a range of connections between print forms and speech forms. These connections, supported by phonological sensitivity, are critical factors in reading acquisition (Bradley and Bryant, 1983; Ehri and Sweet, 1991; Juel, Griffith and Gough, 1986; Share and Stanovich, 1995; Tunmer, Herriman and Nesdale, 1988).

The practical questions of teaching reading can become complex when competing goals are juggled. Certainly, it is important to cultivate the child's developing interest in learning to read – to build on the child's 'emerging literacy' (Sulzby, 1985). It is critical to give meaning a central role. And it is important to continue to strengthen the child's oral language expression and comprehension. If all these are seen as 'alternative approaches' or as alternating emphases, it adds greatly to a teacher's burden. If they are viewed as interlocking parts of learning to read, with learning how the writing system works as the focused goal, that eases the burden.

Conclusion: What about Comprehension?

I have argued that four well-established and important classes of research results challenge misconceptions and inform reading instruction. I appear, however, to have ignored comprehension. The reason is not a lack of clear research on comprehension. Indeed, models of text comprehension (Kintsch, 1988), studies of goal-directed reading and inferences (Trabasso and van den Broek, 1985), studies of comprehension monitoring (Baker, 1979; 1985; Baker and Anderson, 1982) – to mention only a few of many – have contributed greatly to understanding of reading processes. But these comprehension discoveries either have been well disseminated into educational thinking or have only the vaguest of implications, or both. They deserve attention in a fuller account of reading, but not in a focused search for critical results.

The four research results discussed in this chapter deserve focused attention because (1) they converge on clear principles of reading pedagogy, and (2) they appear to be under represented in the education of reading teachers. They do not, in my view, point to a particular method of teaching. However, they do point to a general goal of reading education that can be met in a variety of ways that give a central place to learning about written words. This general goal is that children learn how their writing system works. This means, for alphabetic writing systems, making sure they learn the alphabetic principle, something that requires some attention to fostering students' phonemic awareness.

The other basic facts I have stressed support the importance of this conclusion. There is no shortcut to reading words. Words are read more than skipped, and context doesn't alter this fact much. Besides, an emphasis on context is easily misplaced. Children learn to use context readily, even when they are not good at reading. Helping students develop text problem solving skills, such as using contexts to figure out interpretations, intentions, conclusions, etc., is a good idea. But getting good at word identification is an important goal in setting the stage for the successful use of such comprehension strategies.

Because it turns out that phonology is so pervasive in skilled word reading, it is counterproductive to think of phonology antagonistically. It is a central fact of ordinary word identification. Its use originates in a strong connection that is learned between the written forms of words and their pronunciations.

Finally, it is interesting to consider again the case of Chinese. As I noted, Chinese reading involves more phonology than previously assumed. Full writing systems build on speech, not on meanings only. Especially interesting is the fact that Chinese education acknowledges the value of alphabetic reading. Chinese students start out not with characters but with an alphabetic script (pin yin). There is systematic instruction over the first eight weeks of school in letter–sound correspondences. A Chinese student masters the reading of this alphabetic script and then moves on to characters (which are first presented above pin yin spellings). The only purpose this pin yin stage serves is to help the student later learn to read his or her own script. In effect, Chinese students learn a system like English (but more regular) just to make their own system easier. This emphasis on letter–phoneme learning where it is, ultimately, not necessary is in striking contrast to its avoidance in the training of English-language teachers. One would imagine that because the alphabetic principle is necessary rather than merely convenient in the reading of English, teaching it – in whatever manner – should be the prime goal of early reading instruction. Comprehension is not sacrificed by an intelligent approach to this goal.

References

Baker, L. (1979) Comprehension monitoring: Identifying and coping with text confusions. *Journal of Reading Behavior, 11*, 365–74.

Baker, L. (1985) Differences in the standards used by college students to evaluate their comprehension of expository prose. *Reading Research Quarterly, 20*, 297–313.

Baker, L., and Anderson, R. I. (1982) Effects of inconsistent information on text processing: Evidence for comprehension monitoring. *Reading Research Quarterly, 22*, 281–94.

Berent, I., and Perfetti, C. A. (1995) A rose is a REEZ: The two-cycles model of phonology assembly in reading English. *Psychological Review, 102*, 146–84.

Bradley, L., and Bryant, P. E. (1983) Categorizing sounds and learning to read – a causal connection. *Nature, 301*, 419–21.

Brady, S. A., and Shankweiler, D. (eds) (1991) *Phonological Processes in Literacy: A Tribute to Isabelle Y. Liberman.* Hillsdale, NJ: Lawrence Erlbaum Associates.

Coltheart, M. (1978) Lexical access in simple reading tasks. In G. Underwood (ed.), *Strategies of Information Processing,* New York: Academic Press, pp. 151–216.

DeFrancis, J. (1989) *Visible Speech: The Diverse Oneness of Writing Systems.* Honolulu: University of Hawaii.

Ehri, L. C., and Sweet, J. (1991) Fingerpoint-reading of memorized text: What enables beginners to process the print. *Reading Research Quarterly, 26*, 442–62.

Ehrlich, S. F., and Rayner, K. (1981) Contextual effects on word perception and eye movements during reading. *Journal of Verbal Learning and Verbal Behavior, 20*, 641–55.

Fox, B., and Routh, D. K. (1976) Phonemic analysis and synthesis as word-attack skills. *Journal of Educational Psychology, 68*, 70–4.

Gelb, I. J. (1952) *A Study of Writing*. Chicago: University of Chicago Press.

Glaser, R. (1976) Components of a psychology of instruction: Toward a science of design. *Review of Educational Research, 46,* 1–24.

Glaser, R. (1982) Instructional psychology: Past, present, and future. *American Psychologist, 37,* 292–305.

Gleitman, L. R., and Rozin, P. (1977) The structure and acquisition of reading, I: Relations between orthographies and the structure of language. In A. S. Reber and D. L. Scarborough (eds), *Toward a Psychology of Reading: The Proceedings of the CUNY Conferences,* Hillsdale, NJ: Lawrence Erlbaum Associates (distributed by Wiley), pp. 1–54.

Juel, C., Griffith, P. L., and Gough, P. B. (1986) Acquisition of literacy: A longitudinal study of children in first and second grade. *Journal of Educational Psychology, 78,* 243–55.

Just, M. A., and Carpenter, P. A. (1987) *The Psychology of Reading and Language Comprehension*. Boston: Allyn and Bacon.

Just, M. A., Carpenter, P. A., and Masson, M. E. J. (1982) *What Eye Fixations Tell Us about Speed Reading and Skimming* (eyelab tech. report). Pittsburgh: Carnegie-Mellon University.

Kintsch, W. (1988) The role of knowledge in discourse processing: A construction–integration model. *Psychological Review, 95,* 163–82.

Liberman, I. Y., Shankweiler, D., Fischer, F. W., and Carter, B. (1974) Explicit syllable and phoneme segmentation in the young child. *Journal of Experimental Child Psychology, 18,* 201–12.

Lukatela, G., and Turvey, M. T. (1990) Automatic and pre-lexical computation of phonology in visual word identification. *European Journal of Cognitive Psychology, 2,* 325–44.

Lundberg, I., Olofsson, A., and Wall, S. (1980) Reading and spelling skills in the first school years predicted from phonemic awareness skills in kindergarten. *Scandinavian Journal of Psychology, 21,* 159–73.

Lundberg, I., and Torneus, M. (1978) Nonreaders' awareness of the basic relationship between spoken and written words. *Journal of Experimental Child Psychology, 25,* 404–12.

Mann, V. A. (1991) Phonological abilities: Effective predictors of future reading ability. In L. Rieben and C. A. Perfetti (eds), *Learning to Read: Basic Research and its Implications,* Hillsdale, NJ: Lawrence Erlbaum Associates, pp. 121–33.

Morais, J., Bertelson, P., Cary, L., and Alegria, J. (1986) Literacy training and speech segmentation. *Cognition, 24,* 45–64.

Morais, J., Cary, L., Alegria, J., and Bertelson, P. (1979) Does awareness of speech as a sequence of phones arise spontaneously? *Cognition, 7,* 323–31.

National Research Council (1988) *Preventing Reading Difficulties in Young Children*. Washington, DC: National Academy of Sciences Press.

Paap, K. R., and Noel, R. W. (1991) Dual-route models of print and sound: Still a good horse race. *Psychological Research*, *53*, 13–24.

Perfetti, C. A., Beck, I., Bell, L., and Hughes, C. (1987) Phonemic knowledge and learning to read are reciprocal: A longitudinal study of first grade children. *Merrill-Palmer Quarterly*, *33*, 283–319.

Perfetti, C. A., Bell, L., and Delaney, S. (1988) Automatic phonetic activation in silent word reading: Evidence from backward masking. *Journal of Memory and Language*, *27*, 59–70.

Perfetti, C. A., Goldman, S. R., and Hogaboam, T. W. (1979) Reading skill and the identification of words in discourse context. *Memory and Cognition*, *7*, 273–82.

Perfetti, C. A., and Roth, S. F. (1981) Some of the interactive processes in reading and their role in reading skill. In A. M. Lesgold and C. A. Perfetti (eds), *Interactive Processes in Reading*, Hillsdale, NJ: Lawrence Erlbaum Associates, pp. 269–97.

Perfetti, C. A., and Zhang, S. (1995) The universal word identification reflex. In D.L. Medin (ed.), *The Psychology of Learning and Motivation*, vol. 33. San Diego: Academic Press.

Perfetti, C. A., and Zhang, S. (1996) What it means to learn to read. In M. F. Graves, B. M. Taylor, and P. van den Broek (eds), *The First R: Children's Right to Read*, New York: Teachers College Press, pp. 37–60.

Perfetti, C. A., Zhang, S., and Berent, I. (1992) Reading in English and Chinese: Evidence for a 'universal' phonological principle. In R. Frost and L. Katz (eds), *Orthography, Phonology, Morphology, and Meaning*, Amsterdam: North-Holland, pp. 227–48.

Pinker, S. (1984) *Language Learnability and Language Development*. Cambridge, MA: Harvard University Press.

Rayner, K., and Pollatsek, A. (1989) *The Psychology of Reading*. Englewood Cliffs, NJ: Prentice-Hall.

Rieben, L., and Perfetti, C. A. (eds) (1991) *Learning to Read: Basic Research and its Implications*. Hillsdale, NJ: Lawrence Erlbaum Associates.

Rozin, P., Bressman, B., and Taft, M. (1974) Do children understand the basic relationship between speech and writing? The Mow-Motorcycle test. *Journal of Reading Behavior*, *6*, 327–34.

Seidenberg, M. S., Waters, G. S., Barnes, M. A., and Tanenhaus, M. K. (1984) When does irregular spelling or pronunciation influence word recognition? *Journal of Verbal Learning and Verbal Behavior*, *23*, 383–404.

Share, D. L., and Stanovich, K. E. (1995) Cognitive processes in early reading development: Accommodating individual differences into a model of acquisition. *Issues in Education*, *1*, 1–57.

Stanovich, K. E. (1980) Toward an interactive–compensatory model of individual differences in the development of reading fluency. *Reading Research Quarterly*, *16*, 32–71.

Stanovich, K. E. (1981) Attentional and automatic context effects in reading. In A. M. Lesgold and C. A. Perfetti (eds), *Interactive Processes in Reading*, Hillsdale, NJ: Lawrence Erlbaum Associates, pp. 241–67.

Stanovich, K. E., Cunningham, A. E., and Cramer, B. (1984) Assessing phonological awareness in kindergarten children: Issues of task comparability. *Journal of Experimental Child Psychology*, *38*, 175–90.

Stanovich, K. E., and West, R. F. (1981) The effect of sentence context on on-going word recognition: Tests of a two-process theory. *Journal of Experimental Psychology: Human Perception and Performance*, *7*, 658–72.

Sulzby, E. (1985) Children's emergent reading of favorite storybooks: A developmental study. *Reading Research Quarterly*, *20*, 458–81.

Trabasso, T., and van den Broek, P. (1985) Causal thinking and the representation of narrative events. *Journal of Memory and Language*, *24*, 612–30.

Treiman, R., and Baron, J. (1983) Phonemic-analysis training helps children benefit from spelling–sound rules. *Memory and Cognition*, *11*, 382–9.

Tunmer, W. E., Herriman, M. L., and Nesdale, A. R. (1988) Metalinguistic abilities and beginning reading. *Reading Research Quarterly*, *23*, 134–58.

Van Orden, G. C., Pennington, B., and Stone, G. (1990) Word identification in reading and the promise of subsymbolic psycholinguistics. *Psychological Review*, *97*, 488–522.

Vellutino, F. R., and Scanlon, D. M. (1991) The effects of instructional bias on word identification. In L. Rieben and C. A. Perfetti (eds), *Learning to Read: Basic Research and its Implications*, Hillsdale, NJ: Lawrence Erlbaum Associates, pp. 189–203.

Yuill, N., and Oakhill, J. (1991) *Children's Problems in Text Comprehension: An Experimental Investigation*. Cambridge: Cambridge University Press.

Chapter Four

Constructing Meaning: The Role of Decoding

PHILIP B. GOUGH AND SEBASTIAN WREN

The idea that reading is a process of constructing meaning is gaining popularity among reading educators. This is a useful metaphor. It reminds us of the fact that all that exists on the printed page is dried ink, so that meaning must emerge in the mind of the reader. It also suggests that the reader actively contributes to this process, that what he or she knows and thinks will contribute to that meaning.

But as a description of reading, the metaphor is obviously incomplete. For one thing, it tells us nothing of *how* meaning is constructed. In particular, it makes no mention of the role of the printed word in constructing meaning. (Indeed, it does not even offer a hint as to how reading might differ from other ways of constructing meaning, like thinking.)

The reason, we suspect, is that advocates of this view (largely proponents of Whole Language) would de-emphasize the role of decoding (word recognition) in the reading process. They tend to believe that print is only one of several cueing systems which the reader makes use of in constructing meaning. The standard view (Goodman, 1993; Goodman, 1996) has it that there are three cueing systems, the semantic, the syntactic, and the graphophonic. As Routman (1988, p. 41) diagrams it, the reader makes use of the three cueing systems in equal proportion.

Empirical support for this position can be found in a large body of research on *miscue analysis* (e.g., Goodman and Burke, 1973), that is, the qualitative and quantitative description of oral reading errors.

What we take to be the central result of this research is that oral reading errors (miscues) are often syntactically and semantically appropriate, even though they may depart wildly from the text, indicating that they must have been derived from the syntactic and semantic cueing systems.

This is important evidence; in fact, it provides the cornerstone of research support for the Whole Language position. But it should be noted that it depends upon the existence of miscues. To obtain miscues, the miscue analyst will routinely ask the student to read a passage which is challenging (i.e., slightly too difficult) for him or her. This led us to wonder how common miscues are among college students reading college-level materials.

The Miscues of Skilled Readers

As part of a larger study of the miscues of skilled readers (Gough, Wren, Watts, Deneen-Bell, and Lee, in preparation), we asked 101 students in introductory psychology to read aloud the first page of Ken Goodman's *Phonics Phacts* (Goodman, 1993, p. 1); reprinted in figure 4.1). We recorded their miscues (defined as an uncorrected departure from text; if the reader corrected his or her error, we did not consider it a miscue), and timed their reading of the passage with a stopwatch.

On average, our 101 students read the 259 words in 106 seconds, an oral reading rate of approximately 147 words per minute. The 101 readers made a total of 223 miscues. The nature of those miscues is summarized in table 4.1. The lion's share of them (76 per cent) were substitution errors (e.g., the student read 'reach' when the word was *read*). Of these substitution errors, the vast majority were orthographically similar to the target (e.g., 'word' for *work*, 'phonetics' or 'phonemics' for *phonics*, or 'definition' for *definitive*). Orthographically dissimilar words (e.g., 'anyone' for *everybody*) constituted only 4 per cent of the substitution errors (and 3 per cent of all errors). The next most common error was omission, accounting for 16 per cent of all miscues; the remaining 8 per cent were insertions.

We also categorized the miscues as meaning-preserving or meaning-changing. We were surprised to see (given previous miscue research) that nearly half (48 per cent) of the miscues were meaning-

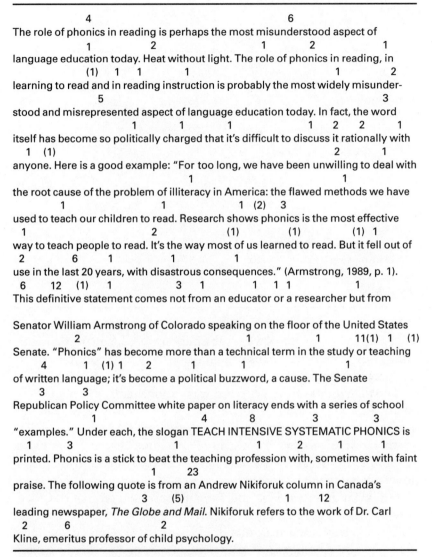

(Numerals in parentheses over spaces between words indicate the number of insertions made at that point in the passage. Errors made on the reference '(Armstrong, 1989, p. 1)' and on the proper name 'Nikiforuk' were not counted for this study.)

Figure 4.1 Reprint of the first page of Ken Goodman's *Phonics Phacts* (Goodman, 1993, p. 1); numbers indicate the total number of miscues made by 101 subjects on each word in the passage

Table 4.1 Summary of the nature of the miscues made by 101 students
reading aloud the first page of Ken Goodman's *Phonics Phacts*

Type of miscue	Number	Percent of total	Percent of class
Substitution:	**169**	**76%**	
Meaning Changing:	107	48%	63%
Meaning Consistent:	62	28%	37%
Omission	**36**	**16%**	
Meaning Changing:	6	3%	17%
Meaning Consistent:	30	13%	83%
Insertion:	**18**	**8%**	
Meaning Changing:	5	2%	28%
Meaning Consistent:	13	6%	72%
Total Miscues:	**223**		

changing. Most of these were substitutions (e.g., 'equator' for *educator*, 'insensitive' for *intensive*); omissions and insertions tended not to change meaning.

The number of errors per word was exponentially distributed (see figure 4.2) with a mode of 0; 167 of the 259 words were read correctly by all 101 students. Only 92 words were ever misread, and 54 of these were misread by no more than one reader. Four words (*definitive* 12, *or* 11, *an* 23, and *work* 12) accounted for the majority of the remaining miscues.

But what impressed us more than the quality of our readers' miscues was their quantity: there were very few of them. Our 101 college students each read aloud 259 words (we ignored the reference cited by Goodman – '(Armstrong, 1989, p. 1)' – because many of our readers chose not to read it aloud, and *Nikiforuk*, as we don't know its correct pronunciation), a total of 26,159 words. They made a total of 223 miscues, an error rate of 0.0086. Looked at positively, they correctly named 25,797 of the 26,020 words, an accuracy rate of 0.9914. The distribution of their errors is presented in figure 4.3. It shows a nearly exponential distribution, with the vast majority of students making 0 or 1 errors; the worst made 11 (0.04).

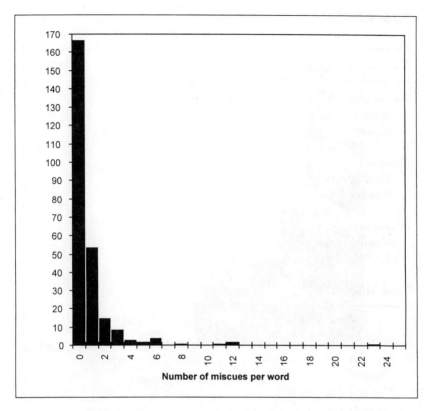

Figure 4.2   Number of miscues per word in the first page of Ken Goodman's *Phonics Phacts*

It appears that college students reading college-level material make very few miscues. Clearly, we could induce more miscues by using more demanding material. But as we see it, this would be inauthentic. The fact seems to be that skilled readers, reading a text like those they usually read, do so very accurately.

How are we to account for this amazing accuracy? (We acknowledge that some of it may be attributed to Ken Goodman, who writes very readably, but we have obtained similar results with a variety of texts.) Supporters of Whole Language would presumably argue that it was the skilful integration of the multiple cueing systems which led to this success. In particular, they would downplay the role of print in this process. As Ken Goodman (1993, p. 97) describes it, 'The

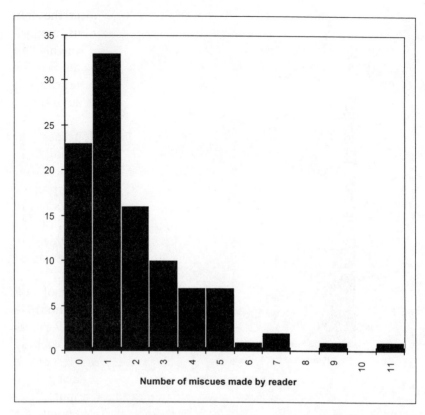

Figure 4.3   Number of miscues made by each of 101 students reading the
first page of Ken Goodman's *Phonics Phacts*

brain, the organ of human intelligence, is engaged in far more than
recognizing known entities. It actively seeks meaning. It controls the
sensory organs and uses them to select and sample from available
input, print in the case of reading.'

Thus the Whole Language advocate underplays the recognition
of letters and words ('known entities') in constructing meaning. As
Goodman (1996, p. 91) writes, 'An *efficient* reader uses only enough
information from the published text to be *effective*.' This led us
next to wonder how well readers would recognize words if the 'information from the published text' was reduced.

In previous research (e.g., Gough, Alford and Holley-Wilcox,
1981; Gough, 1983) we have *completely* eliminated the text. We have

provided the prior context and asked readers to predict the next word. In the case of function words (articles, conjunctions, prepositions, auxiliary verbs, and pronouns, which account for roughly half the words in running text), readers can correctly anticipate roughly 0.4 of them. With content words (adjectives, nouns, and verbs, which account for the remaining half), our subjects could manage only 0.1, and the mode was 0.

This condition is clearly too extreme. Goodman concedes that readers do 'select and sample' from the print, so that depriving them of all print is unfair. But what would give them a fair shot? If we knew what the reader would 'select and sample', we could provide that and see if the other letters are irrelevant (as Goodman's model would predict). But we obviously cannot anticipate this, so we decided to examine the effect of two graphophonic cues which we believed (along with many teachers) must be useful cues: the word's first letter, and its length.

As part of a broader examination of the predictability of text (Gough, Wren, Watts, Deneen-Bell, and Larson, in preparation) we asked 60 readers to anticipate (predict) each of the first 119 words of Ray Monk's (1996) fascinating biography of Bertrand Russell by typing it into a computer. The computer recorded their responses, applauding them if their response was correct, and replacing it by the correct word in the event they were wrong; the computer also provided all punctuation. Thus the reader had, at every point, the entire preceding context (i.e., both the syntactic and semantic cueing systems) to aid him or her in anticipating the next word. Half of our readers were also provided with the first letter of that word; orthogonally, half of our readers were given the length of the word. Thus one-fourth (15) of our readers had only the prior context, one-fourth had the prior context plus the first letter of the word to be predicted, one-fourth had the prior context plus the word's length, and the remaining fourth had the prior context plus the word's first letter and its length.

The proportions of correct identifications in each of the four conditions are presented in table 4.2, divided into content words and function words.

As we have repeatedly observed, function words were more identifiable (across all conditions, mean = 0.51) than content words (0.23), and this held true in each of the four conditions as well.

Table 4.2 The proportions of correct identifications in each of the cue conditions (no cue, first letter cue, word length cue, and both word length and first letter cues)

Function Words

	No length hint given	Length hint given	Average
First letter hint given	0.57	0.69	0.63
No first letter hint given	0.34	0.43	0.38
Average	0.455	0.56	0.51

Content Words

	No length hint given	Length hint given	Average
First letter hint given	0.25	0.40	0.325
No first letter hint given	0.11	0.17	0.14
Average	0.18	0.285	0.23

Without any cues except prior context, our students correctly predicted 0.34 of the function words and 0.11 of the content words, a result similar to what we have previously reported. But with both content and function words, adding the first letter significantly increased their identification, by about 20 per cent. Providing the word's length increased its predictability another 10 per cent. (While we collected no data to support this, our impression was that providing the target's length greatly increased the latency of the subject's guess: while it increased accuracy, it retarded reading rate.) Yet even with both cues, the readers averaged only 70 per cent correct identification of function words, and only 40 per cent of the content words, far short of the 99.14 per cent they averaged (across all words) when given the full word.

It might be objected that the real reader not only has prior context but following context as well. This is a reasonable objection; had we provided this information, correct identifications would surely have increased (cf. Potter, Stiefbold and Moryadas, 1998). But using later context to identify a preceding word must retard reading; it is far easier to recognize a word than to reconstruct it. It would seem that the most useful information we could have provided would be the letters of the word to be identified.

These results suggest to us that the reader relies on the printed word far more than Goodman and other advocates of Whole Language would lead us to believe. Our results seem to indicate that the graphophonic system plays a central role in constructing meaning. How else are we to explain why the speed and accuracy of reading isolated words (and even *pseudowords*) correlates almost perfectly with reading comprehension in the early grades (Gough, Hoover and Peterson, 1996), and still substantially in college students (Cunningham, Stanovich and Wilson, 1990)? How else are we to explain why an inability to decode is found in the vast majority of disabled readers (Rack, Snowling & Olson, 1992)?

We are inclined to agree with Marilyn Adams (1990, p. 105), who asserts that 'the single immutable fact about skillful reading is that it involves relatively complete processing of the individual letters in print'.

Ken Goodman (1993, p. 94) completely disagrees. He holds that this claim was refuted by an experiment conducted by Frederick Gollasch (1980). Gollasch asked seventh-graders and university juniors to read the passage presented in figure 4.4. Half the readers in each group were told in advance that there were errors in the text; the other half were not. After reading the text, all readers were asked to write down the story, and list any errors they had noticed in the text.

There are six errors in the passage. According to Gollasch, the college students found more errors (42 per cent) than did the seventh-graders (32 per cent). But in both groups, those readers who had been warned that the passage contained errors reported only slightly more than three (none found all six), while those who had not been informed found even fewer. Evidently only about half of the errors

---

The Boat in the Basement

A woman was building a boat in
her basement. When she had finished the
the boot, she discovered that it was
too big to go though the door. So he
had to take the boat a part to get
it out. She should of planned ahead.

Figure 4.4   Passage used by Gollasch in a study of error identification

were noticed. Importantly, despite the presence of these errors the readers still understood the story; as Goodman puts it, 'They all got the meaning. . . .'

Goodman's reasoning seems to be that since the readers did not report the errors, those errors did not affect their reading. We wondered whether this was correct. So we decided to compare the reading times on Gollasch's error-filled passage with reading times on an error-free ('clean') version of the same text.

We (Gough, Wren, Watts, Deneen-Bell, and Lee, in preparation) asked 65 undergraduates to read the Gollasch passage, and 65 others to read an error-free version of the same passage. The passage was presented line by line on a computer screen. The subject advanced from one line to the next by pressing the space bar and the computer recorded how long the reader spent on each line. When the reader finished the passage, he or she was given a copy of the Gollasch version of the text and asked to indicate any errors he or she had noticed. (We did not bother to ask for a retelling, assuming that our readers, like Gollasch's, would 'all get the meaning'.)

Our students reading Gollasch's passage noticed even fewer errors (mean 1.56) than his did, as exhibited in table 4.3. But our reading-time data (figure 4.5) indicated that the errors did have an effect on the reading process. While readers of the Gollasch passage read the error-free title and first line of the passage slightly faster than the controls, on each line containing an error they were slower.

It might be objected that these differences could be attributed to those readers who noticed the errors. To eliminate this possibility, we examined the reading times on each line only of those readers who

Table 4.3   Number and proportion of readers who reported each error in the Gollasch text

	Number of readers	Proportion of readers
THE THE line	4	6%
BOAT BOOT line	40	59%
TH(R)OUGH line	4	6%
(S)HE line	30	44%
A( )PART line	14	21%
SHOULD HAVE/OF line	10	15%

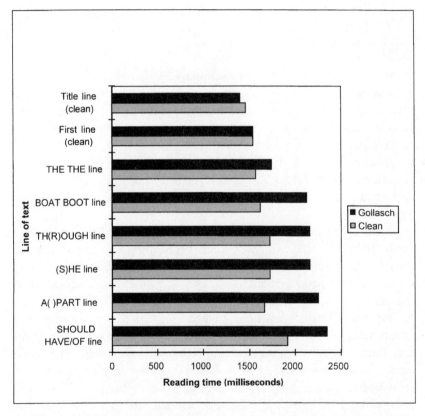

Figure 4.5   Comparison of reading times on each line of text between subjects reading the 'Gollasch' version and those reading the 'clean' version of the text

Table 4.4   A comparison of the reading times on each line of text, comparing only the reading times of those readers who failed to report each error with the reading times for subjects reading the same line of the error-free passage

	Clean	*Gollasch*	*N in Gollasch condition*
Title line (clean)	1459	1406	68 subjects
First line (clean)	1549	1547	68 subjects
THE THE line	1579	1760	64 subjects
BOAT BOOT line	1625	1742	28 subjects
TH(R)OUGH line	1723	2132	64 subjects
(S)HE line	1723	1942	38 subjects
A( )PART line	1661	2145	54 subjects
SHOULD HAVE/OF line	1916	2256	58 subjects

failed to report that error, and compared them to the reading times for the error-free passage. Again, we compared each difference with any difference observed on the first two lines of the passage (which contained no error in either version). These data are presented in table 4.4.

What we found was that in every case, reading times were greater on the erroneous line than on its error-free counterpart; five of these differences were statistically significant, and the sixth approached significance.

What these results indicate is that, whether or not an error is reported, it slows down the reader. While they still are able to see past (or through) those errors and arrive at a correct interpretation of the story, those errors do make meaning construction more difficult.

We conclude that decoding – word recognition – is an important component of reading. It is important to note that we are not equating reading with decoding. Having recognized the words, the reader must then comprehend them. Thus we see reading as the product of two dissociable factors, decoding and comprehension. If we think of reading (R), decoding (D), and comprehension (C) as variables ranging from 0 to 1, then $R = D \times C$. Both decoding and comprehension are necessary; neither is sufficient. We have defended this Simple View elsewhere (Gough, Hoover and Peterson, 1996; Gough and Tunmer, 1986; Hoover and Gough, 1990), arguing that it provides a very parsimonious description of reading skill and reading disability.[1]

Goodman (1996, p. 61) has likened our view to the pre-Copernican view of astronomy: 'In the pre-Copernican world of understanding reading we thought accurate, rapid letter and/or word recognition was the center of the process and somehow comprehension followed.'

This does not quite describe our view. We do think that word recognition is *a* central process in reading, and that comprehension *usually* follows word recognition. But we concede that there may be occasions on which the comprehension of a word may precede its

---

[1] First, it is clear that the decoding and comprehension can be dissociated. In fact, they can be doubly dissociated: it is easy to find individuals who can decode without comprehending (for example, most of us can decode Italian but understand almost none of it), and even easier to find children who can comprehend without decoding (the typical five-year-old, for example).

Second, we have found that if you measure the two skills separately, their product predicts reading comprehension all but perfectly (Hoover and Gough, 1990).

Third, the Simple View helps us understand the changing relationships between the three variables, R, D and C. For example, the relations between R and D, and R and C, change in a predictable way with development. In the beginning, when what we ask children to read is easily comprehended (i.e., C is close to 1.0), decoding accounts for almost all of the variance in reading comprehension. But as decoding skill increases (and D approaches 1.0), the correlation between R and D decreases, while the correlation between R and C increases (cf. Gough, Hoover, and Peterson, 1996).

It also sharpens our understanding of the relation between D and C. In the general population, D and C are positively correlated. The child who is a good comprehender tends to be a good decoder, and vice versa. But among the reading disabled, the opposite must be the case. Consider a hypothetical reader for whom R = 0.9. If this reader is a good decoder (D = 1.0), then he must be a poor comprehender (C = 0.09). If he is a good comprehender (C = 1.0), then he must be a poor decoder (D = 0.09). Thus the Simple View explains why, among the reading disabled, the correlation between D and C may turn negative (cf. Hoover and Gough, 1990).

recognition. We suspect, however, that this happens only when the word is highly predictable. When this is the case (e.g., when the predictability of a word is 0.93), Ehrlich and Rayner (1981) report that the reader will skip the word about half the time, and that when that word is fixated, the fixation duration is shortened. Still, Zola (1984) has shown that when a predictable word *is* fixated, all of its letters will be examined, for misspelling the word increases its fixation duration.

But as we have noted time and again, few content words are so predictable. Instead, the typical content word is all but completely *un*predictable. Therefore the reader cannot anticipate it, but must simply recognize it. So while we would not deny that word recognition is occasionally 'top-down', we would maintain that with respect to content words, it is primarily 'bottom up'.

Ken Goodman concludes his attack on Marilyn Adams by saying that 'the real world of reading is making sense of print, not recognizing words'. We would conclude that the real world of reading is making sense of print *by* recognizing words. Our results indicate that decoding is far more important than Whole Language advocates would have us believe.

It is widely believed that reading is interactive. There is no question that comprehension is. Comprehension clearly depends on Whole Language's three cueing systems. Context determines the pronunciation (and thus the identity) of polyphonic words like *bow*, it determines the meaning of polysemic words like *foot*, it determines the form class (and thus the syntax) of words like *like*. But what about decoding?

Literally hundreds of studies have shown that context can facilitate the recognition of a word (see Stanovich, 1991). But we believe that its role in word recognition has been greatly exaggerated.

First, context aids poor readers more than good (Nicholson, 1991; Stanovich, 1980), mainly because good readers are so good at reading words in isolation that context cannot help them much.

Second, the effects of context vary inversely with stimulus quality (e.g., Meyer, Schvaneveldt and Ruddy, 1975); the more degraded a word, the greater the effect of context on the recognition of that word. Put more positively, the clearer the print, the less context affects its recognition. So context's effects are minimized when clear print is read in good light.

Third, and most important to our argument, the effect of context varies with the word's predictiveness. The more predictable the target, the greater the effect of context on its recognition. But the less predictable the target, the less the effect of context on its recognition. In fact, Fischler and Bloom (1979) have argued that predictability must be near 0.9 before context can facilitate a word's recognition. The fact is that very few content words reach this level. As we have indicated, the typical (modal) content word is all but completely unpredictable. It would be a waste of the reader's time to try to predict them; he or she is better off simply recognizing them. Thus we are led to believe that the majority of content words are simply read bottom-up.

We conclude that Goodman, Routman, and other advocates of Whole Language are wrong about the role of the graphophonic cueing system. We concede that the semantic and syntactic cueing systems play a central role in comprehension. But with respect to decoding, we contend that their role is very limited. The three cueing systems are certainly equally important to reading, but we contend that they make their contributions to different parts of the reading process: the graphophonic system is far and away the most important cueing system in decoding.

We hope no one will take our results and conclusions as a total indictment of the Whole Language approach to teaching reading, or as an endorsement of intensive, systematic phonics instruction. As we see it, the questions of the importance of decoding to reading, and the role letter–phoneme correspondences play in decoding, are distinct from (and should not be equated or conflated with) the question of how those correspondences should be taught.

While we believe that Whole Language is quite wrong about the role of decoding in constructing meaning, we feel that there is much to be admired about Whole Language instruction. For one thing, we tend to agree with Whole Language advocates that the child learns to read mainly by reading (though we probably disagree about what it is the child learns). Consider once again the Simple View, that reading equals the product of decoding and comprehension. It seems clear to us that the child comes to the task of learning to read with a fairly complete comprehension system. (We are speaking here of native-language learners.) We recognize that there will be large differences among children in this skill: in vocabulary, in background knowledge, etc. (cf. Hart and Risley, 1995). But the vast majority of children entering first grade will have mastered the syntax, semantics, and phonology of their native language better than most college students with two years of courses in that language as a second language. (We recognize that learning to read a language other than the native language offers a different and more difficult challenge.) If the child can already comprehend, then what the child must learn is how to decode.

How do they do this? The basis of decoding skill (in an alphabetic orthography like English) is mastery of the cipher, the system of letter–phoneme correspondences. Knowing that system is not enough; the child must also internalize a great deal of specific lexical information (e.g., that *shoe* rhymes with *moo* not *mow*, that *rough* rhymes with *tough*, not *bough* or *cough*). But Gough and Walsh (1991) have shown that such knowledge cannot be assembled without the cipher; the cipher is the foundation of skilled decoding.

How does the child acquire the cipher? Here we come to the question of the role of phonics. Advocates of phonics believe that the cipher can (some would say must) be installed through direct instruction. We are sceptical: there are too many connections to be taught, and phonics instruction does not always lead to the cipher. There is no doubt that phonics provides a useful tool, for, as we have previously suggested (Gough and Hillinger, 1980), it provides the child with the ability to identify an unfamiliar word. But we would argue that there are three important differences between the rules taught in phonics and the cipher.

First, the rules (if they are such) of the cipher are far more numerous than the rules of phonics. Most phonics programmes attempt to teach the child 80–100 rules. Mastery of the cipher involves hundreds more. If the latter are learned through induction, why not suppose that many (even a majority) of the former might also be mastered in this way?

Second, the rules of the cipher are largely unconscious, while the rules taught in phonics are conscious. What child (or adult, for that matter) can state the rule which tells the reader whether *th* is voiced or not, or when *ch* is pronounced /k/ vs /tʃ/ vs /ʃ/)?

Third, the cipher is applied automatically and swiftly, whereas the rules of phonics are applied only with conscious effort. The difference between the skilled reader's rapid and effortless pronunciation of a pseudoword like *spiff* or *clard* and the child's laborious sounding out of a novel word should be obvious to anyone.

How, then, does the child internalize the cipher? In order for the child to internalize the cipher, two things are required. One is phonemic awareness: in order to connect the letters with the phonemes, the child must be aware that the word is composed of phonemes. The other is practice. As we currently see it, what the child must form are connections between letters and phonemes, mediated by hidden units (cf. Plaut, McClelland, Seidenberg and Patterson, 1996). The only way to do that is through experience (i.e., *reading*).

Almost certainly, some phonics instruction is necessary, if only to lead the child to the alphabetic principle (i.e., that printed letters map onto the phonemes of spoken words). Good Whole Language teachers do teach phonics; we don't know how much. But we don't know how much phonics instruction is necessary; we suspect that no one else does, either. In any event, we would argue that phonics instruction may instil the cipher; it does not install it. Instead, the child must induce it: he or she must internalize these correspondences by reading. But reading will lead to this result only if the child has phonemic awareness.

In this connection, we admire Whole Language's integration of reading and writing instruction. We can think of no activity (other than direct instruction) which better promotes phonemic awareness than writing.

We also admire Whole Language's emphasis on engaging the child in authentic tasks; we share their distaste for drills and worksheets. Actually, this principle antedates the Whole Language movement. Bond and Wagner (Bond and Wagner, 1966, pp. 72–3) wrote that 'A child learns to read well only when what he is asked to do seems both useful and vital, both compelling and authentic.'

We also concur with Whole Language that the aim of reading is to make sense of the print. But we obviously do not agree that learners should by taught to do so by relying on the three cueing systems equally. We worry, for example, about the practice of using predictable books, for two reasons. One is that, since we know that children perform better on such books than on novel texts, children's performance on these books may lead the teacher to overestimate the child's ability to deal with novel text. Second, predictable books almost certainly lessen the child's attention to print; moreover, they may lead the child to unrealistic expectations about text.

We conclude that one of the cueing systems is far more important than the others to decoding. Since decoding is necessary (if not sufficient) for constructing meaning, early reading instruction should focus on this skill. Whole Language instruction would be better if it would discard its disdain for print.

References

Adams, M. J. (1990) *Beginning to Read: Thinking and Learning about Print.* Cambridge, MA: MIT Press.

Bond, G. L., and Wagner, E. B. (1996) *Teaching the Child to Read.* New York: Macmillan.

Cunningham, A. E., Stanovich, K. E., and Wilson, M. R. (1990) Cognitive variation in adult college students differing in reading ability. In C. T. H. and B. A. Levy (eds), *Reading and its Development,* New York: Academic Press, pp. 81–128.

Ehrlich, S. F., and Rayner, K. (1981) Contextual effects on word perception and eye movements during reading. *Journal of Verbal Learning and Verbal Behavior, 20,* 641–55.

Fischler, I., and Bloom, P. A. (1979) Automatic and attentional processes in the effects of sentence contexts on word recognition. *Journal of Verbal Learning and Verbal Behavior, 18,* 1–20.

Gollasch, F. V. (1980) *Readers' Perception in Detecting and Processing Embedded Errors in Meaningful Text* (UMI no. AAC 81-07445). Tucson, AZ: University of Arizona.

Goodman, K. S. (1993) *Phonics Phacts.* Portsmouth, NH: Heinemann.

Goodman, K. (1996) *On Reading.* Portsmouth, NH: Heinemann.

Goodman, K. S., and Burke, C. L. (1973) *Theoretically Based Studies of Patterns of Miscues in Oral Reading Performance* (Final Report OEG-0-9-320375-4269). Washington, DC: US Office of Education.

Gough, P. B. (1983) Context, form, and interaction. In K. Rayner (ed.), *Eye Movements in Reading: Perceptual and Language Processes,* New York: Academic Press.

Gough, P. B., Alford, J. A., Jr, and Holley-Wilcox, P. (1981) Words and contexts. In O. J. L. Tzeng and H. Singer (eds), *Perception of Print,* Hillsdale, NJ: Lawrence Erlbaum, pp. 85–102.

Gough, P. B., and Hillinger, M. L. (1980) Learning to read: An unnatural act. *Bulletin of the Orton Society*, 30, 179–96.

Gough, P. B., Hoover, W. A., and Peterson, C. (1996) Some observations on the Simple View of reading. In C. Cornoldi and J. Oakhill (eds), *Reading Comprehension Difficulties*, Hillsdale, NJ: Lawrence Erlbaum.

Gough, P. B., and Tunmer, W. E. (1986) Decoding, reading, and reading disability. *Remedial and Special Education*, 7, 6–10.

Gough, P. B., and Walsh, M. A. (1991) Chinese, Phoenicians, and the orthographic cipher of English. In S. Brady and D. Shankweiler (eds), *Phonological Processes in Literacy*, Hillsdale NJ: Erlbaum.

Gough, P. B., Wren, S., Watts, J., Deneen-Bell, N., and Lee, C. H. The miscues of skilled readers. In preparation.

Gough, P. B., Wren, S., Watts, J., Deneen-Bell, N., and Larson, K. The effect of typographical errors on reading time. In preparation.

Hart, B., and Risley, T. R. (1995) *Meaningful Differences*. Baltimore: Paul H. Brookes.

Hoover, W. A., and Gough, P. B. (1990) The simple view of reading. *Reading and Writing*, 2, 127–60.

Juel, C., Griffith, P. L., and Gough, P. B. (1986) Acquisition of literacy: A longitudinal study of children in first and second grade. *Journal of Educational Psychology*, 78, 243–55.

Meyer, D. E., Schvaneveldt, R. W., and Ruddy, M. (1975) Loci of contextual effects in visual word recognition. In P. M. A. Rabbitt and S. Dornic (eds), *Attention and Performance*, New York: Academic Press.

Monk, R. (1996) *Bertrand Russell: The Spirit of Solitude*. London: Jonathan Cape.

Nicholson, T. (1991) Do children read words better in context or in lists? A classic study revisited. *Journal of Educational Psychology*, 83 (4), 444–50.

Plaut, D. C., McClelland, J. L., Seidenberg, M. S., and Patterson, K. (1996) Understanding normal and impaired word reading: Computational principles in quasi-regular domains. *Psychological Review*, 103 (1), 56–115.

Potter, M. C., Stiefbold, D., and Moryadas, A. (1998) Word selection in reading sentences: Preceding versus following contexts. *Journal of Experimental Psychology: Learning, Memory and Cognition*, 24 (1), 68–100.

Rack, J. P., Snowling, M. J., and Olson, R. K. (1992) The nonword reading deficit in developmental dyslexia: A review. *Reading Research Quarterly*, 27 (1), 28–53.

Routman, R. (1988) *Transitions*. Portsmouth, NH: Heinemann.

Stanovich, K. (1991) Word recognition: Changing perspectives. In R. Barr, M. L. Kamil, P. B. Mosenthal, and P. D. Pearson (eds), *Handbook of Reading Research*, New York: Longman, vol. 2, pp. 418–52.

Stanovich, K. E. (1980) Toward an interactive–compensatory model of individual differences in the development of reading fluency. *Reading Research Quarterly*, 16, 32–71.

Zola, D. (1984) Redundancy and word perception during reading. *Perception and Psychophysics*, 36, 277–84.

Chapter Five

Phases of Development in Learning to Read Words

LINNEA C. EHRI

One of the great mysteries confronting literacy researchers is how mature readers are able to read written materials so rapidly and fluently yet with full comprehension (Adams, 1990; Barron, 1986; Chall, 1983; Perfetti, 1985; Rayner and Pollatsek, 1989). A capability that has proved central in explaining this feat is the ability to read single words rapidly and automatically by accessing the words in memory, also referred to as sight word reading (Ehri, 1992; LaBerge and Samuels, 1974). Readers are able to look at the written forms of familiar words and immediately recognize their pronunciations and meanings without expending any attention or effort decoding the words. In fact, readers' minds will process and recognize familiar words despite their best intentions to ignore the words, as evidenced in tasks where the presence of distracting words slows readers down in naming a series of pictures (Guttentag and Haith, 1978). A major task for researchers has been to explain how beginners acquire the ability to recognize words rapidly and automatically by sight. Recent studies have challenged the conventional view that sight word reading is a process of memorizing the visual forms of whole words. Rather, as explained below, mature readers read sight

The present chapter is an expanded version of the paper by Ehri (1994). Gratitude is expressed to Sandra McCormick who co-authored a related paper (Ehri and McCormick, 1998) and who contributed in elaborating the implications of phase theory for instruction.

words by remembering how the configuration of letters in the spellings of individual words symbolizes sounds or phonemes in their pronunciations.

In addition to reading words from memory or sight, mature readers have available three other ways to read words that are also central to their skill as readers: decoding, analogizing, and predicting. Whereas reading words from memory is the primary means of recognizing words that have been read before, these other ways of reading words are the means of identifying and learning new words not known by sight. As readers practise reading new words, the words are retained in memory and added as sight words. Another function of these other ways of reading words is to provide a backup check on the accuracy of words recognized by sight, that is, to verify that a word read from memory is likely to be that word (Ehri, 1991; 1994).

One way to read words, referred to as decoding, phonological recoding, or word attack, involves transforming graphemes into phonemes and blending the phonemes into pronunciations. Graphemes are single letters or letter combinations that represent phonemes, which are the smallest sounds in words (Venezky, 1970). For example, the spelling CHECK has 3 graphemes, CH, E, CK, representing 3 phonemes, initial /tʃ/, medial vowel /ɛ/, and final /k/. A more advanced form of decoding requires readers to have knowledge of spelling patterns. With this knowledge, readers can decode sequences of letters as single units, for example, -TION, -MENT, -OCK. Knowledge of spelling patterns makes it easier to read multisyllabic words. A common way to assess readers' decoding ability is to have them read a list of pseudowords that have not been read before (e.g., CIBE, FOD, DISBOCKING).

Another way to read words is by analogy. This refers to the process of using known words to read unknown words that share letters, for example, reading BLIGHT by analogy to NIGHT, or FABLE by analogy to TABLE (Cunningham, 1976; Gaskins et al., 1988; Goswami and Bryant, 1990; Marsh et al., 1981). Findings indicate that it is easier to analogize between words that share rime stems (e.g., BEAK–PEAK sharing the rime-EAK) than between words sharing other parts (e.g., BEAK–BEAN sharing BEA) (Goswami, 1986). Beginners may display some ability to analogize if the known words are visible, to prompt the reading of the new analogous words.

However, mature forms of analogizing require readers to hold and access known words from memory to read unfamiliar words (Ehri and Robbins, 1992; Muter, Snowling and Taylor, 1994).

A final way to read words is by prediction, that is, by generating educated guesses about the identities of unfamiliar written words based on pictures accompanying the words, or text that has preceded the words, or partial letters appearing in the words. Beginners are often able to read words more successfully when they appear in a text than when they appear in isolation, indicating the use of context cues to read words (Goodman, 1965; Nicholson, 1991). The errors or miscues that pupils make as they read text orally reveal the operation of prediction. Typically when pupils misread words, the words that they produce are syntactically and semantically consistent with the text up to that point.

Although mature readers have available various means of reading words, they utilize sight word reading whenever possible. One reason is that reading words from memory operates more rapidly and automatically than the other processes. Also sight word reading operates unobtrusively, allowing readers' attention to focus without interruption on the meaning of print, in contrast to the other ways, which require shifting attention to word forms.

It is important to dispel misconceptions about sight word reading. It is not true that only irregularly spelled words are read by sight. Rather, all words, even easily decoded words, become sight words once they have been read enough times to be stored in memory. Also, it is not true that sight word reading refers to the flashcard method of teaching pupils to read words. Sight word reading refers not to a method of teaching reading but to the *process* of reading words by accessing them in memory (Ehri, 1992).

Another misconception is that sight word learning involves memorizing the shapes of words or other visual features and has nothing to do with their letter–sound correspondences. This is not true. The research we have conducted over the years reveals that effective forms of sight word learning are alphabetic and phonological at root (Ehri, 1978; 1980; 1984; 1987; 1992). Use of non-alphabetic visual features to memorize how to read words is attempted only by immature beginners who lack knowledge of letters. Because this approach works poorly, these beginners have great difficulty remembering how to read words.

The concept of sight words that is addressed in this chapter involves words that readers have read accurately several times and retained in memory. Readers recognize the words by remembering how they were read previously. The term 'sight' indicates that sight of the word triggers that word in memory, including information about its spelling, pronunciation and meaning.

How to explain this capability is not easy. An adequate account must explain how readers are able to look at specific printed words they have read before and immediately locate their pronunciations and meanings in memory while bypassing thousands of other words, including those with very similar spellings or meanings, for example, distinguishing easily among *stick, stink, slink, stint* (Ehri, 1992). Moreover, an adequate explanation must cover how readers are able to store and remember new words easily after very few encounters reading the words (Ehri, 1980; Reitsma, 1983). According to Experiment 3 in Reitsma's study, beginning readers may retain information about words in memory after reading words as few as four times.

The kind of process thought to be at the heart of sight word learning is a *connection-forming* process. Connections are formed that link the written forms of words to their pronunciations and meanings in memory. This information is stored in the reader's word memory bank, or lexicon. In studying the course of development of sight word learning, we have found that different types of connections predominate at different points in development (Ehri, 1991; 1994). To capture these differences, we have distinguished four developmental phases characterized by the degree of involvement of the alphabetic system. This system refers to the regularities that underlie the written forms of English words and that all learners must internalize in order to build a fully functioning sight vocabulary. The term 'alphabetic' indicates not simply that words consist of letters but that the letters function as symbols for phonemes and phoneme blends in the words. The four phases are: pre-alphabetic, partial alphabetic, full alphabetic, and consolidated alphabetic. Each phase is labelled to reflect the predominant type of connection that links the written forms of sight words to their pronunciations and meanings in memory. An overview of the properties of each phase will be given, followed by a more detailed consideration of each phase along with implications for instruction.

Sight word learning beings as a non-alphabetic or *pre-alphabetic* process involving memory for connections between selected visual cues and words, for example, using red and white colour cues to remember that a street sign says 'stop'. However, once learners acquire some knowledge about the alphabetic writing system, sight word learning becomes an alphabetic process involving connections between letters in written words and sounds in their pronunciations. At first, readers form *partial alphabetic* connections linking the most salient letters to sounds. For example, beginners might connect only the initial letter S in STOP to the initial sound in its pronunciation to remember how to read the word. When readers acquire more complete knowledge of the alphabetic system, *full alphabetic* connections are formed between graphemes in spellings and phonemes in the pronunciations of words, for example, connecting all four letters in STOP to four phonemes in its pronunciation. As sight words accumulate in memory in fully analysed forms, letter patterns recurring in different words become consolidated into units symbolizing phonological blends, for example, *-op, -eed, -ack*. These *consolidated alphabetic* units are used to form connections in learning sight words.

Our phase theory of word reading differs from Frith's (1985) stage theory in several respects. First, ours is centred around the development of sight word reading whereas hers describes development more generally. Second, our view of sight word learning involves forming graphophonological connections whereas she views sight word learning as a non-phonological process. Third, we postulate phases rather than stages to avoid the extra claims that accompany the assertion of stages, for example, that each stage is a prerequisite for the next stage, that stages are discrete, non-overlapping periods of development. Fourth, our notions about the first and fourth phases differ from Frith's notions. We refer to the first phase as pre-alphabetic rather than logographic, and to the fourth phase as consolidated alphabetic rather than orthographic.

The term 'logographic' is possibly misleading. English-speaking children in the pre-alphabetic phase do not read words like mature readers of logographic orthographies such as Chinese. True logographic readers remember the full visual forms of sight words as unified wholes or gestalts, whereas children remember only selected visual cues to read sight words, perhaps even a visual cue lying beside rather than inside the written word (Gough, Juel and Griffith, 1992).

The term 'orthographic' is considered inadequate for two reasons. One is that a variety of meanings have been imposed on it by researchers, hence rendering the term too general and ambiguous (Wagner and Barker, 1994). Another is that the link to phonology is marginalised. Labelling the phase 'consolidated alphabetic' is more accurate and precise. It reflects the fact that the units and connections have evolved from an earlier phase and retain a phonological function.

Information about phases of development in learning to read words has practical value. It can assist teachers in interpreting the word-reading behaviours of their pupils. Rather than concluding that a reader is behaving abnormally, a teacher might recognize the behaviour as characteristic of an earlier phase of development. Also, knowledge about phases can provide teachers with realistic expectations about the next steps in acquisition: what pupils might be able to learn, and what might be too advanced. Knowing about phases can help teachers plan instruction that is appropriate for pupils, for example, providing letter instruction to pre-alphabetic readers rather than pushing them to memorize words and read text independently. As teachers gain experience relating their methods of instruction to pupils' phases of development, they should become better able to understand how to facilitate reading acquisition and what factors underlie difficulties encountered by pupils along the way (Ehri and McCormick, 1998; Ehri and Williams, 1995).

Pre-alphabetic Phase

The first phase is referred to as pre-alphabetic because children do not use alphabetic knowledge to read words. As a result, decoding and analogizing as well as independently reading print are far beyond their reach. They have access to only two ways of reading words: by memorizing selected visual cues to remember how to read words, and by prediction. These ways are adopted not by choice but by default because children lack more effective ways of reading words (Byrne, 1992).

During this phase, beginners remember how to read words by forming connections between selected non-alphabetic visual features of words and their pronunciations or meanings and storing these connections in memory. Gough and Hillinger (1980) describe this as a process of paired associate learning. We have called this visual cue reading (Ehri and Wilce, 1985). Gough, Juel and Griffith (1992) showed that pre-alphabetic readers select single salient visual cues to remember words. In one case, a thumbprint appearing next to a word proved to be the salient cue. When it accompanied the word, children could read the word. When it did not, the word was not recognized. Other examples of salient visual cues that readers might use to form connections are the two round eyes in 'look', the tail dangling at the end of 'dog', two humps in the middle of 'camel' (Gough, Juel and Roper-Schneider, 1983). Of course, most words lack salient semantic cues such as these for forming memorable connections. For most words, the visual connections available are arbitrary and hence hard to remember.

When pre-alphabetic phase readers are observed to read print in their environment, such as stop signs and fast-food restaurant signs, they do this by remembering visual cues accompanying the print rather than the written words themselves, for example, the golden arches behind the 'McDonald's' sign rather than the initial M in the name. In various studies, when children were shown environmental print without logos or without distinctively appearing letters, many were unable to read the words, indicating their dependence upon these non-alphabetic cues (Dewitz and Stammer, 1980; Goodman and Altwerger, 1981; Harste, Burke and Woodward, 1982; Heibert, 1978; Mason, 1980).

Masonheimer, Drum and Ehri (1984) selected preschoolers who could read environmental print and showed them the print with one letter altered, for example, 'PEPSI' changed to 'XEPSI'. Children failed to notice the change, even when given a hint that there might be a problem. Their failure occurred, not because they had not paid any attention to letters in the signs (McGee, Lomax and Head, 1988), but because they had not stored the letters in memory as part of the connections that supported their reading of the signs.

One interesting consequence of the fact that pre-alphabetic connections do not involve ties between letters and sounds is that readers are not held to specific pronunciations of printed words. In studies by Goodman and Altwerger (1981) and Harste et al. (1982), children were observed to connect print with ideas and to produce variable rather than exact wordings, for example, reading

CREST as 'brush teeth' or 'toothpaste', reading DYNAMINTS as 'fresh-a-mints'. This lack of correspondence at the phonological level but equivalence at the semantic level indicates that at this phase the connections formed in lexical memory are between salient visual cues and meanings of words. This contrasts with later phases where the involvement of letter–sound connections restricts the word accessed in memory to a single pronunciation linked to the word's spelling.[1] Children who look at the word SNOW and say 'winter', or who look at the word APPLE and say 'orange', do not have wires crossed in their brains but rather are using primitive semantically based connections to remember how to read these words because they lack more advanced means of forming alphabetic connections.

One instructional technique used with young children is for the teacher to read and reread predictable text while pointing to the words in the text. Pre-alphabetic readers who have heard the story sufficiently often are able to 'pretend read' the text, that is, to recite it from memory. However, they have great difficulty learning to point to the words they are reciting. Pauses corresponding to the empty spaces between written words are absent in speech, so these cannot be used to match print to speech (Ehri, 1975; 1979; Holden and MacGinitie, 1972). Studies of fingerpoint reading ability reveal that to learn to do this effectively requires some alphabetic knowledge and phonemic awareness (Morris, 1992; 1993; Ehri and Chun, 1996; Ehri and Sweet, 1991). To be capable of noticing whether the initial letters in words being pointed to match the words being spoken, readers need to have awareness of initial sounds in words plus some letter–sound knowledge. Moreover, to remember how to read words

[1]   It is interesting to note that in non-alphabetic systems such as Chinese, written characters symbolize words at a semantic level but not at a phonemic level. As a result, readers may assign variable pronunciations to Chinese characters when they read text aloud. In the extreme, speakers of two different dialects of Chinese, for example, Mandarin and Cantonese, assign to Chinese characters totally different pronunciations that are incomprehensible to speakers of the other dialect. This results in a situation where the two speakers cannot communicate with each other in speech but they can communicate meanings and ideas in writing because the print–meaning relationships are the same across the two dialects.

being pointed to so they can be recognized in new contexts, readers need alphabetic knowledge. Pre-alphabetic readers are thus precluded from acquiring these reading behaviours.

Findings of these studies underscore the point that the word reading and text reading experiences of children in the pre-alphabetic phase do not really help children advance in their ability to process print, although story reading experiences may contribute in other ways, for example, expanding their vocabulary, world knowledge, and familiarity with the syntax of print. For the purpose of acquiring word reading skills, however, these experiences simply strengthen ways of reading that become defunct at the next phase of development. It is not until children acquire some working knowledge of the alphabetic system that a path leading to mature forms of word reading is initiated.

It is easy to spot children who are in the pre-alphabetic phase. Usually they cannot name many letters, they lack much phonemic awareness, they know few if any words by sight, and they are unable to read text that has not been memorized. Basically, they are non-readers. Preschoolers and kindergartners who have not received any instruction in reading are likely to be in this phase.

Studies conducted with young children entering school have revealed that the best predictors of their success in learning to read during the first two years of instruction are letter knowledge and phonemic awareness (Share, Jorm, Maclean & Matthews, 1984). Thus, to help pre-alphabetic children become alphabetic readers, they need to be taught the shapes, names and sounds of letters; they need to be taught to attend to and analyse sounds in words; they need to be taught to link those sounds to letters they have learned. Directed exercises such as teaching children to use their letter knowledge to spell sounds they hear in words can help them build the knowledge needed at the next phase.

Partial Alphabetic Phase

To move into the partial alphabetic phase, children need to learn the shapes and names or sounds of upper- and lower-case letters. Also they need to acquire phonological awareness that includes segmenting words into the more salient sounds and recognizing the identity

of these sounds across different words, for example, recognizing
that *bird* and *boat* begin with the same sound (Byrne and Fielding-
Barnsley, 1989). At this phase, children are limited to reading words
by sight and by prediction. Decoding unfamiliar words as well
as analogising are difficult because both require more working
knowledge of the alphabetic system than partial alphabetic readers
possess.

Readers in this phase remember how to read sight words by
forming partial alphabetic connections between one or a few letters
in written words and sounds detected in their pronunciations.
Because first and final letters and sounds are especially salient, these
are often selected as the cues to be remembered. We have called this
phonetic cue reading. To remember sight words in this way, partial
alphabetic readers need to know the relevant letter–sound correspondences and they need to be able to segment sounds in words represented by the letters. For example, to remember how to read
'spoon', beginners need to look at the word while saying it, and recognize that at least one letter can be linked to a sound in the word,
perhaps S and initial /s/, or N and final /n/. Recognizing these connections is facilitated by the fact that the *names* of these letters
contain the relevant sounds (i.e., 'ess' and 'en') (Ehri, 1983; Templeton and Bear, 1993; Treiman, 1993). These connections are retained
in memory and enable learners to remember how to read 'spoon' the
next time they see it. Of course, if readers have remembered only the
initial and final letter–sound connections, they may misread other
words as 'spoon', for example, SKIN and SUN.

The reason why the connections formed are partial rather than
complete is that readers lack full knowledge of the spelling system,
particularly vowels, and also how to segment speech into phonemic
units that match up with the array of graphemic units. This partial
knowledge of the alphabetic system is observable in the spellings they
invent for unfamiliar words. The words they write display letters
for only some sounds, typically initial and final consonants but
not medial vowels or consonant blends (Ehri, 1986; Morris and
Perney, 1984; Read, 1971; 1975; Templeton and Bear, 1993;
Treiman, 1993).

Ehri and Wilce (1985) have provided evidence supporting the
distinction between the pre- and partial alphabetic phases of sight
word learning. They compared kindergartners' ability to learn to

read words exhibiting two types of spellings: visually distinctive spellings having unique visual forms with letters bearing no relationship to sounds (e.g., 'WcB' for 'elephant'), and simplified phonetic spellings containing cues linking letters to salient sounds in words (e.g., 'LFT' for 'elephant'). They found that readers in the pre-alphabetic phase remembered how to read the visually distinctive words better than the phonetic words, whereas readers in the partial alphabetic phase remembered how to read phonetic spellings better than visual spellings. This finding was replicated by De Abreu and Cardoso-Martins (1998) with Portuguese-speaking children in Brazil.

Rack, Hulme, Snowling and Wightman (1994) confirmed the phenomenon of phonetic cue reading in children. They showed that beginners remembered how to read words better when the spellings provided alphabetic connections that were phonetically close rather than distant. For example, beginners were taught to read either of two simplified spellings of 'garden', KDN or BDN. Phonemes symbolized by the initial letters in both spellings, /k/ and /b/, differ from the initial phoneme in 'garden', but /k/ is closer phonetically to /g/ than /b/ is to /g/. This is because /k/ and /g/ are articulated at the same place in the mouth, in the back, whereas /b/ and /g/ are articulated at different places in the mouth. (Say /k/ and /g/ to yourself to detect the similarity.) Results showed that beginners learned to read KDN as the word 'garden' more easily than BDN. This occurred despite the fact that both spellings contained incorrect initial letters. The explanation is that KDN provided more relevant phonetic cues than BDN, hence easing children's task of forming connections to remember how to read the word as 'garden'.

Byrne and Fielding-Barnsley (1989, 1990) studied what type of training was required to move readers from the pre-alphabetic phase to the partial alphabetic phase. Pupils had to be taught to perceive the identity of initial sounds in different words, to segment initial sounds in the pronunciations of words, and to recognize how letters symbolized initial sounds in words. These three skills had to be acquired in combination to enable beginners to deduce and transfer alphabetic information from training words to the reading of transfer words.

There is an advantage to forming connections out of partial phonetic cues rather than visual cues. Ehri and Wilce (1985) and also

Mason (1980) found that phonetic cue readers remembered how to read words they had been taught much better than visual cue readers, who forgot most of the words after 15 minutes. This is because phonetic cue readers possess a connection-forming system that supports long-term memory. Knowing the alphabetic system enables beginners to form and remember letter–sound connections linking written words to their pronunciations. In contrast, visually based connections are idiosyncratic rather than systematic and are often arbitrary, making them much harder to remember.

In reading unfamiliar words, partial phase readers might use prediction by combining partial letters with context cues to guess words. For example, if shown a picture of a dinner plate containing a stuffed bird that might be called 'turkey' or 'chicken', seeing a word beginning with T beneath the picture would cause them to read the unfamiliar word as 'turkey'. In contrast, pre-alphabetic readers would not be influenced by letters in guessing the word.

Partial phase readers might be observed to read words backwards, for example, *was* for *saw*, or *no* for *on*. However, they are not really seeing these words backwards but rather are processing the words using partial cues that lack a left-to-right orientation (Vellutino, 1979). It is not uncommon for partial phase readers to confuse similarly shaped letters, for example, 'b' and 'd', upper-case 'I' and lower-case 'l', 'h' and 'n'. This occurs not because these readers have faulty vision but rather because they have not fully learned to discriminate the identities of these letters.

At this phase, children have difficulty reading words by analogy because they possess insufficient memory for the spellings of sight words to recognize how known and new words are both similar and different. Rather than reading a new word by analogy to a known word (e.g., *beak* and *bean*), a reader is apt to mistake the new word for the known word because the two words share the phonetic cues that activate the known word in memory (e.g., *be-*) (Ehri and Robbins, 1992).

Several different age groups might exhibit reading behaviours putting them in the partial alphabetic phase: preschoolers who have rudimentary working knowledge of letter–sound relations; kindergartners and first-graders who have not received explicit code-emphasis instruction; or older disabled readers whose working knowledge of the alphabetic system is poorly developed.

There are several ways to spot partial alphabetic readers. Their invented spellings, although exhibiting relationships between letters and sounds, are typically inaccurate or incomplete. Salient boundary sounds may be represented with letters but medial sounds are left out unless they are heard as letter names. Conventional vowel spellings are poorly known. Consonant clusters are under-represented. Letter choices may be unconventional, for example, H to represent /ch/, Y to represent /w/, with choices reflecting pupils' use of letter names to select letters. They have poor memories for the correct spellings of words. Likewise, they have difficulty decoding unfamiliar pseudo-words and may give up trying or may substitute a real word sharing some letters with the pseudoword. In reading words in isolation, they may misread words as other words they know when the spellings are similar. When given practice learning to read a list of similarly spelled words, they mix up the words and have difficulty mastering the list.

Basically, instruction needs to be directed at improving pupils' working knowledge of the alphabetic system, particularly the spelling of vowels, consonant blends, and digraphs. Pupils may need help discriminating confusable letters. Rather than guessing the identities of words on the basis of partial letter cues, pupils need to learn how to analyse all the letters in words to determine their pronunciations and to remember their spellings. Writing as well as reading instruction and practice can facilitate these ends. It is important for teachers to recognize that pupils will have difficulty remembering the correct spellings of words until they acquire substantial knowledge of the alphabetic system. For pupils who do not recognize systematic graphophonemic relationships in words, having them try to memorize spellings will prove frustrating and futile.

Studies conducted with German-speaking beginning readers have indicated that they may move very quickly into the full alphabetic phase of word reading and spend little time as partial alphabetic readers (Wimmer, 1993; Wimmer and Goswami, 1994; Wimmer and Hummer, 1990). This is attributed to two factors: grapheme–phoneme correspondences that are more systematic and less variable in the German writing system than in English; and code-emphasis instruction that implants working knowledge of the alphabetic system in pupils from the outset.

Full Alphabetic Phase

During the full alphabetic phase, beginners remember how to read sight words by forming complete connections between letters seen in the written forms of words and phonemes detected in their pronunciations. This is possible because readers understand how most graphemes symbolize phonemes in the conventional spelling system (Venezky, 1970). In applying this knowledge to form connections for sight words, spellings become amalgamated or bonded to pronunciations of words in memory (Ehri, 1992; Perfetti, 1992). For example, in learning to read 'spoon', full alphabetic readers recognize how the five letters correspond to four phonemes in the word, including how OO symbolizes /u/.

Figure 5.1 displays the connections that full alphabetic readers might form to remember how to read several words by sight. They recognize that graphemes may consist of two letters symbolizing one phoneme. Digraphs may involve vowels as well as consonants. They recognize that some letters may not correspond to any phonemes in words. Sometimes silent letters are predictable, for example, final E in words containing 'long vowels'. Sometimes silent letters must be learned as a feature characterizing a particular word, for example, the T in *listen*. All readers may not utilize the same connections in learning particular words. For example, some readers may consider the final E in *little* silent while others may regard it as symbolizing the 'schwa' vowel in the second unstressed syllable. Some readers might consider WR in *write* and *KN* in *know* to be digraphs, while other readers might regard the initial letters as silent. However, what is common to readers at this phase is that they have a systematic way of analysing graphophonemic units to form complete connections in memory. To what extent this analysis is performed consciously or unconsciously is unclear. It may be that once readers acquire working knowledge of the alphabetic system, connections are formed automatically between spellings and pronunciations of words.

One advantage of representing sight words more completely in memory is that word reading becomes much more accurate. Whereas phonetic cue readers' memory for initial and final letters may cause them to confuse SPOON with SOON, SPIN, and SUN, full alphabetic readers' representatons eliminate confusion because their

S P OO N
| | | |
/s/ /p/ /uː/ /n/

S T O P
| | | |
/s/ /t/ /ɒ/ /p/

TH A N K
| | | |
/θ/ /æ/ /ŋ/ /k/

C A K E
| | |
/k/ /eɪ/ /k/

L I ST E N
| | | | |
/l/ /ɪ/ /s/ /ə/ /n/

K I NG
| | |
/k/ /ɪ/ /ŋ/

L I TT L E
| | | |
/l/ /ɪ/ /t/ /l/

L I TT L E
| | | ✕
/l/ /ɪ/ /t/ /ə/ /l/

KN OW
| |
/n/ /əʊ/

K N OW
| |
/n/ /əʊ/

WR I   T E
| | |
/r/ /aɪ/ /t/

WR I T E
| | |
/r/ /aɪ/ /t/

I SL A N D
| | | | |
/aɪ/ /l/ /ə/ /n/ /d/

S W O R D
| | |
/s/ /ɔː/ /d/

S I G N
| | |
/s/ /aɪ/ /n/

T A L K
| | |
/t/ /ɔː/ /k/

Note. Capital letters separated by blank spaces designate graphemes. Lower-case letters or phonetic symbols between diagonal slashs designate phonemes. Vertical lines between graphemes and phonemes designate connections. Symbols represent standard British pronunciation.

Figure 5.1   Connections formed between graphemes and phonemes during the full alphabetic phase

representations are sufficiently complete to distinguish easily among similarly spelled words. This difference in the tendency to confuse similarly spelled words was apparent in a study comparing partial and full alphabetic readers performed by Ehri and Wilce (1987) (see below).

Another characteristic distinguishing full phase from partial phase readers is the ability to decode words never read before, that is, to transform unfamiliar spellings of words into recognizable pronunciations. It is this knowledge that enables full phase readers to fully connect spellings to pronunciations of words in remembering how to read them. In a study by Ehri and Wilce (1987), partial phase readers received one of two different treatments. The experimental group was taught to process all of the letters in words much as full phase readers would do. The control group was given isolated letter–sound training, supporting their status as phonetic cue readers. Following training, subjects practised learning to read a list of 15 similarly spelled words, for example, *stab*, *stamp*, *stand*, *drip*, *drum*, *dump*. The full phase readers mastered the list within three trials whereas the partial phase readers read only 40 per cent of the words after seven learning trials. The difficulty exhibited by partial phase readers was in confusing words that contained similar letters. These results reveal the great advantage to word reading that occurs at the full alphabetic phase.

Although full phase readers are able to decode words, this process is supplanted by sight word reading for words that are practised sufficiently often. According to Reitsma's (1983) study, four practice trials may be sufficient for readers to retain information about sight words in memory. The advantage of sight word reading over decoding is that sight word reading operates much faster. In a study by Ehri and Wilce (1983), pupils in the first, second, and fourth grades read familiar sight words much faster than simply-spelled nonsense words. In fact, good readers were able to read the sight words as rapidly as they could name single digits, indicating that the words were read as single unified wholes rather than as letters identified sequentially. Unitization is taken to indicate that spellings of sight words are fully bonded to their pronunciations in memory.

Sight word reading enables readers to recognize words that are difficult to decode accurately because they contain some unexpected letters (Adams and Huggins, 1985). According to our theory, the same types of connections are formed for irregular words as for regular words since most of the letters in these words can be connected to sounds, for example, all but one letter in the following words: S in *island*, W in *sword*, G in *sign*, L in *talk*. In dealing with exceptional letters, full phase readers may flag them as silent (Ehri and Wilce, 1982), or create in memory a special spelling pronunciation that includes the silent letter (Drake and Ehri, 1984). In contrast, readers at the next phase may process exceptional letters as part of a consolidated spelling pattern if that pattern recurs in different words, for example, -ALK or -IGHT.

Readers' lexicons of sight words grow steadily and substantially during this phase as they are exposed to more and more words in their text reading. Practice reading text is essential for acquiring word reading skill, especially in English, which involves retaining the specific forms of words in memory to read them effectively (Ehri, 1992; Share and Stanovich, 1995).

All forms of word reading become possible in the full alphabetic phase. In contrast to previous phases, decoding becomes part of the reader's repertoire. Readers are able to read new words by analogy to words they know by sight, although analogizing is more commonly used by readers in the next phase (Bowey and Hansen, 1994; Leslie and Calhoon, 1995). Also, readers in the full alphabetic phase find it much easier to spell words correctly, not only because they have better knowledge of the alphabetic system but also because this general knowledge along with their improved memory for sight words makes it easier to store the spellings of specific words in memory.

Readers in this phase can be distinguished from readers in the previous phase by their ability to read pseudowords, by their ability to learn to read a set of similarly spelled words easily, and by their ability to generate spellings of words that contain conventional letter choices and are graphophonemically complete. The main difficulty confronting full phase readers is dealing effectively with multisyllabic words. Although they can learn multisyllabic words as sight words, they may have problems decoding them or remembering their correct spellings.

To move to the next phase, readers need much reading and spelling practice so that they become familiar with the spellings of different words and can detect common patterns. A method of instruction that may promote the detection of patterns is one developed by teachers at Benchmark School in Pennsylvania (Gaskins et al., 1988; Gaskins et al., 1996–7). In this programme, beginning readers are taught a set of about 90 key words over the course of a year. These key words contain a variety of common vowel spellings and spelling patterns that recur in many other words. Examples of key words taught during the first three weeks of the programme are: *in, and, up, king, long, jump, let, pig, day*. The instruction that pupils receive helps them retain the words as fully analysed spellings in memory. For example, they are taught to segment the words into their constituent phonemes and then to match up letters in the words' spellings to these phonemes. They also practise writing the words from memory by accessing these remembered connections. The main reason for learning these key words is to practise using them to read other words by analogy. Pupils are given plenty of practice doing this. According to our phase theory, one would expect that sensitizing pupils to shared patterns among words and teaching them to use known words to read new words should facilitate movement to the next phase of word reading because it draws attention to letter patterns recurring in different words.

Consolidated Alphabetic Phase

The consolidated alphabetic phase actually begins during the preceding phase. As full alphabetic phase readers retain complete information about the spellings of a growing number of sight words in memory, they are in a position to detect letter patterns that recur across words. As words with shared letters are retained in memory, the letters become consolidated into multi-letter units representing morphemes, syllables, or subsyllabic units such as onsets and rimes, and the units become part of readers' generalized knowledge of the spelling system.

Knowing larger letter patterns and their connections to phonological units is valuable for sight word reading because it reduces the memory load involved in storing sight words in memory. For example, -EST might emerge as a consolidated unit in a reader's memory from its occurrence in several sight words known by the reader – *nest, pest, rest, test, vest, west, crest.* Knowing -EST as a consolidated unit means that the graphemes and phonemes have been analysed and bonded. Knowing this should ease the task of forming connections to learn the new word *chest*, as a sight word. Whereas full phase readers would need to form four separate connections linking CH, E, S, T to the phonemes /ʃ/, /ɛ/, /s/, /t/, respectively, a consolidated phase reader would need to form only two separate connections, CH, and EST linked to /tʃ/ and /est/, respectively. If a reader knew units such as EST, TION, IN, and ING as consolidated units, the task of learning longer sight words such as 'question' and 'interesting' would be easier. Another contribution of consolidated units to sight word reading is that they speed up the process of accessing words by facilitating letter identification (Juel, 1983; Venezky and Massaro, 1979).

A number of studies have shown that older readers are more sensitive to letter co-occurrence patterns than beginning readers. For example, Leslie and Thimke (1986) gave first- and second-graders a word-search task and found that pupils reading at a second-grade level were sensitive to the difference between legally sequenced and illegally sequenced letters in nonwords whereas first-graders were sensitive only to the difference between familiar and unfamiliar real words. This suggests that second grade is when children's sight vocabularies grow large enough to support the consolidation of frequently occurring letter patterns into units.

Also, there is evidence that words containing more familiar letter patterns are read more accurately by pupils than words containing unfamiliar patterns even when the words are constructed out of the same grapheme–phoneme correspondences (Treiman, Goswami and Bruck, 1990). Such effects are more apparent in advanced beginning readers than in novice beginners, indicating the contribution of a larger sight vocabulary to knowledge of common spelling patterns (Bowey and Hansen, 1994; Leslie and Calhoun, 1995).

However, few studies have been conducted to demonstrate the facilitative effects of consolidated units on sight word learning. In a study by Ehri and Robbins (1992), first-graders who displayed some decoding skill were taught to read one set of words and then received practice learning to read a second set of words. For some pupils, the second set contained the same rime spellings as the first set (e.g., *feed*

– *seed*). For other pupils, the second set had the same letter–sound correspondences across words but not the same rime patterns as the first set. Pupils learned to read the analogous words faster than the non-analogous words, indicating that shared letter patterns facilitate the process of remembering how to read words, that is, building a sight vocabulary.

A study by Juel (1983) showed that knowledge of letter patterns enabled more mature readers to read familiar words faster. She found that fifth-graders read words that shared letter patterns with many other words more rapidly than words having less common letters. However, this factor made little difference to second-graders, who were influenced primarily by the decodability of the words. Thus, word reading speed may be facilitated by knowledge of letter patterns sometime after second grade.

Signs that average readers are using consolidated units in their reading become apparent typically in second grade (Bowey and Hansen, 1994; Ehri, 1991; Juel, 1983; 1991). Acquisition of more complex relationships may continue to mature through at least eighth grade (Juel, 1991; Venezky, 1976; Venezky and Johnson, 1973). It is important for readers to continue building their knowledge of spelling regularities characterizing multisyllabic words because this knowledge is thought to ease the difficulty of remembering the spellings of these words (Ehri, 1997). For example, a reader who recognizes that the E in words such as *pigeon*, *sergeant*, and *vengeance* performs the function of marking the preceding G as soft rather than hard stands a better chance of remembering that these words include this letter than readers who do not recognize this pattern.

Programmes have been developed by Henry (1988) and Calfee (in press) to teach additional regularities to pupils in this phase by distinguishing the linguistic roots of spellings and the patterns associated with each type of root:

Anglo-Saxon patterns such as *-hood*, *-ful*, *-ness*, *-ship*, and *-ish*;
Latin patterns such as *-tion*, *-ture*, *-scrib*, *-struct*, and *-rupt*;
Greek patterns such as *tele-*, *-graph*, *-ology*, *-phon*, and *auto-*.

Learning these patterns helps to expand pupils' knowledge of the alphabetic system, which in turn contributes to their word reading and word spelling skills.

Summary and Conclusions

To portray the course of development in learning to read words, we have distinguished four phases, each characterized by the involvement of learners' working knowledge of the alphabetic system. Characteristics of the four phases are summarized in table 5.1. Children in the pre-alphabetic phase lack much knowledge of letter–sound relations, so they utilize non-alphabetic, visually salient features of

Table 5.1   Characteristics and capabilities of pupils at various phases of word reading development

Pre-alphabetic Phase
- Able to read sight words by remembering one or two distinctive visual cues in or around the word and ignoring all other cues.
    Example: reading YELLOW by remembering the two tall posts in the middle
- Other characteristics and capabilities of pupil:
    - Lacks much knowledge of letters
    - Forgets sight words easily
    - Reads text by memorizing it (pretend reading)
    - Unable to read text independently
    - Unable to decode
    - Reads environmental print by remembering visual cues, not letters

Partial Alphabetic Phase
- Able to read sight words by remembering one or a few salient letters in words as they correspond to sounds detected in pronunciations.
    Example: reading KITTEN by detecting and remembering the presence of initial K for the sound /k/ and final N for the sound /n/ but failing to remember much about other letters in the word
- Other characteristics and capabilities of pupil:
    - Knows most alphabet letters
    - Invents partially phonetic spellings of words
    - Has difficulty remembering the correct spellings of words
    - Mistakes similarly spelled words in reading them
    - Has difficulty decoding unfamiliar words; misreads them as real words
    - Able to read text composed of familiar words independently
    - Able to use context to read unfamiliar words in text

Table 5.1   (cont.)

Full Alphabetic Phase
- Able to read sight words by remembering their spellings as distinct, letter-analysed forms bonded fully to their pronunciations.
    Example: reading WENT and WANT, or QUITE, QUIET, QUICK by accessing connections in memory, i.e., remembering the 4 letters in WENT as symbols for its 4 sounds; reading these similarly spelled words accurately upon seeing them, without confusion and without the aid of any context cues
- Other capabilities of pupil:
    - Knows letter names and sounds
    - Able to segment words into the smallest sounds, phonemes
    - Invents fully phonetic spellings of words
    - Remembers the correct spellings of shorter, regularly spelled words
    - Able to decode unfamiliar words
    - Able to use known words to read unknown words
    - Reads practised words accurately and automatically
    - Reads text comprised of familiar, decodable, or predictable words independently

Consolidated Alphabetic Phase
- Able to read sight words by analysing and remembering chunks of letters symbolizing blends of sounds when these syllabic units are familiar spelling patterns whose letter–sound relations have been consolidated. Learning is easier at this phase because fewer connections are involved than at the alphabetic phase, particularly for multisyllabic words.
    Example: remembering how to read STRING by forming connections between 2 letter chunks, STR and –ING, and their respective blends; remembering how to read INTERESTING by forming connections between 4 letter chunks symbolizing the syllables 'in', 'ter', 'est', 'ing'.
- Other characteristics and capabilities of pupil:
    - Knows spelling patterns as they symbolize syllabic and subsyllabic units
    - Decodes multisyllabic words by chunking letters
    - Decodes unfamiliar words and nonwords rapidly
    - Uses known words skilfully to read unknown words
    - Remembers the correct spellings of words

---

words to remember how to read them. Once children learn about letter names and sounds, they use alphabetic information to remember how to read words. They do this by forming connections between letters seen in spellings of words and sounds detected in their pronunciations. Initially the connections formed are partial, limited to those in salient positions. However, as beginners learn more about the spelling system, particularly vowel spellings, they become able to analyse and connect all of the graphemes seen in spellings to phonemes detected in pronunciations. This enables their sight vocabularies to grow rapidly. As more words are stored in memory, letter patterns that recur in different words are detected and consolidated to symbolize units larger than phonemes, including affixes, syllables, and subsyllabic units. Having available consolidated units for forming connections improves the efficiency of the sight word learning process, particularly for multisyllabic words.

Not only sight word reading but also other ways to read words are linked to the phases of development. Making informed guesses about the identities of words is possible during all phases. Semantic contextual cues inform predictions during the pre-alphabetic phase; letter cues begin to inform predictions during the partial phase; during the full and consolidated phases, readers rely primarily on other means for recognizing words and use prediction as a check on the accuracy of their identifications (Stanovich, 1986). Decoding words does not become possible until the full alphabetic phase; it becomes an automatic process during the consolidated phase. Reading new words by analogy to known words becomes possible during the full phase but increases in use during the consolidated phase.

Developmental relationships between adjacent phases differ. Word reading processes used during the pre-alphabetic phase occur by default and are not precursors of processes used during subsequent phases. That is, a child who never does visual cue reading suffers no disadvantage at the next phase. Acquisitions begun during the partial phase, however, provide the foundation for all other phases, most importantly, left-to-right orientation, knowledge of letters, and phonological awareness. Use of partial graphophonic cues to read and spell words provides a temporary, immature approach that enables beginners to perform these literacy tasks albeit in a fashion that is prone to error. The sooner this form of processing words is replaced by processing at the full phase, the sooner mature forms of word reading get under way. Word reading at the full alphabetic phase is essential for the formation of consolidated units that allow movement into the next phase. In other words, readers must become full alphabetic phase readers before they can become consolidated alphabetic phase readers.

The phase theory of word reading development carries important implications for reading instruction. It reveals that the attainment of mature word reading skill is possible only if pupils acquire working knowledge of the alphabetic system. Beginners need to know the shapes and names or sounds of letters before they can be expected to make any progress in learning to read words. Also, beginners need to be tuned into the phonological level of language so that they can recognize the sounds that letters symbolize in words. Without this knowledge, pupils will regard text reading as a frustrating and incomprehensible process.

There are several ways to assess readers' knowledge of the alphabetic system and the extent of their development as readers: examining pupils' accuracy and speed in naming letters or in writing letters, having pupils generate spellings of words that are unfamiliar in print, giving pupils pseudowords to decode, giving them graded lists of words and graded passages to read. All of these provide information suggestive of pupils' phase of development. With this information teachers are in a better position to understand the source of pupils' errors and to anticipate the type of instruction that is most appropriate.

References

Adams, M. (1990) *Beginning to Read: Thinking and Learning about Print*. Cambridge, MA: MIT Press.

Adams, M., and Huggins, A. (1985) The growth of children's sight vocabulary: A quick text with educational and theoretical implications. *Reading Research Quarterly*, 20, 262–81.

Barron, R. W. (1986) Word recognition in early reading: A review of the direct and indirect access hypotheses. *Cognition*, 24, 93–119.

Bowey, J., and Hansen, J. (1994) The development of orthographic rimes as units of word recognition. *Journal of Experimental Child Psychology*, 58, 465–88.

Byrne, B. (1992) Studies in the acquisition procedure for reading: Rationale, hypotheses and data. In P. Gough, L. Ehri, and R. Treiman (eds), *Reading Acquisition*, Hillsdale, NJ: Erlbaum, pp. 1–34.

Byrne, B., and Fielding-Barnsley, R. (1989) Phonemic awareness and letter knowledge in the child's acquisition of the alphabetic principle. *Journal of Educational Psychology*, *81*, 313–21.

Byrne, B., and Fielding-Barnsley, R. (1990) Acquiring the alphabetic principle: A case for teaching recognition of phoneme identity. *Journal of Educational Psychology*, *82*, 805–12.

Calfee, R. (1998) Phonics and Phonemes: Learning to decode and spell in a literature-based program. In J. Metsala and L. Ehri (eds), *Word Recognition in Beginning Literacy*, Mahwah, NJ: Erlbaum, pp. 315–40.

Chall, J. S. (1983) *Stages of Reading Development*. New York: McGraw Hill.

Cunningham, P. (1976) Investigating a synthesized theory of mediated word identification. *Reading Research Quarterly*, *11*, 127–43.

De Abreu, M., and Cardoso-Martins, C. (1998) Alphabetic access route in beginning reading acquisition in Portuguese: The role of letter-name knowledge. *Reading and Writing: An Interdisciplinary Journal*, *10*, 85–104.

Dewitz, P., and Stammer, J. (1980) *The Development of Linguistic Awareness in Young Children from Label Reading to Word Recognition*. Paper presented at the National Reading Conference, December, San Diego, CA.

Drake, D. A., and Ehri, L. C. (1984) Spelling acquisition: Effects of pronouncing words on memory for their spellings. *Cognition and Instruction*, *1*, 297–320.

Ehri, L. (1975) Word consciousness in readers and prereaders. *Journal of Educational Psychology*, *67*, 204–12.

Ehri, L. (1978) Beginning reading from a psycholinguistic perspective: Amalgamation of word identities. In F. B. Murray (ed.), *The Development of the Reading Process* (International Reading Association Monograph, no. 3), Newark, DE: International Reading Association, pp. 1–33.

Ehri, L. (1979) Linguistic insight: Threshold of reading acquisition. In T. G. Waller and G. E. MacKinnon (eds), *Reading Research: Advances in Theory and Practise*, New York: Academic Press, vol. 1, pp. 63–114.

Ehri, L. (1980) The development of orthographic images. In U. Frith (ed.), *Cognitive Processes in Spelling*, London, England: Academic Press, pp. 311–38.

Ehri, L. (1983) Summaries and a critique of five studies related to letter-name knowledge and learning to read. In L. Gentile, M. Kamil, and J. Blanchard (eds), *Reading Research Revisited*, Columbus, Ohio: C. E. Merrill, pp. 131–53.

Ehri, L. (1984) How orthography alters spoken language competencies in children learning to read and spell. In J. Downing and R. Valtin (eds), *Language Awareness and Learning to Read*, New York: Springer Verlag, pp. 119–47.

Ehri, L. (1986) Sources of difficulty in learning to spell and read. In M. Wolraich and D. Routh (eds), *Advances in Developmental and Behavioral Pediatrics*, Greenwich, CT: Jai Press, pp. 121–95.

Ehri, L. (1987) Learning to read and spell words. *Journal of Reading Behavior, 19*, 5–31.

Ehri, L. (1991) Development of the ability to read words. In R. Barr, M. Kamil, P. Mosenthal, and P. Pearson (eds), *Handbook of Reading Research*, New York: Longman, vol. II, pp. 383–417.

Ehri, L. (1992) Reconceptualizing the development of sight word reading and its relationship to recoding. In P. Gough, L. C. Ehri, and R. Treiman (eds), *Reading Acquisition*, Hillsdale, NJ: Erlbaum, pp. 107–43.

Ehri, L. (1994) Development of the ability to read words: Update. In R. Ruddell, M. Ruddell, and H. Singer (eds), *Theoretical Models and Processes of Reading* (4th edn), Newark, DE: International Reading Association, pp. 323–58.

Ehri, L. (1997) Learning to read and learning to spell are one and the same, almost. In C. Perfetti, L. Rieben, and M. Fayol (eds), *Learning to Spell: Research, Theory and Practice across Languages*, Mahwah, NJ: Erlbaum, pp. 237–69.

Ehri, L. (1995) Phases of development in learning to read words by sight. *Journal of Research in Reading, 18*, 116–25.

Ehri, L., and Chun, C. (1996) How alphabetic/phonemic knowledge facilitates text processing in emergent readers. In J. Shimron (ed.), *Literacy and Education*, Cresskill, NJ: Hampton, pp. 69–93.

Ehri, L., and McCormick, S. (1998) Phases of word learning: Implications for instruction with delayed and disabled readers. *Reading and Writing Quarterly, 14*, 135–63.

Ehri, L., and Robbins, C. (1992) Beginners need some decoding skill to read words by analogy. *Reading Research Quarterly, 27*, 12–26.

Ehri, L., and Sweet, J. (1991) Fingerpoint reading of memorized text: What enables beginners to process the print? *Reading Research Quarterly, 26*, 442–62.

Ehri, L., and Wilce, L. (1982) The salience of silent letters in children's memory for word spellings. *Memory and Cognition, 10*, 155–66.

Ehri, L., and Wilce, L. (1983) Development of word identification speed in skilled and less skilled beginning readers. *Journal of Educational Psychology, 75*, 3–18.

Ehri, L., and Wilce, L. (1985) Movement into reading: Is the first stage of printed word learning visual or phonetic? *Reading Research Quarterly*, 20, 163–79.

Ehri, L., and Wilce, L. (1987) Cipher versus cue reading: An experiment in decoding acquisition. *Journal of Educational Psychology*, 79, 3–13.

Ehri, L., and Williams, J. (1995) Learning to read and learning to teach reading. In F. Murray (ed.), *The Teacher Educator's Handbook: Building a Knowledge Base for the Preparation of Teachers*, San Francisco, CA: Jossey-Bass, pp. 231–44.

Frith, U. (1985) Beneath the surface of developmental dyslexia. In K. E. Patterson, J. C. Marshall, and M. Coltheart (eds), *Surface Dyslexia: Neuropsychological and Cognitive Studies of Phonological Reading*, London: Erlbaum, pp. 301–30.

Gaskins, I., Downer, M., Anderson, R., Cunningham, P., Gaskins, R., Schommer, M., and the Teachers of Benchmark School (1988) A metacognitive approach to phonics: Using what you know to decode what you don't know. *Remedial and Special Education*, 9, 36–41.

Gaskins, I., Ehri, L., Cress, C., O'Hara, C., and Donnelly, K. (1996–7) Procedures for word learning: Making discoveries about words. *The Reading Teacher*, 50, 312–27.

Goodman, K. (1965) A linguistic study of cues and miscues in reading. *Elementary Journal*, 42, 639–43.

Goodman, K. (1976) Reading: A psycholinguistic guessing game. In H. Singer and R. Ruddell (eds), *Theoretical Models and Processes of Reading* (2nd edn), Newark, DE: International Reading Association, pp. 497–508.

Goodman, Y., and Altwerger, B. (1981) *Print Awareness in Preschool Children – A Working Paper: A Study of the Development of Literacy in Preschool Children* (Occasional Paper no. 4). Tucson, AZ: University of Arizona, Program in Language and Literacy.

Goswami, U. (1986) Children's use of analogy in learning to read: A development study. *Journal of Experimental Child Psychology*, 42, 73–83.

Goswami, U., and Bryant, P. (1990) *Phonological Skills and Learning to Read*. Hillsdale, NJ: Erlbaum.

Gough, P., and Hillinger, M. (1980) Learning to read: An unnatural act. *Bulletin of the Orton Society*, 30, 180–96.

Gough, P., Juel, C., and Griffith, P. (1992) Reading, spelling and the orthographic cipher. In P. Gough, L. C. Ehri, and R. Treiman (eds), *Reading Acquisition*, Hillsdale, NJ: Erlbaum, pp. 35–48.

Gough, P., Juel, C., and Roper-Schneider, D. (1983) Code and cipher: A two-stage conception of initial reading acquisition. In J. A. Niles and L. A. Harris (eds), *Searches of Meaning in Reading /Language Processing and Instruction* (32nd Yearbook of the National Reading Conference), Rochester, NY: National Reading Conference, pp. 207–11.

Guttentag, R., and Haith, M. (1978) Automatic processing as a function of age and reading ability. *Child Development, 49,* 707–16.

Harste, J., Burke, C., and Woodward, V. (1982) Children's language and world: Initial encounters with print. In J. Langer and M. Smith-Burke (eds), *Bridging the Gap: Reader Meets Author,* Newark, DE: International Reading Association, pp. 105–31.

Henderson, E., Templeton, S., and Bear, D. (eds) (1993) *Development of Orthographic Knowledge: The Foundations of Literacy,* Hillsdale, NJ: Erlbaum.

Henry, M. (1988) Beyond phonics: Integrated decoding and spelling instruction based on word origin and structure. *Annals of Dyslexia, 38,* 258–75.

Hiebert, E. (1978) Preschool children's understanding of written language. *Child Development, 49,* 1231–4.

Holden, M., and MacGinite, W. (1972) Children's conceptions of word boundaries in speech and print. *Journal of Educational Psychology, 63,* 551–7.

Juel, C. (1983) The development and use of mediated word identification. *Reading Research Quarterly, 18,* 306–27.

Juel, C. (1991) Beginning reading. In R. Barr, M. Kamil, P. Mosenthal, and P. Pearson (eds), *Handbook of Reading Research,* New York: Longman, vol. II, pp. 759–88.

LaBerge, D., and Samuels, J. (1974) Toward a theory of automatic information processing in reading. *Cognitive Psychology, 6,* 293–323.

Leslie, L., and Calhoon, A. (1995) Factors affecting children's reading of rimes: Reading ability, word frequency, and rime-neighborhood size. *Journal of Educational Psychology, 87,* 576–86.

Leslie, L., and Thimke, B. (1986) The use of orthographic knowledge in beginning reading. *Journal of Reading Behavior, 18,* 229–41.

Marsh, G., Freidman, M., Welch, V., and Desberg, P. (1981) A cognitive-development theory of reading acquisition. In T. G. Waller and G. MacKinnon (eds), *Reading Research: Advances in Theory and Practise,* New York: Academic Press, vol. 3, pp. 199–221.

Mason, J. (1980) When *do* children begin to read: An exploration of four-year-old children's letter and word reading competencies. *Reading Research Quarterly, 15,* 203–27.

Masonheimer, P. E., Drum, P. A., and Ehri, L. C. (1984) Does environmental print identification lead children into word reading? *Journal of Reading Behavior, 16,* 257–72.

McGee, L., Lomax, R., and Head, M. (1988) Young children's written language knowledge: What environmental and functional print reading reveals. *Journal of Reading Behavior, 20,* 99–118.

Morris, D. (1992) Concept of word: A pivotal understanding in the learning to read process. In S. Templeton and D. Bear (eds), *Development of Orthographic Knowledge: The Foundations of Literacy*, Hillsdale, NJ: Erlbaum, pp. 53–77.

Morris, D. (1993) The relationship between children's concept of word in text and phoneme awareness in learning to read: A longitudinal study. *Research in the Teaching of English*, 27, 133–54.

Morris, D., and Perney, J. (1984) Developmental spelling as a predictor of first grade reading achievement. *Elementary School Journal*, 84, 441–57.

Muter, V., Snowling, M., and Taylor, S. (1994) Orthographic analogies and phonological awareness: Their role and significance in early reading development. *Journal of Child Psychology and Psychiatry*, 35, 293–310.

Nicholson, T. (1991) Do children read words better in context or in lists? A classic study revisited. *Journal of Educational Psychology*, 83, 444–50.

Perfetti, C. (1985) *Reading Ability*. New York: Oxford University Press.

Perfetti, C. (1992) The representation problem in reading acquisition. In P. Gough, L. C. Ehri, and R. Treiman (eds), *Reading Acquisition*, Hillsdale, NJ: Erlbaum, pp. 107–43.

Rack, J., Hulme, C., Snowling, M., and Wightman, J. (1994) The role of phonology in young children learning to read words: The direct-mapping hypothesis. *Journal of Experimental Child Psychology*, 57, 42–71.

Rayner, K., and Pollatsek, A. (1989) *The Psychology of Reading*. Englewood Cliffs, NJ: Prentice-Hall.

Read, C. (1971) Pre-school children's knowledge of English phonology. *Harvard Educational Review*, 41, 1–34.

Read, C. (1975) *Children's Categorization of Speech Sounds in English*. Urbana, IL: National Council of Teachers of English, Research Report no. 17.

Reitsma, P. (1983) Printed word learning in beginning readers. *Journal of Experimental Child Psychology*, 75, 321–39.

Share, D., Jorm, A., Maclean, R., and Matthews, R. (1984) Sources of individual differences in reading achievement. *Journal of Educational Psychology*, 76, 1309–24.

Share, D., and Stanovich, K. (1995) Cognitive processes in early reading development: Accommodating individual differences into a model of acquisition. *Issues in Education: Contributions from Educational Psychology*, 1, 1–57.

Stanovich, K. E. (1986) Matthew effects in reading: Some consequences of individual differences in the acquisition of literacy. *Reading Research Quarterly*, 21, 360–406.

Templeton, S., and Bear, D. (eds) (1993) *Development of Orthographic Knowledge and the Foundations of Literacy: A Memorial Festschrift for Edmund H. Henderson*. Hillsdale, NJ: Erlbaum.

Treiman, R. (1985) Onsets and rimes as units of spoken syllables: Evidence from children. *Journal of Experimental Child Psychology, 39,* 161–81.

Treiman, R. (1986) The division between onsets and rimes in English syllables. *Journal of Memory and Language, 25,* 476–91.

Treiman, R. (1993) *Beginning to Spell.* New York: Oxford University Press.

Treiman, R., Goswami, U., and Bruck, M. (1990) Not all nonwords are alike: Implications for reading development and theory. *Memory and Cognition, 18,* 559–67.

Vellutino, F. (1979) *Dyslexia: Theory and Research.* Cambridge, MA: MIT Press.

Venezky, R. L. (1970) *The Structure of English Orthography.* The Hague: Mouton.

Venezky. R. (1976) *Theoretical and Experimental Base for Teaching Reading.* The Hague: Mouton.

Venezky, R., and Johnson, D. (1973) Development of two letter–sound patterns in grades one through three. *Journal of Educational Psychology, 64,* 109–15.

Venezky, R. L., and Massaro, D. W. (1979) The role of orthographic regularity in word recognition. In L. Resnick and P. Weaver (eds), *Theory and Practise of Early Reading,* Hillsdale, NJ: Erlbaum, pp. 85–107.

Wagner, R., and Barker, T. (1994) The development of orthographic processing ability. In V. Berninger (ed.), *The Varieties of Orthographic Knowledge, I: Theoretical and Developmental Issues,* Dordrecht, Netherlands: Kluwer Academic, pp. 243–76.

Wimmer, H. (1993) Characteristics of developmental dyslexia in a regular writing system. *Applied Psycholinguistics, 14,* 1–33.

Wimmer, H., and Goswami, U. (1994). The influence of orthographic consistency on reading development: Word recognition in English and German children. *Cognition, 51,* 91–103.

Wimmer, H., and Hummer, P. (1990) How German-speaking first graders read and spell: Doubts on the importance of the logographic stage. *Applied Psycholinguistics, 11,* 349–68.

Chapter Six

Learning to Read Words Turns Listeners into Readers: How Children Accomplish this Transition

MORAG STUART, JACKIE MASTERSON AND
MAUREEN DIXON

The act of reading can be broadly defined as accessing meaning through printed words. Even skilled fluent readers can, in certain circumstances (e.g., trying to follow complex ideas expressed by writers whose areas of expertise do not coincide with their own) become painfully aware of the efforts they are having to make to understand the meaning of texts. Yet skilled readers are seldom aware of making any effort to decipher the words on the page which act as the vehicle for that meaning: the print seems a transparent window through which we look to the meanings of the text. In the same way, in conversations, we attend consciously to the meanings, intents and purposes of speakers, and unless dialects, accents or speech impediments interfere, we are unaware of the spoken forms which act as vehicles for the expression of thought. Speech also seems a transparent window through which we look to the meaning of the speaker.

We acknowledge the support of ESRC grant no. 000234380 for the work discussed in this chapter. We should like to thank A. & C. Black, Mammoth Books, Oxford University Press, Ginn and Penguin Books, who donated materials to our database project; and Reed International, Lion Books, Nelson, Ladybird, Walker Books and Longman, for allowing us access to their texts.

In terms of the broad definition of reading given above, learning to read must involve learning to access meaning through printed words. In this chapter we shall discuss recent work which investigates how children develop fluent and automatic processing systems for recognizing, understanding and pronouncing printed words: processing systems which are necessary to, but not sufficient for, accessing the meanings of printed texts.

At the heart of this development lies a paradox. One thing which has become abundantly clear from psychological research conducted over the past two decades (for recent reviews, see Perfetti, 1995; Stanovich and Stanovich, 1995) is that, if children are to become skilled and fluent readers, able to look through the transparent window of print to the meaning of a text, the window of speech must first have become opaque. The children who learn to read easily are those who have early on become aware of the word as object, who can focus *on* the window of speech as well as looking through it to meaning. Many young children are unable to do this, as the phonological awareness and pre-reading literatures demonstrate. Their judgements about spoken words are semantically rather than phonologically based. So, for example, in a rhyme production task, they might produce 'stick' as a rhyme for 'drum', or 'saucer' as a rhyme for 'cup' (Stuart, 1986). In writing, they might announce that they will write their father's name 'with bigger letters because daddy is big', or that 'a cow needs more letters than a fly, because it is bigger' (Ferreiro and Teberovsky, 1982). Because of this lack of awareness of spoken words as sound patterns, they find it difficult to make rhyme judgements (see, for example, Bowey and Francis, 1991; Bradley and Bryant, 1983; Knafle, 1974) and to perform phoneme segmentation tasks (see, for example, Nesdale, Herriman and Tunmer, 1980; Stuart and Coltheart, 1988). Yet well-controlled studies in several different language communities (Ball and Blachman, 1991; Bradley and Bryant, 1983; Byrne and Fielding-Barnsley, 1991; 1993; 1995; Cunningham, 1990; Lundberg, Frost and Petersen, 1988) have shown that there is a consistent relationship between success on phonological awareness tasks and the ease with which young children develop word recognition skills in reading. In order to become fluent readers, it is now clear that children must be able to decentre from meaning and pay attention to sound.

In a longitudinal study of reading development in a group of children from four-year-old pre-readers to the end of their primary school career at age eleven (Stuart, 1993; Stuart and Coltheart, 1988; Stuart and Masterson, 1992) it was shown that the disparity in reading age between two groups of children classified as either phonologically aware or unaware at the age of four grew from a difference of six months when they were five years old to a difference of over three years when they were eleven years old: that is, the phonologically unaware children fell further and further behind as time went on, demonstrating the Matthew effect (Stanovich, 1986). The children's views of themselves as readers likewise diverged, with the struggling children becoming ever less enthusiastic about reading, and increasingly unwilling to indulge in it. The strugglers' ability to engage with the rest of the school curriculum was affected too, leading to a general lowering of their self-esteem.

Some of the tests used to measure reading age at different points in this longitudinal study were lists of single words to read aloud, measuring only the children's word recognition skills. But when the children were eleven, the Neale test, which gives both a word recognition accuracy score and a text comprehension score, was also used. There was a highly significant (0.82) correlation between accuracy and comprehension scores: by and large, children who were good at word recognition understood what they read, and children with poor word recognition skills were unable to access the meaning of the text. This was further explored by measuring the children's listening comprehension, and by asking them to read aloud random lists of words from the Neale text passages. In a stepwise multiple regression analysis, with children's IQ scores entered as the first step, their listening comprehension scores as the second step, and their ability to read aloud the words from the text passages as the third step, each of the three predictor variables made a significant contribution to reading comprehension scores, together accounting for almost 90 per cent of the variance (Stuart, in preparation). So, more intelligent children with good listening comprehension skills and good printed word recognition skills show better understanding of the texts they read. This evidence supports the simple view of reading propounded by Hoover and Gough (1990): understanding what we read depends on being able to read the words on the page, as well as on the general comprehension skills we bring to the reading task. When inability to recognize the printed word impairs its transparency, we cannot look through it to meaning.

But how does phonological awareness, the ability to focus on the form of the spoken word, influence the development of fluent printed word recognition skills? Recent research suggests that it works in two ways: first, it allows children to make sense of the alphabetic system; and, second, it facilitates acquisition of sight vocabulary. Evidence describing the role of phonological awareness in each of these aspects of the development of printed word recognition is discussed in turn below.

Making Sense of the Alphabetic System

Alphabets are systems of rules for mapping between printed symbols (graphemes) and speech sounds (phonemes). Alphabetic systems are efficient because they allow us to represent in writing all the thousands of words in our spoken vocabulary, using a very small set of printed symbols. Sometimes, as in English, the set of printed symbols is rather too small to allow consistent one-to-one mappings between a printed symbol and the sound it represents. English has only 26 letters of the alphabet with which to represent a set of about 44 different phonemes.

It has sometimes been argued (e.g., Smith, 1971) that it is an impossibly difficult task to teach children all the possible grapheme–phoneme correspondences used in English. It may be difficult to teach them, but it is not necessarily difficult to learn them: many children become fluent readers with minimal exposure to phonics teaching. The phonologically aware four-year-olds from our longitudinal study are a case in point. The only phonics they were taught at school were the single sounds of letters of the alphabet, whereby the letter A is always /a/ as in 'cat', B is /b/, C is /k/, D is /d/, E is /ɛ/ as in 'egg', etc. Nevertheless, by the age of eleven, they knew most of the major secondary vowel correspondences identified by Venezky (1970): the vowel digraphs ai, oa, ea, etc. Their comments when asked as seven-year-olds to give the sounds of vowel digraphs when these were presented to them singly on cards were illuminating: presented with a printed 'oy' digraph, one child said, 'Oh, yes, it's in "joy" and "boy" . . .' before pronouncing it correctly;

presented with a printed 'igh' trigraph, another child said, 'It's in "light" and "night", it must be /ai/.' These children were able to infer grapheme–phoneme correspondences from their sight vocabulary.

In a recent study (Stuart, Masterson, Dixon and Quinlan, in press) we explored whether children with up to two years' experience of learning to read were able to use the sight vocabulary they had acquired from their reading experience as a database from which they could infer grapheme–phoneme correspondences. We first made a database of the printed word vocabulary which the children in our experiment had experienced in their reading, so that we could count the frequency with which they had experienced different vowel digraphs, and so that we could check to see which digraphs they had experienced as consistently representing a single pronunciation. We planned to work with Year 2 (six- to seven-year-old) children, who were in their third year at school. We first consulted their reading records (booklets filled in by teachers and parents, where each book read by a child was recorded), and scanned or typed into the computer all the texts which the children had read. The database was compiled from these texts and consisted of a word frequency table, a book table (which listed all the books in the database and allowed words to be located in particular books) and a child table (which listed all contributing children and allowed children to be identified as readers of particular books). Thus, from the database, we could discover which words were in which books, how many times they occurred, and which children had read them. The accuracy of the reading vocabulary represented within the database was checked by a structured interview and questionnaire given to parents of participating children at the school, during which they were asked how widely their child read outside school. Results indicated that most parents relied on books sent home from school (and hence recorded at school and entered into the database) for their children's reading material, although they read *to* the children from a much wider variety of texts (Stuart, Dixon, Masterson and Quinlan, 1998).

We decided to make up nonwords containing vowel digraphs for the children to read, because we knew they were not being taught these correspondences in school: if they could read them correctly, they must have learned to do so from their reading experience. We used our database to compile a list of all the major vowel digraphs and their frequency counts in the children's reading experience. We hypothesized that if children were inferring vowel digraph pronunciations from their reading experience, then they should be more likely to have inferred highly frequent digraphs than more uncommon ones which they had seldom come across. We also hypothesized that vowel digraphs with a one-to-one mapping between print and sound should be easier to infer than those with a one-to-many mapping. That is, 'ee says /i/' must be easier to infer than 'ea says /i/', because 'ee' always represents the sound /i/ (e.g., 'feel', 'see', 'meet'), but 'ea' can also represent /ɛ/ (e.g., 'bread') and /eɪ/ (e.g., 'great'). Therefore, from the list, we chose four vowel digraphs, according to frequency of occurrence and consistency of pronunciation, to give one high frequency consistent digraph (EE); one high frequency inconsistent digraph (EA); one low frequency consistent digraph (OY); and one low frequency inconsistent digraph (EI).

We also hypothesized that children who are good readers and proficient at phoneme segmentation tasks should be better able to infer sublexical correspondences from their reading experience, because they will have built up a larger sight vocabulary (Stuart and Masterson, 1992) from which to make these inferences, which also depend on segmentation ability.

The children were first given a reading test (BAS single word test, Elliott, Murray and Pearson, 1983) and a phoneme segmentation test, and then asked to read aloud a set of 44 monosyllabic nonwords, 24 experimental items containing 6 examples of each digraph in medial position (e.g., veek, heam, reil, woyd), and 20 filler items containing a variety of other vowel digraphs (e.g., paik, roum, gorb, sood).

Since we were interested in whether or not they gave the correct pronunciation to the vowel digraph in each nonword, rather than in their ability to pronounce the nonwords correctly, we gave one point for each correct pronunciation of the four vowel digraphs under test, to a maximum of 6 points in each of the four conditions. For the inconsistent digraphs, all possible correct pronunciations were counted as correct: hence, for both inconsistent digraphs there were three possible correct pronunciations (EI = /eɪ/, /aɪ/ or /i/; EA = /eɪ/, /ɛ/ or /i/). Means and standard deviations for each group are shown in table 6.1.

Table 6.1   Means and standard deviations for scores (max = 6) in each
experimental condition, by reading quotient group

Reading quotient (RQ) group		RQ	HFC ee	HFI ea	LFC oy	LFI ei
			(n = 6)	(n = 6)	(n = 6)	(n = 6)
High	Mean	1.19	4.95	3.70	4.05	0.35
	sd	0.17	1.43	2.27	2.24	0.67
Low	Mean	0.91	0.70	0.30	1.30	0.10
	sd	0.05	1.25	0.67	1.16	0.32

Key: HFC high frequency consistent.
        HFI   high frequency inconsistent.
        LFC low frequency consistent.
        LFI   low frequency inconsistent.

We analysed these scores in a repeated measures analysis of variance with one between-subjects factor (reading quotient group) and two within-subjects factors (frequency and consistency). We entered phoneme segmentation scores as a covariate in the analysis. There were significant main effects of group ($F_{1,30} = 29.6$, $p < 0.001$) and of frequency ($F_{1,31} = 7.2$, $p < 0.012$). Children with high reading quotients read more vowel digraphs correctly overall, and high frequency digraphs were overall more likely to be read correctly than low frequency. However, there was no significant main effect of consistency ($F_{1,31} = 1.22$, n.s.): possibly an unavoidable consequence of allowing three times as many possible correct responses for inconsistent as for consistent items. There was a significant effect of the covariate (beta = 0.28, $t = 2.4$, $p < 0.03$): phoneme segmentation ability made a significant contribution to vowel digraph reading. There was also a significant two-way interaction between group and frequency ($F_{1,31} = 4.36$, $p < 0.05$): children with high reading quotients were more affected by frequency. No other interactions reached significance.

The results show clearly that six- to seven-year-old children who are reading well for their age are able to infer grapheme–phoneme correspondences from exposure to printed words in their reading experience. The children had not been taught correspondences between digraphs and the vowel phonemes they represented, yet they were able to give the correct pronunciation to digraphs in nonwords. Similar results are reported by Duncan, Seymour and Hill (1997).

Working with younger children, Stuart (1995) found that rising fives with good initial phoneme segmentation skills and sound-to-letter mapping knowledge invariably were reading well by the age of six. By six, they were able to read aloud some simple three-letter nonwords, which none of the poor readers in the group could do. Typically, the poor readers responded by naming some of the letters on the page, or by giving a visually similar real word, for example, responding 'pig' to 'sig'. When the children were retested after a seven-month interval, some of the poor readers had become able to read three-letter nonwords correctly, while others remained in their earlier state of letter naming or real-word responding. The children who had begun to develop phonological recoding skills had improved their reading age on average by twelve months, compared with an average improvement of only three months by those who had not. Development of phonological recoding skills appeared to accelerate development of word recognition skills, an acceleration already noted in a much earlier study by Davies and Williams (1974): what was not revealed in the earlier study was the deceleration of progress towards fluent word recognition apparent here following failure to develop phonological recoding skills.

It seems to be generally the case that six-year-olds who can read well have begun to develop these skills. For example, Masterson, Laxon and Stuart (1992) found a strong positive correlation (0.80) in a sample of five- and six-year-olds between reading ability and the proportion of errors that were made in response to irregular words. The better readers were more likely to read regular words correctly, and to make more errors in irregular words, which, if unfamiliar, cannot be read correctly by applying grapheme–phoneme correspondence rules.

Stuart, Masterson and Dixon (in preparation) further explored the nature of regularity effects in six- to seven-year-olds. Using the database mentioned above, we worked out individual word frequency counts from the individual reading vocabularies of 35 children in their third year at school. We used these frequency counts to compile a set of up to 80 words for each child to read, divided equally into two subsets of high frequency (30–120 exposures)

Table 6.2 Means and standard deviations of scores on all experimental
tests, by reading quotient group
(Word reading scores are mean %.)

Test	Reading quotient group			
	High		Low	
	Mean	sd	Mean	sd
Reading quotient (RA/CA)	1.17	0.15	0.87	0.1
High Frequency Regular word	96.63	6.7	77.34	25.18
High Frequency Irregular word	94.25	9.2	69.21	32.9
Low Frequency Regular word	92.25	9.9	39.69	23.2
Low Frequency Irregular word	87.13	11.4	38.5	16.5
Phoneme segmentation	29.3	3.28	19.7	9.8

and low frequency (2–20 exposures) words. Within each frequency
level, half the words were regular (i.e., conformed to the most
frequent grapheme–phoneme correspondence rules as categorized
by Venezky, 1970), and half were irregular. Each child was tested
on their own set of words, and on a phoneme segmentation test, and
the BAS single word reading test (Elliott et al., 1983). We again
grouped children by their reading quotients, making one group of
children who were reading well for their age, and one of children
who were under-achieving in relation to their age. Means and
standard deviations for scores by each group on each test are shown
in table 6.2.

We analysed the data for each reading group in two separate analyses of variance with two factors of frequency and regularity, and
entered phoneme segmentation scores as covariate. The children who
were reading well for their age showed significant effects of both
regularity (F 1,19 = 7.3, p < 0.02) and frequency (F 1,19 = 8.8,
p < 0.01), but the interaction between regularity and frequency did
not approach significance. Phoneme segmentation was significant as
a covariate (beta = 0.47, t = 2.2, p < 0.04). The children who were
already under-achieving relative to their age showed only a highly
significant effect of frequency (F 1,13 = 43.3, p < 0.0001), but
no effect of regularity (F 1,13 = 0.36, p = 0.6) and no regularity by

frequency interaction. Phoneme segmentation was not significant as a covariate (beta = 0.17, t = 0.64, p = 0.5).

These results again suggest strongly that children who are reading well by the age of six are those who have developed phonological recoding processes: the advantage for regular over irregular words is taken to indicate a contribution to word recognition from sublexical grapheme–phoneme translation, which allows the correct reading of regular but not irregular words. Children whose reading age is beginning to fall behind their chronological age show only effects of frequency, suggesting a strong reliance in this group on learned sight vocabulary: they are much more likely to be successful with the high frequency words, which they have experienced many times.

It is thus clear that early phonological awareness, together with knowledge of single letter–sound correspondences, contributes to children's ability to exploit the alphabetic principle. This allows them to set up phonological recoding systems which, according to many accounts of skilled reading (see, for example, Coltheart, Curtis, Atkins and Haller, 1993), contribute to recognition of familiar words and are essential for reading unfamiliar words.

Learning Sight Vocabulary

Recent theories of the development of word recognition procedures in children have begun to indicate a second role for phonological awareness and letter–sound correspondence knowledge. For example, Ehri (1980; 1992; 1995), Stuart and Coltheart (1988), Goswami (1993) and Rack, Hulme, Snowling and Wightman (1994) all suggest that children's sight vocabulary acquisition is also based in their phonological analyses of spoken words. We recently tested this suggestion in a training experiment with five-year-olds in their first term at school. We hypothesized that, if phonological analyses underpin the acquisition of sight vocabulary, then phonologically aware five-year-olds should learn sight vocabulary faster than those who are unaware.

We mimicked the school conditions under which the children were expected to acquire a printed word vocabulary by preparing two story books, which we repeatedly read with pairs of children. Embedded in the two books were sixteen words which we hoped the children would learn, eight per book. Each word to be learned was printed in red among the otherwise black print, and appeared four times in the book at the rate of one red word per page. The sixteen words comprised four subsets: four nouns with regular spellings (e.g., 'camel'), four nouns with irregular spellings (e.g., 'onion'), four function words with regular spellings (e.g., 'myself') and four function words with irregular spellings (e.g., 'enough'). We used our database to determine that none of the words to be learned appeared in any of the books the children had read: they were all therefore of zero frequency for the children. We included regular and irregular spellings because, if the earliest role of children's phonological analyses consists of a contribution to sight vocabulary development rather than to phonological recoding, irregular words should be learned and subsequently read correctly as easily as regular words. We included nouns and function words because previous research with adult acquired dyslexic patients (i.e., patients who have difficulties following brain damage) has shown lexical storage and retrieval to be subject to effects of word class and imageability (see, for example, Funnell, 1983; Patterson and Shewell, 1987). We therefore expected nouns to be easier to learn than function words.

We departed from the normal school procedures experienced by the children, in that we made it clear to them from the outset that we wanted them to try to remember the red words. We reinforced this message by testing each child with flashcards of the red words after each reading session.

Twenty five-year-olds were selected for training on the basis of their ability to identify the initial phonemes of spoken words, and choose from a set of three letters the correct letter to write each identified initial sound. The ten phonologically unaware children were completely unable to identify any initial sounds, and performed at chance on the letter selection task. The ten phonologically aware children performed at or near ceiling on both tasks. Both groups were also given a visual memory test (Goulandris and Snowling, 1991): groups did not differ in visual memory scores ($t = 0.38$, $p = 0.54$). The trainer who repeatedly read the books with the children was not involved in this screening, and did not know which children were phonologically aware or unaware.

Acquisition of sight vocabulary for all twenty children was a much slower process than the previous (albeit scanty) literature on this subject had led us to expect. For example, Reitsma (1983) claimed from the results of three experiments with Dutch schoolchildren that only a few training trials are necessary to familiarize children with the printed form of a word. This study has also been interpreted by Adams (1990) as indicating 'remarkably sponge-like word acquisition' by children, as long as they are familiar with letters of the alphabet. However, the children in Reitsma's first experiment were already in the third grade, and had therefore been learning to read for some time. As can be seen from table 6.2 (above), of the six- to seven-year-old readers we discussed previously, those who were reading well for their age were able to read words which they had only experienced in their reading from 2 to 20 times with 92 per cent accuracy (regular spellings) and 87 per cent accuracy (irregular spellings), which appears to support Reitsma's claim. But, six- to seven-year-olds who were not reading well for their age showed a much lower success rate for these low frequency items, reading the regular spellings with 39 per cent accuracy, and the irregular with 38 per cent. Thus, the sponge-like acquisition of new reading vocabulary seems to be confined to older children who read well, and to depend perhaps more on phonological recoding ability than on entering new items into sight vocabulary: Reitsma's second experiment involved reading nonwords, which is usually considered to require the application of phonological recoding processes.

Given the expectations raised in us by Reitsma's work, we were considerably surprised that even after 36 exposures to each word to be learned, no child had learned all sixteen words. Nevertheless, there were differences in the learning achieved by phonologically aware and unaware five-year-olds: the mean for phonologically aware children was 6.8 words learned (standard deviation 2.6), for phonologically unaware the mean was 3.1 words learned (standard deviation 2.4), a significant difference ($F_{1,18} = 10.95$, $p < 0.004$).

We did seem to be tapping sight vocabulary learning uncontaminated by use of phonological recoding processes, as there was no significant effect of regularity on word learning ($F_{1,18} = 0.24$, $p = 0.63$), and a highly significant effect of word type ($F_{1,18} = 12.5$, $p < 0.003$), with nouns more likely to be learned than function words, especially by phonologically aware children. It is also of interest that, although there was no significant difference in visual memory scores between the two groups of children, the visual memory scores of the phonologically unaware group were highly and significantly correlated (r = 0.79) with their word learning scores, but no such correlation was apparent in the phonologically aware group (r = −0.11). This perhaps might suggest that different factors underlie successful learning in the two groups, with phonologically aware children using their phonological analysis ability to set up partial links between sounds and letters in words to be learned. Phonologically unaware children are unable to do this, and so their word learning depends more on having a good visual memory, which perhaps aids registration of letter patterns and thus increases recall of the essentially arbitrary relations between letter patterns and word meanings.

What picture of the successful beginning reader emerges from these findings? We suggest the successful beginner is a child who, at the start of formal reading tuition, is already aware that words are patterns of sound, and whose awareness has developed beyond this hardwon initial insight (evidenced by ability to perform rhyme detection and production tasks) to include the ability to identify initial phonemes in spoken words. In our experience, it is extremely unusual to find children who can identify initial phonemes who are not also able to perform at above chance levels when asked to choose, from a set of three, the letter which represents each initial phoneme. Our successful beginner also therefore has good knowledge of the sounds of letters of the alphabet, which Stuart and Coltheart (1988) define as knowing the sounds of at least thirteen letters.

These 'graphophonic' abilities underlie both sight vocabulary acquisition and the establishment of phonological recoding processes. Sight vocabulary becomes a database from which more complex and conditional sublexical correspondences between print and sound are inferred. This continuing enlargement of the child's rule system in turn enables the child to work out the pronunciations (and hence gain access to the meanings) of unfamiliar words encountered in their text reading, which can then be entered into sight vocabulary. The continuing enlargement of sight vocabulary increases the database available to the child for further correspondence inferences, and also increases the accuracy of the weighting system which we assume is applied to the rules formed from inference. The self-teaching mechanism proposed by Share (1995) becomes an extremely powerful tool if instantiated in this way.

We have assumed that segmentation ability is crucial to the inference procedure, and the fact that in our studies phoneme segmentation is invariably a significant predictor supports this assumption. We set out to test the further assumption, expressed both by Stuart and Coltheart (1988) and by Ehri (1992), that successful beginning readers' early internal representations of words in sight vocabulary will be partial, and will include the boundary letters of those words. Since children are first able to segment initial and then final phonemes in words (Stanovich, Cunningham and Cramer, 1984; Stuart, 1990), we hypothesize that they will first look to these positions in the printed word for information about the word, and link the observed boundary letters to their segmented sounds.

We tested this in another training experiment (Dixon, Stuart and Masterson, in preparation) with naive five-year-old beginning readers, screened for visual memory, initial and final phoneme segmentation and sound-to-letter mapping ability. This screening was used to identify three groups of children. Group 1 consisted of ten children who were near ceiling at both initial and final phoneme segmentation (mean 90 per cent and 88 per cent correct respectively). Group 2 consisted of ten children who were good at initial phoneme segmentation (mean 85 per cent correct) but could not segment final phonemes (mean 0 per cent correct). Group 3 consisted of eight children who were at floor on initial phoneme segmentation (mean 1 per cent correct).

We aimed to teach the children ten words, presented singly on flashcards. Because we wanted to see which *letters* children stored as a basis for their subsequent word recognition, we chose ten six-letter bisyllabic words to be learned. This abolished any word length cues the children might have used. We also printed each word in upper case, to abolish any word shape cues; and we made five pairs of two words which started with the same letter, so that use of just the initial letter would not work well as a learning strategy. All the words were concrete nouns, to make this difficult task as easy as possible. The stimuli were then illustrated on cards to make sure that children first understood their meanings when the words were spoken: SANDAL, SIGNAL, RASCAL, ROCKET, TICKET, TURNIP, CARTON, COBWEB, PICNIC, PENCIL. Once we were certain children understood these meanings, we repeatedly presented the words on flashcards in several sessions, four presentations per session, until children reached our criteria for successful learning of all ten words correctly on two consecutive trials, or until a maximum of fourteen training sessions had been reached.

We then presented the children with eight alternative spellings of the words learned in a forced-choice recognition task. These alternatives included the correct spelling, and seven spellings which either substituted or transposed consonants. For example, the word SANDAL was presented with PANDAL (substitute first letter of word), SANDAN (substitute last letter of word), SARDAL (substitute last letter of first syllable), SANCAL (substitute first letter of second syllable), NASDAL (transpose first and last letters of first syllable), SANLAD (transpose first and last letters of second syllable), and SADNAL (transpose middle consonants across syllable boundary). We asked each child, 'Which of these do you think looks most like the word (e.g.) SANDAL that we've been learning?' The child's choice was noted and removed, and the child was then asked 'Can you see any others which could be (e.g.) SANDAL?' This procedure was repeated until the child refused to make any more choices, or until all eight alternatives had been chosen. We gave a score of 1 to each choice made by each child regardless of whether or not it was correct. Thus, if a child chose the correctly spelled item for all item sets, the correct spelling would achieve the maximum score of 10; if a child also chose the medial transposition item for all item sets, that too would achieve the maximum score of 10.

We anticipated that only children in Group 1, who could segment both initial and final phonemes, would show the boundary letter effect. That is, we expected only children in this group to make fewer choices of alternatives like SANDAN and SANLAD as well as of PANDAL and NASDAL. Children in Group 2, who could segment just initial phonemes, should be misled by the former but not the latter pair.

As a preliminary analysis the number of items that a child picked from the item set was investigated. The maximum score was eight (seven incorrect and one correct version) and this was achieved when a child picked all the items from the set as an appropriate representation of the target word. The mean number of responses for children in Group 1 was 3.36 (standard deviation = 1.36), for Group 2 was 5.89 (standard deviation = 0.76, and for Group 3 was 6.54 (standard deviation = 0.84). Inspection of these means reveals that the children in Group 1 were much more likely to choose fewer alternatives than the other two groups. An analysis of variance revealed that this effect of phonological awareness group was highly significant ($F_{2,22} = 19.17$, $p < 0.0005$ by subjects; $F_{1,9} = 403.57$, $p < 0.00005$ by items). Post hoc comparisons revealed that the difference between Group 1 and the other two groups was highly significant, but that there was no significant difference between Groups 2 and 3. This result demonstrates that children who are aware of boundary consonants in spoken words are overall less likely to be misled by misspelt versions of words learned.

We then turned to our primary area of interest, that is, which alternative misspellings were most likely to be wrongly accepted as correct representations of a word? Initial inspection of the results revealed that there was no significant difference between scores for the two medial substitutions (SARDAL vs SANCAL), and these two scores were averaged to create a single score for medial substitution. Means and standard deviations for each alternative by the three groups of children are shown in table 6.3. We analysed these data in by-subjects and by-items analyses of variance. In the subject analysis, we entered type of error choice (substitution vs transposition) and position of error (initial vs final vs medial) as within-subjects variables, and phoneme segmentation group (group 1 vs group 2 vs group 3) as the between-subjects variable. In the item analysis, the three factors were entered as within-items variables.

The between-subjects variable of groups was highly significant in both subject and item analyses ($F_{2,20} = 18.8$, $p < 0.0005$ by subjects; $F_{2,18} = 280.9$, $p < 0.0005$ by items).

Type of error choice failed to reach significance in the subject analysis ($F_{1,20} = 1.69$, $p = 0.21$), but was significant in the item analysis ($F_{1,19} = 495.8$, $p = 0.036$). This showed a slight tendency for the transposition items to be more acceptable misspellings than the substitution items, where letters appeared which were not in the original (correct) learned version.

Position of error was highly significant across both subject and item analyses ($F_{2,40} = 81.88$, $p < 0.0005$ by subjects; $F_{2,18} = 343.93$, $p < 0.0005$ by items). Further investigation of the position of error effect revealed a highly significant linear trend from initial to final to medial position ($F_{1,20} = 138$, $p < 0.0005$ by subjects; $F_{1,9} = 323.55$, $p < 0.0005$ by items).

Table 6.3 Means and standard deviations for scores of each alternative choice, by three groups of children differing in phoneme segmentation ability

Group	Correct Spelling (n = 10)	Substitution			Transposition		
		Initial (PANDAL)	Final (SANDAN)	Medial (SARDAL SANCAL)	Initial (NASDAL)	Final (SANLAD)	Medial (SADNAL)
Group 1	8.60	0.30**	3.50**	4.85**	0.40**	4.00**	7.00*
	(1.71)	(0.67)	(3.30)	(2.96)	(0.70)	(3.56)	(2.58)
Group 2	9.88	1.00**	9.12	9.50	1.25**	9.13	9.63
	(0.35)	(1.60)	(1.73)	(1.41)	(1.28)	(2.10)	(1.06)
Group 3	10	3.60*	9.60	9.90	3.40*	9.20	10
	(0)	(4.04)	(0.89)	(0.23)	(3.91)	(1.79)	(0)

*   significantly different from choice of the correct spelling at $p < 0.05$.
** significantly different from choice of the correct spelling at $p < 0.001$.

There was also a significant interaction between group and position of error ($F_{4,40} = 3.54$, $p < 0.02$ by subjects; $F_{4,36} = 3161.26$, $p < 0.0005$ by items). This suggests that the linear effect only operates in Group 1, in children able to segment both initial and final phonemes, with Groups 2 and 3 only showing a difference for errors in initial position. That is, only if the first letter of the word was changed were they significantly less likely to choose it as an acceptable spelling of the word. This was supported by a series of post hoc investigations using Tukey's HSD, which confirmed that only children in Group 1 were able to reject as misspellings items containing final (e.g., SANDAN for SANDAL) or medial (e.g., SARDAL or SANCAL) substitutions, and final (e.g., SANLAD) or medial (e.g., SADNAL) transpositions. Group 1 were also significantly better able than Group 3 to reject as misspellings items containing initial substitutions (e.g., PANDAL) and transpositions (e.g., NASDAL). There were no significant differences between the ability of Groups 1 and 2 to reject as misspellings items containing initial substitutions and transpositions. This suggests that, in this difficult task, those children who were able to segment the initial phoneme were able to make use of initial letter information when asked to choose the correct spelling.

Thus, as we had anticipated, children who were able to segment both initial and final phonemes seemed to have incorporated the boundary letters representing phonemes in these positions into their mental representations of the words. Their earliest representations in sight vocabulary incorporated boundary letters. Children only able to segment initial phonemes incorporated letters representing initial phonemes. The fact that, as shown in table 6.3, children who were unable to segment initial phonemes were also less likely to accept as correct spellings items where the initial letter was changed is, at first sight, puzzling. However, it is possible that these two groups were using the initial letters in different ways. We suggest that children able to segment initial phonemes are making links between the initial letter and the initial phoneme, whereas children unable to segment phonemes at all are using the initial letter as a visual cue. Further work is necessary to investigate this suggestion, but in its tentative support we would like to refer back to our earlier training study with five-year-olds. In this earlier study, we had found a significant correlation between visual memory scores and number of words learned, which was restricted to the group of children who were unable to segment initial phonemes. We suggested then that children who cannot link letters to sounds may learn sight vocabulary differently from children who can, and do so by relying on their visual memory.

Conclusions

We hope to have shown in this chapter that recent psychological investigations into normal reading development, controlled and circumscribed as they necessarily are, have begun to lift the curtain on the secret of how children learn to read well. We are now well beyond the stage of saying 'children learn to read when there is something they want to read and an adult who takes time and trouble to help them' (Meek, 1983). It has been possible to identify some of the specific skills and knowledge required for children to undergo a smooth and painless transition from non-reader to reader. There are clear implications for the teaching of reading. As children come into school (and into nursery classes where these are available) they should be engaged in lots of enjoyable activities and games to develop an awareness of rhyme and of the phonemic structure of speech. Four- and five-year-olds are also capable of, enjoy, and benefit from learning all about letters: what they look like, what their names are, how to write them, what sounds map onto them. They need to understand not only that the print is what carries the message, but also that in order to become a reader one needs to pay attention to the words on the page, to commit them and their meanings and sounds to memory, so that they can be re-recognized in any different context. Those much maligned flashcards are an excellent and efficient way of providing children with the right kind of experience in solving the problems of how to distinguish one printed word from another. Practice is needed in listening to sounds in spoken words, and writing down what you can hear. Practice is also needed in sounding out and blending simple short words. All of this work is accessible to most five-year-olds, and should certainly be accomplished by all six-year-olds. It is never too early to intervene with children who are failing to make progress. Five-year-olds who arrive at school unable to detect and produce rhymes are already potentially in trouble with their reading. Six-year-olds who cannot read aloud three-letter nonwords are too. Proactive diagnostic and structured teaching is essential if we are to make readers of all our children: just providing a literate environment is not enough.

References

Adams, M. J. (1990) *Beginning to Read: Thinking and Learning about Print.* Cambridge, MA: MIT Press.

Ball, E. W., and Blachman, B. A. (1991) Does phoneme awareness training in kindergarten make a difference in early word recognition and spelling? *Reading Research Quarterly, 26,* 49–66.

Bowey, J. A., and Francis, J. (1991) Phonological analysis as a function of age and exposure to reading instruction. *Applied Psycholinguistics, 12,* 91–123.

Bradley, L., and Bryant, P. E. (1983) Categorising sounds and learning to read: A causal connection. *Nature, 301,* 419–21.

Byrne, B., and Fielding-Barnsley, R. (1991) Evaluation of a program to teach phonemic awareness to young children. *Journal of Educational Psychology, 83,* 451–55.

Byrne, B., and Fielding-Barnsley, R. (1993) Evaluation of a program to teach phonemic awareness to young children: A one-year follow-up. *Journal of Educational Psychology, 85,* 104–11.

Byrne, B., and Fielding-Barnsley, R. (1995) Evaluation of a program to teach phonemic awareness to young children: A two- and three-year follow-up and a new preschool trial. *Journal of Educational Psychology, 87,* 488–503.

Coltheart, M., Curtis, B., Atkins, P., and Haller, M. (1993) Models of reading aloud: Dual-route and parallel-distributed-processing approaches. *Psychological Review, 100,* 589–608.

Cunningham, A. E. (1990) Explicit versus implicit instruction in phonemic awareness. *Journal of Experimental Child Psychology, 50,* 429–44.

Davies, P., and Williams, P. (1974) *Aspects of Early Reading Growth: A Longitudinal Study.* Oxford: Blackwell.

Duncan, L. G., Seymour, P. H. K., and Hill, S. (1997) How important are rhyme and analogy in beginning reading? *Cognition, 63,* 171–208.

Ehri, L. C. (1980) The development of orthographic images. In U. Frith (ed.), *Cognitive Processes in Spelling,* London: Academic Press.

Ehri, L. C. (1992) Reconceptualizing the development of sight word reading and its relationship to recoding. In P. Gough, L. C. Ehri, and R. Treiman (eds), *Reading Acquisition,* Hillsdale, NJ: Erlbaum.

Ehri, L. C. (1995) Phases of development in learning to read words by sight. *Journal of Research in Reading*, 18, 116–25.

Elliott, C. D., Murray, D. J., and Pearson, L. S. (1983) *British Ability Scales.* Windsor, England: NFER-Nelson.

Ferreiro, E., and Teberovsky, A. (1982) *Literacy before Schooling.* London: Heinemann.

Funnell, E. (1983) Phonological processes in reading: New evidence from acquired dyslexia. *British Journal of Psychology*, 74, 159–80.

Goswami, U. (1993) Towards an interactive analogy model of reading development: Decoding vowel graphemes in beginning reading. *Journal of Experimental Child Psychology*, 56, 443–75.

Goulandris, N., and Snowling, M. (1991) Visual memory deficits: A plausible cause of developmental dyslexia? Evidence from a single case study. *Cognitive Neuropsychology*, 8, 127–54.

Hoover, W. A., and Gough, P. B. (1990) The simple view of reading. *Reading and Writing*, 2, 127–60.

Knafle, J. D. (1974) Children's discrimination of rhyme. *Journal of Speech and Hearing Research*, 17, 367–72.

Lundberg, I., Frost, J., and Petersen, O. P. (1988) Effects of an extensive program for stimulating phonological awareness in preschool children. *Reading Research Quarterly*, 23, 263–84.

Masterson, J., Laxon, V., and Stuart, M. (1992) Beginning reading with phonology. *British Journal of Psychology*, 83, 1–12.

Meek, M. (1983) *Achieving Literacy: Longitudinal Studies of Adolescents Learning to Read.* London: Routledge & Kegan Paul.

Nesdale, A. R., Herriman, M., and Tunmer, W. E. (1980) The development of phonological awareness. *Education Research and Perspectives, vol. 7*, 20–31.

Patterson, K., and Shewell, C. (1987) Speak and spell: Dissociations and word-class effects. In M. Coltheart, G. Sartori, and R. Job (eds), *The Cognitive Neuropsychology of Language*, London: Erlbaum.

Perfetti, C. A. (1995) Cognitive research can inform reading education. *Journal of Research in Reading*, 18, 106–15.

Rack, J., Hulme, C., Snowling, M., and Wightman, J. (1994) The role of phonology in young children learning to read words: The direct-mapping hypothesis. *Journal of Experimental Child Psychology*, 39, 161–81.

Reitsma, P. (1983) Printed word learning in beginning readers. *Journal of Experimental Child Psychology*, 36, 321–39.

Share, D. L. (1995) Phonological recoding and self-teaching: *sine qua non* of reading acquisition. *Cognition*, 55, 151–218.

Smith, F. (1971) *Understanding Reading.* New York: Holt, Rhinehart & Winston.

Stanovich, K. E. (1986) Matthew effects in reading: Some consequences of individual differences in the acquisition of literacy. *Reading Research Quarterly*, *21*, 360–406.

Stanovich, K. E., Cunningham, A. E., and Cramer, B. B. (1984) Assessing phonological awareness in kindergarten children: Issues of task comparability. *Journal of Experimental Child Psychology*, *38*, 175–90.

Stanovich, K. E., and Stanovich, P. J. (1995) How research might inform the debate about early reading acquisition. *Journal of Research in Reading*, *18*, 87–105.

Stuart, K. M. (1986) Phonological awareness, letter–sound knowledge, and learning to read. Unpublished PhD thesis, University of London.

Stuart, M. (1990) Factors influencing word recognition in pre-reading children. *British Journal of Psychology*, *81*, 135–46.

Stuart, M. (1993) Learning to read: A longitudinal study. *Education, 3–13*, *21*, 19–25.

Stuart, M. (1995) Prediction and qualitative assessment of 5- and 6-year-old children's reading: A longitudinal study. *British Journal of Educational Psychology*, *65*, 287–96.

Stuart, M., and Coltheart, M. (1988) Does reading develop in a sequence of stages? *Cognition*, *30*, 139–81.

Stuart, M., Dixon, M., Masterson, J., and Quinlan, P. (1998) Learning to read at home and at school. *British Journal of Educational Psychology*, *68*, 3–14.

Stuart, M., and Masterson, J. (1992) Patterns of reading and spelling in 10-year-old children related to prereading phonological abilities. *Journal of Experimental Child Psychology*, *54*, 168–87.

Stuart, M., Masterson, J., Dixon, M., and Quinlan, P. (in press) Interacting processes in the development of printed word recognition. In T. Nunes (ed.), *Learning to Read: An Integrated View from Research and Practice*, Kluwer Academic Publishers (in press).

Venezky, R. L. (1970) *The Structure of English Orthography*. The Hague: Mouton.

Chapter Seven

Dyslexia: Core Difficulties, Variability and Causes

CARSTEN ELBRO

The Problem

Some children do not develop reading and spelling abilities at a reasonable rate. They have not yet become independent readers when schools expect them to be able to learn from texts. In some cases such children eventually catch up with their peers, in other cases children appear to be almost resistant to even the best qualified, most considerate, and individually tailored instruction that the school can provide. Recent longitudinal studies have found that a majority of children with slow initial development of reading do *not* catch up with their peers later on (Foorman, Francis, Shaywitz, Shaywitz and Fletcher, 1997; Francis, Shaywitz, Stuebing, Shaywitz and Fletcher, 1994; Jacobson and Lundberg, in press). Hence many children do appear to have deficits in reading and spelling, while a minority of poor readers show a (mere) developmental delay. Children who experience severe, continuing deficits in reading and spelling are prototypical cases of developmental dyslexia, provided that there is no simple cause for this developmental arrest, such as uncorrected far sightedness, severe attentional deficits, or very poor mastery of the language in which the child is supposed to learn to read.

Problems with initial reading and spelling development which may be unnoticed or unacknowledged by the school are rarely unnoticed by the children who have them (e.g. Downing and Leong, 1978, chapter 11). Children usually come to school with a strong

expectancy to learn to read, write, and calculate almost instanta-
neously. So when a child finds it hard to learn to read while his or
her classmates develop skills in reading seemingly effortlessly, the
child starts to wonder why. Since reading and writing are such important aspects of learning in school, an obvious conclusion for the child
is that he or she is simply incapable of learning anything in school.
The child will, depending on his or her way of handling such defeats,
react with a negative attitude towards school and/or him or herself
as a learner.

With an increasing knowledge of the early abilities of importance
to the development of reading, early *prediction* of dyslexia and
assignment of children to early non-stigmatizing, *preventive* programmes will, one hopes, become a part of everyday school practices
(Blachman, 1997, part IV; Singleton, 1997; Turner, 1998). The development and implementation of such programmes depends on many
things, but first of all on reliable knowledge and teacher resources,
both of which are indispensable. The present chapter highlights
central aspects of recent insights into dyslexia: the core problem in
reading and spelling, some types of variability of dyslexia, some proximal and underlying causes, and early prevention. A substantial part
of the empirical sources for the chapter comes from a recent comprehensive Danish study of dyslexia in adults and in their children,
but references are included to many other studies that have provided
similar results. Given the relative brevity of the presentation, the
emphasis will be on clarity and simplicity rather than on details and
controversies about the nature and causes of dyslexia.

The Core: Phonological Processing Difficulties in Reading

Since only some children experience genuine deficits in learning to
read and write, a first task for research would be to characterize the
core of the most persistent problems. One way to do this is to study
adults who experienced severe difficulties in learning to read during
childhood at school, i.e. to study the adult outcome of reading
difficulties in childhood. The idea behind this method is that *some*
difficulties in reading and associated skills may still be found among
the adults even though the problems with initial reading and spelling
development lie many years back in the past.

There is now considerable evidence that adults with a history of difficulties in learning to read differ strongly from adults without such a history in terms of *certain aspects* of reading skills. In particular, large differences in the reading of novel words, typically pronounceable nonwords, have been reported (Bruck, 1990; Elbro, Nielsen and Petersen, 1994; Pennington, Van Orden, Smith, Green and Haith, 1990; compare with Rack, Snowling and Olson, 1992, with respect to younger disabled readers). Some adults may appear to be fairly normal readers when it comes to comprehension of everyday texts. Yet, their difficulties with *phonological processing* in reading and spelling appear to be very long lasting. Even as adults they continue to misspell words – sometimes in ways that are in discord with the sound structure of the spoken words (e.g., *strong* spelled 'stong' or *theatre* spelled 'threater'). Similarly, in reading they may also assign unconventional pronunciations to novel words, e.g., *spraken* pronounced 'spaker' or *norevang* as 'noring'.

Elbro et al. (1994) compared groups of adults with (N = 102) and without (N = 56) a childhood history of reading difficulties on several measures of reading. The differences in nonword reading skills were impressive: the two groups had almost non-overlapping distributions of skills, only 10 per cent of the adults with a history of reading difficulties read at a level of a 'normal' reader. The remaining 90 per cent read at levels below the poorest of the adults without a history of difficulties in learning to read. The difficulties with nonwords also showed up in a pseudo-homophone task. In this task the adults were shown a list of nonwords (e.g., *kise flite spile froone*) and asked to select the one that might sound like a real word if read aloud (e.g., *flite = flight*). Furthermore, the group differences observed in reading *comprehension* disappeared completely when differences in nonword reading were taken into account. This result suggests that the phonological recoding difficulties picked up by the nonword reading test may be the cause of the differences in reading comprehension. The opposite was not the case: the group differences found in reading comprehension did not entirely account for the differences in nonword reading.

In addition to the persistent difficulties with phonological recoding in reading and spelling, Elbro et al. (1994) reported that adults with a history of reading difficulties also showed signs of phonological processing problems with spoken words. The adults performed poorly in a phonological analysis task where they were asked to search for a specified speech sound in pictured words (e.g., which of the following words has an [m] sound in the same position as in *bomb*: *smile, home, shell, milk*?). Similar results have been found in groups of young adults who had managed to compensate for their reading difficulties (Pennington et al., 1990). These results suggest that the long-lasting problems with phonological processing observed in reading may extend to phonological processing of oral language, and that the reading difficulties should be understood from a linguistic perspective.

Difficulty with phonological processing in reading is also a powerful predictor of the choice of education after school. In a longitudinal study, Danish teenagers were studied with reading and spelling tests just before they left school (Elbro, Haven and Jandorf, 1997). One year later they were contacted and interviewed again. The poorest readers (below approximately the 8th percentile) were compared with a group of average readers, and large differences were found in choice of further education and associated social indicators. Among the poor readers not a single participant was enrolled into upper secondary school, whereas more than half of the average readers were. These differences were *not* explained by differences in the socio-economic backgrounds of the teenagers, that is, the educational level, job, and status of their parents. In fact, the best predictor of choice of education among the teenagers was the *reading ability* of their parents – in terms of presence or absence of reading difficulties. Even after two years, only 2 per cent of the poor readers had entered upper secondary school. Somewhat surprisingly, the single best predictor of choice of education was phonological recoding in reading (pseudo-homophone detection) – not reading comprehension.

In sum, a definition of dyslexia based on poor phonological recoding in reading is reliable, stable over time, valid, and educationally and socially relevant.

Variability in Dyslexia

Teachers frequently observe that dyslexics use somewhat different strategies in reading. The most commonly observed difference is that between a more word-by-word oriented strategy and that of a painstaking letter-by-letter recoding strategy (e.g., Boder, 1971; Elbro, 1990; Seymour, 1986; Stanovich, Siegel, Gottardo, Chiappe and Sidhu, 1997). There is only a small amount of evidence that the individual differences in developmental dyslexia are any greater than, or different from, those found among normal beginning readers. The variability observed seems to exist only at low levels of reading skills, at the 'foundation level' of reading ability (Seymour and Evans, 1996). Yet, Elbro (1990) found that some severely dyslexic teenagers, probably among the 1 per cent most severely affected, displayed a more pronounced word-by-word reading strategy than any of the reading-level matched normal controls (from the 2nd and 3rd grades). This finding is perhaps not so surprising given that dyslexics have such great difficulties with phonological processing in reading. After years of struggling with letter–sound correspondences, some dyslexics may give up and try to rely almost exclusively on a whole-word recognition strategy. In this perspective their extreme strategies in reading are nothing but a reflection of their extreme difficulties with an essential subcomponent of reading.

Conversely, dyslexics who continue to use a letter-by-letter reading strategy would seem to be the ones who use a peculiar strategy ill-suited to their abilities. Hence, dyslexics who continue to read like typical beginning readers at the entry of the 'alphabetic phase' of development (Frith, 1985) may be those whose reading stragegy is truly counterproductive and in need of an explanation. The reportedly very slow development of dyslexics with a continued tendency to use a letter-by-letter recoding strategy (e.g. Gjessing, 1980) fits well with the view that they may have a 'double deficit' (Wolf, 1986; 1997): they may have an additional problem on top of their primary problem with phonological recoding in reading. We shall return to this suggestion in a moment.

Some researchers (e.g., Castles and Coltheart, 1993) have attempted to draw parallels between variations in developmental dyslexia and acquired dyslexia, i.e. reading difficulties following brain damage. They have compared developmental dyslexia based on letter-by-letter reading to so-called acquired 'surface' dyslexia. Both types of reading disabilities are characterized by slow but relatively accurate nonword reading in contrast to poor reading of irregularly spelled words. Conversely, developmental dyslexics with a tendency to read words as wholes have been compared to adults with acquired 'phonological' dyslexia. Such comparisons can only be illustrative, however (see Bryant and Impey, 1986). An analogy with walking difficulties, for instance, can illustrate the problems of such comparisons: small children may have difficulties learning to walk for a variety of reasons which are quite distinct from the reasons that usually cause *adult* problems with walking. Obviously, in the case of developmental walking difficulties it is highly unlikely that research in acquired walking difficulties will be of any real importance. As concerns developmental dyslexia, comparisons with acquired dyslexia still have to show their usefulness in terms of an improved understanding of the neurological and neuropsychological bases of the difficulties.

Several researchers have suggested that dyslexics with a pronounced letter-by-letter decoding strategy may have problems with visual word form memory (e.g., Boder, 1971; Gjessing, 1980). This seems an obvious possibility. Some dyslexics continue to be letter-by-letter readers because they have some kind of visual–perceptual or memory deficit which prevents them from setting up orthographic representations of whole words in long-term memory. However compelling it may sound, this visual hypothesis has never received any empirical support. So far no one has shown that differences in visual–perceptual skills are reliably associated with differences in dyslexic reading strategies. Even single case studies of visually based reading difficulties are rare. Consequently, terms like 'visual' or 'dyseidetic' dyslexia suggest causes of special strategies in dyslexia which are, so far, in most cases *not* based on empirical findings.

Candidate causes are more likely to be verbal. Psycholinguistic studies of dyslexia have provided some indication that letter-by-letter reading may be associated with poor access to whole-word phonology (Elbro, 1993). Dyslexics with a tendency to read letter-by-letter (while they rely on isolated letter sounds) have been found to be relatively slow in picture naming. This relation has been found in groups of both Danish and American dyslexics. The correlation between picture naming and reading strategies may be explained in terms of access to whole-word phonology in the following way: a poor decoder who is struggling with single letter–sound correspondences will typically have to guess a lot of the time. He or she may successfully assign a pronunciation to the first few letters of an unknown word and then attempt a guess at the identity of the whole word. If suitable words are retrieved only slowly (as indicated by slow picture naming), there is nothing much the dyslexic can do but continue to spell out the word letter-by-letter.

The hypothesis of a deficit in retrieval of whole-word phonology also fits with the 'double deficit' hypothesis. This latter hypothesis is based upon the finding that some dyslexics are slow at rapid automatized naming, i.e. naming of series of colours, figures, digits, and letters. Such dyslexics appear to have a naming difficulty in addition to their poor phonological recoding abilities, and in this sense they have a double deficit. They are among the most severely affected dyslexics and they have a poor prognosis in so far as they continue to be slow readers.

Recently, Scarborough and Domgaard (1998) have found that the rapid automatized naming task may have two separable components which both relate to reading skills. One is simple speed of articulation. This is the primary measure of interest in rapid naming of colours. The other is related to vocabulary and higher-order cognitive functions. Both of these components may contribute independent variance to the speed with which the phonological representations of whole words are accessed and pronounced.

Unfortunately, there is no easy 'cure' for word retrieval problems. Words which are familiar and phonologically distinct are retrieved more easily than other words. But there are no shortcuts to become familiar with words; the learner simply has to use the words. Besides the letter-by-letter vs whole-word dimension, there may be other important dimensions along which dyslexics differ in their reading strategies (e.g., Fletcher et al., 1997). One such dimension may be associated with the use of morphological decomposition and recognition in reading and spelling. Morphemes are the smallest significant units of language, i.e., the smallest units with a meaning of their own. For example, there are three morphemes in the word *teach/er/s*, the verbal root *teach*, a noun derivation *-er* and a plural suffix *-s*. Some dyslexic teenagers seem to develop a strategy in reading by which they attempt to identify the (first) root morpheme of unfamiliar words and guess the rest (Elbro, 1990; Elbro and Arnbak, 1996). Such a strategy is associated with a relatively high reading speed at the cost of poor accuracy with derivational and inflectional word endings (suffixes). Awareness of morphemes may be enhanced through teaching with emphasis on the meaning of even abstract morphemes. An increase in morpheme awareness appears to lead to more accurate spelling of polymorphemic words first of all, but perhaps also to improvements in reading comprehension (Elbro and Arnbak, 1996). At present however, it seems unlikely that morphological decomposition in dyslexic reading can be more than a compensatory strategy. It does not remediate the fundamental phonological problems which are the topic of the following sections.

One Step Back: Proximal Causes

The vast majority of studies of causes of dyslexia fall into one of three groups: correlational studies, longitudinal prediction studies, and intervention studies.

Correlational studies are typically ones in which groups of good and poor readers are compared on the candidate causes. Particularly when older dyslexics and normal readers are compared, a large number of differences have been reported. Dyslexics are not only behind their peers in reading and closely related skills, such as spelling and rapid naming of letters; they also appear to be behind in most language abilities, including receptive and productive vocabulary, verbal short-term memory, and awareness of phonemes, rhymes, morphemes, and syntax (e.g., Elbro, Nielsen and Petersen, 1994; Stanovich 1993). Their difficulties even extend into other academic areas, and some reports exist of problems in motor coordination and precise timing mechanisms (e.g., Nicolson and Fawcett, 1994; Wolff, Michel, Ovrut and Drake, 1990). However, these last mentioned results are controversial. Recent failures to replicate differences in non-cognitive areas (e.g., Wimmer, Mayringer, Raberger and Stadler, 1998) suggest that *if* such differences exist they are likely to be quite small.

There are several problems with the interpretation of findings from correlational studies. Most notably, it is impossible to distinguish between causes and consequences of reading difficulties. A difference observed in, for instance, listening comprehension may very well be a consequence of dyslexics having fewer reading experiences than controls – rather than a cause of dyslexia. Indeed, it is even likely to be so (e.g., Juel, 1988). In order to exclude the effects of differences in reading experiences, a *reading-age-match* design has gained increasing popularity. Instead of matching groups on chronological age, the match is based on reading age, that is, the comparison is between older dyslexics and younger normal readers who have similar reading skills (Bryant and Goswami, 1986). With a reading-age-match design, differences between groups are more likely to favour the (older) dyslexic group than the younger controls. So when a difference is found in favour of the younger group, it is likely to be a difference which is at least closely *related* to the causes of problems of the older dyslexics. Such positive findings are rare in comparison with the differences found with the chronological-age-match design. Differences have been reported most consistently with respect to phoneme awareness. Even compensated adult dyslexics show phonological processing problems – in comparison with younger persons with no history of reading problems – when asked to segment spoken words into phoneme-size units or to make Spoonerisms, e.g. *John Lennon* becomes 'lon jennon' (Gallagher, Laxon, Armstrong and Frith, 1996). Such findings are only suggestive of possible causes, though, and they do not provide any estimate of the predictive power of correlates.

In *prediction studies* children are typically followed from before the onset of literacy instruction up to a point when reliable differences in reading development can be detected (Scarborough, 1998, presents a recent overview). The interval between the first and second observation may be as short as six weeks in languages with simple letter–sound correspondences (e.g. Dutch or Finnish) and in educational systems where reading is taught intensively from the start of the school year. However, longer durations are more usual. It is a common finding across languages and educational systems that the ranking of children in terms of reading proficiency does not change much from grade 2 to later grades (Foorman, Francis, Shaywitz, Shaywitz and Fletcher, 1997; Scarborough, 1998). The majority of poor readers in the early grades remain poor readers relative to their peers throughout school. So, although there are late bloomers and children who get stuck at some point, much of the variance in reading to be explained is already present after one or two years of instruction.

The Copenhagen dyslexia study is an example of a longitudinal study of precursors of reading development, and one of very few studies that has focused on early indicators of dyslexia in children at risk, namely, in children of dyslexic parents. The study focused on at-risk children simply because the incidence of dyslexia is much higher in at-risk children than in a random sample of children. Hence, the number of participants could be kept relatively low and yet a number of children would show signs of severe reading difficulties (cf. Scarborough, 1998). The general aim of the study was to assess the relative importance of various environmental and linguistic factors for the development of dyslexia. Groups of at-risk children (N = 87) and not-at-risk children (N = 72) have been followed from the entry of the kindergarten grade (at six years of age in Denmark) to the beginning of the second grade. A follow-up at the beginning of the third grade has recently been completed with the 152 remaining children in the study.

Traditionally, correlational coefficients are used as estimates of the strength of the association between early predictors and reading outcomes. However, correlational coefficients are based on all of the variation associated with each of the variables. The coefficient reflects not only the differences between the poorest readers and the rest, but also the differences between the good readers and the very best readers. This inclusion of all variance associated with each variable has the potential disadvantage of obscuring differences which may be of special interest. In studies of dyslexia the differences of primary interest are, of course, those between the poorest readers and the rest of the readers. The variation among average and superior readers is simply not relevant. As the story of the study unfolds, it will become clear that this point about an inherent danger of computing simple correlations is not only of theoretical interest, but also of practical importance.

Nature has not defined a cut-off point between dyslexia and normal reading. There is no strong evidence that the distribution of reading abilities is anything but normal. In the Copenhagen study a cut-off point was selected at about the 10th percentile in the not-at-risk group. Hence, children with an average score below the 10th percentile in two tests of phonological recoding in reading were considered dyslexic, whereas the rest were labelled 'normal'. This cut-off point corresponds to the percentage of children who are referred to some kind of special education because of reading and/or spelling difficulties in Danish schools. At the beginning of the second grade as many as 31 per cent of the at-risk children could be classified as

Table 7.1 Observed reading abilities at the beginning of grade 2 as a function of predicted group membership based on language measures at the beginning of kindergarten
(Cut-off value p = 0.75; overall prediction rate is 79%.)

Observed	Predicted		Predicted rate
	Dyslexic	Normal	
Dyslexic	18	5	78%
Normal	14	53	79%
Predicted rate	56%	91%	

'dyslexic' (Borstrøm and Elbro, 1997). This highly increased proportion of dyslexics among the at-risk children replicated findings of earlier studies and justified the term 'at risk' (Gilger, Pennington and DeFries, 1991; Scarborough, 1998).

The question now is how well group membership ('dyslexic' versus 'normal' reading) can be predicted by each of the measures taken two years earlier at the beginning of kindergarten. The older half of the children were studied first and results were reported recently. Of sixteen measures of verbal abilities and several measures of home environment, three measures seemed to predict dyslexia best (for details of measures and statistical regression procedures, see Elbro, Borstrøm and Petersen, 1998). The three measures were *knowledge of letter names, phonemic awareness*, and *quality of phonological representations of spoken words*. When these three measures were taken into account, none of the other measures contributed further to the accuracy of the prediction. On the other hand, if any of the three measures was excluded, the accuracy of the prediction was lowered. While the two first-mentioned variables are well known predictors of initial success or failure to learn to read, the third predictor is new. This third predictor further appeared to predict gains in phonemic awareness over the kindergarten year, and it will be introduced and discussed in the following section.

Table 7.1 shows how well dyslexia in the second grade was predicted by three measures of language abilities at the beginning of the kindergarten grade. The 'hit' rate was 78 per cent, which is the proportion of the children with observed reading difficulties who were correctly predicted (also called true positives). Hence, at least three out of every four children with severe reading difficulties could be identified as early as one year *before* they started formal instruction in reading. The expense was that normal reading was also predicted with 79 per cent accuracy, which implies that there were 21 per cent 'false alarms', i.e. cases in which the predicted reading difficulties did not occur (also called 'false positives').

The model underlying table 7.1 put emphasis on keeping the 'hit' rate high and the proportion of 'misses' low, that is, the cut-off value for the predicted at-risk group was selected so as to identify as many as possible of the children who became dyslexic. The cost was, of course, a low 'positive predictive value', that is, there were relatively many children who were identified as at risk by the model, but, fortunately, became normal readers (44 per cent).

In practice, the proportion of children chosen to be considered at risk is determined by educational, economic, and ethical considerations. A high positive predictive value is of the essence in the following circumstances: when the effects of early intervention are (believed to be) poor, when the economic resources are scarce, and when there is little emphasis on attempts to counteract the inequalities among the children's potential for learning to read. Under such conditions it does not matter greatly that a relatively high number of children with potential reading problems are 'missed' by the prediction model. On the other hand, a high 'hit' rate is of the essence where early intervention has greater priority. In this case, it is less important that high-quality preventive programmes are also offered to some children who do not really need them.

Despite their name, most prediction studies are not concerned with true prediction (Scarborough, 1998; Singleton, 1997). They are like 'prediction' of obstacles in the rear-view mirror. Typical 'prediction' studies ask the question: 'how well *might* the observed reading difficulties have been predicted, if we had known what to look for and how much emphasis to put on each "predictor"?' Most so-called predictive studies have attempted to set up the model that best 'predicted' an already observed outcome. Obviously, the resulting prediction model capitalizes on some random variation. No measure is perfect, and no two groups of children are completely alike.

Table 7.2 True prediction in a younger group of children using the regression equation from the older group (table 7.1)
(Cut-off value p = 0.60; overall prediction rate is 69%.)

Observed	Predicted		Predicted rate
	Dyslexic	Normal	
Dyslexic	13	5	72%
Normal	13	28	68%
Predicted rate	50%	85%	

Consequently, prediction rates from retrospective studies are inflated. The prediction rates from true prediction studies are usually much lower than those reported from retrospective studies. Most true prediction rates lie in the range from 50 per cent to 70 per cent (see the surveys in Elbro et al., 1998, and Singleton, 1997).

The Copenhagen dyslexia study comprised two cohorts: an older one on which the initial prediction model was based, and a younger one to which the model was applied in an assessment of its true predictive value. The accuracy of the prediction model in the younger group is shown in table 7.2 (Petersen & Elbro, in press). As expected, the prediction rate was lower in the younger group of children, but not very much lower. The overall prediction rate was about 10 percentage points lower, and the hit rate was still relatively high.

In conclusion, levels of awareness of phoneme-size segments of spoken language is certainly predictive of success and failure in the initial phase of reading development. Certainly, phoneme awareness is not the only predictor. Letter knowledge is another strong predictor. A third predictor may be speed of access to the sounds of words in the mental lexicon – as it is measured in rapid naming tasks (see the survey in Scarborough, 1998). Finally the quality of phonological representations of whole spoken words may be a fourth important predictor (see below).

It is noteworthy that linguistic factors are so strongly predictive of later reading. The strength of the prediction may provide a sense of proportion. An implication of the above findings is that other factors are unlikely to be equally predictive. The list of such relatively less influential factors is, of course, endless but it includes even environmental factors (from age 5–6 and up), factors associated with differences in teaching methods, and other cognitive and related abilities.

However, even strong predictors may be only spuriously related to reading development. There may be a yet unknown third factor underlying the statistical relationship between any predictor and reading development. A better test of the possible causal connections is provided by longitudinal prediction and *intervention* studies in combination. Several such studies have been conducted with phoneme awareness in recent years (Bradley and Bryant, 1983; Lundberg, Frost and Petersen, 1988; Schneider, Küspert, Roth, Visé and Marx, 1997). A typical training programme, such as the one developed by Lundberg and colleagues, aims at directing the attention of the children towards the *form* of spoken language rather than its content (see also Byrne and Liberman, this volume). It proceeds in a highly structured format from listening games and activities with whole words and with rhymes towards activities that direct the attention of the preschool children towards individual phonemes.

This and similar programmes have been demonstrated to have considerable positive impact not only on the phoneme awareness of the children, but also on their subsequent reading and spelling development. This is remarkable in the light of the fact that it is a purely oral programme and does *not* include any letter training. Furthermore, it has been shown to have similarly positive effects in groups of children speaking different languages, including Swedish (Olofsson and Lundberg, 1985), Danish (Lundberg et al., 1988), German (Schneider et al., 1997), and Portuguese (Cary and Verhaeghe, 1994). The programme has recently been translated into English (Adams, Foorman, Lundberg and Beeler, 1998).

Other studies have shown that the effects of phoneme awareness training are greatly enhanced when the training is supported by letters. It might be argued that phoneme awareness training supported by, for example, plastic letters is really just a kind of initial reading instruction. However, as long as the letters are used to help children pay attention to individual phonemes and not as a means to read words, this argument cannot entirely explain away the positive effect of phoneme awareness training.

Fortunately, phoneme awareness training also has preventive effects in groups of at-risk children (Borstrøm and Elbro, 1997; Byrne and Fielding-Barnsley, 1995; Torgesen, Wagner and Rashotte, 1994). In the Copenhagen dyslexia study a group of 36 at-risk children attending 27 different classes received intensive and extensive instruction in phoneme awareness. When their reading development was compared with that of 52 other at-risk children (from 44 different classes) at the beginning of the second grade, a significant reduction in the incidence of possible dyslexia was observed – from 40 per cent in the control group to 17 per cent in the experimental group. Even though the 17 per cent poor readers are more than the 8 per cent in the group of not-at-risk children (N = 44), it is a big step in the right direction (it represents a decrease of the risk (odds) of reading difficulties by more than a factor three).

Unfortunately, the impact of phoneme awareness training appears to be smaller in groups of poor readers than in groups of preschool children (Olson, Wise, Johnson and Ring, 1997). It is possible for poor readers to gain in phoneme awareness, and corresponding gains in phonological recoding (measured by nonword reading) may be found. However, the effects do not appear to generalize to rapid reading of real words. The reason for this difference between the impact of phoneme awareness training in different populations is not known. It is certainly the case that older dyslexics represent a much more selected group than even at-risk preschool children. Older dyslexics have already received the kind of intensive phoneme awareness training that comes with most types of reading instruction – and failed. So it is no surprise that it is harder to teach older dyslexics phonemic awareness. But this does not explain why they do not generalize their letter–sound knowledge to real words and why they do not improve in reading speed following an improvement in phoneme awareness.

The reason for this lack of transfer may be that no phoneme awareness programme can train all phonological segments of importance to reading. Awareness of *single* phonemes may be important for the appreciation of letter–sound correspondences at the single letter–phoneme level. But this level is certainly not the only one of importance in deep orthographies such as English, French, and Danish. There are hundreds of conventions that apply to strings of letters, e.g. so-called letter patterns such as *-ight* pronounced /ait/, or

-all pronounced /ʌːl/. In other words, there are many other important phonological segments to be aware of besides single phonemes. And all these segments are not, and cannot be, taught in a finite training programme.

However, so far this and other suggestions are only speculations. It remains an intriguing possibility that poor phoneme awareness is an indication of a more fundamental language problem. Perhaps only the children with minor problems in this yet unknown area are responsive to training of phoneme awareness. If this were the case, it would be of central practical as well as theoretical importance to study the variation in individual responsiveness to phoneme awareness training. Significant predictors of the individual responsiveness would be good indicators of underlying language problems.

Two Steps Back: Underlying Language Problems

One of the foci of the Copenhagen dyslexia study was the nature and quality of phonological representations of lexical items, i.e. the quality of the representation of the sounds of words in the mental lexicon. The general idea was that children with poorly specified, fuzzy or lacking, representations of the sounds of words might be those who would have difficulties with phoneme awareness – and with reading development later on. This is not a new idea (e.g., Brady, 1997; Fowler, 1991; Reitsma and Wesseling, 1998; Snowling, Wagtendonk and Stafford, 1988). However, it would be wrong to say that it is well researched.

One major problem is that phonological representations cannot be assessed directly. They reside in the mental lexicon of the child. Yet several measures may tap various aspects of phonological representations. Receptive vocabulary tasks are to some extent measures of whether or not specific words are represented. Production tasks are sensitive to the accessibility of phonological representations; a lexical item may be represented with too little detail. This lack of specification may have the consequence that the lexical item is either unretrievable, retrieved incorrectly (Katz, 1986; 1996), or stays at the tip of the tongue for a long time.

The quality of phonological representations was studied with a new measure in the Copenhagen dyslexia study. We simply asked the children to correct a faulty, strongly underspecified pronunciation. On behalf of a hand-held puppet, the experimenter pronounced a pictured object, e.g. a crocodile, at a very low level of distinctiveness, e.g. 'codi'. The task of the child was to correct the puppet – a task that they gladly accepted. The child was instructed to be careful to speak the words as accurately as possible so that the puppet would learn the correct pronunciation. The words were well within the productive vocabulary of the children, and the words were relatively long, allowing for much variation in pronunciation with no great loss of intelligibility. From the responses of each child, several scores were extracted and calculated. The only one mentioned here is the accuracy score, i.e. the percentage of conventional (correct) pronunciations.

Which factors explained variance in the development of phoneme awareness? Who were the children resistant to early prevention? The important task was to predict which children would make substantial gains and which would not. Gains in phoneme awareness were first studied among the 36 at-risk children in the experimental group who received phoneme awareness training. Correlations were calculated between individual gains in phoneme awareness and language abilities at the onset of the training period. It turned out that the quality of the children's phonological representations (as measured in the correction task) correlated the strongest ($r = 0.55$) with gains in phoneme awareness (Elbro, Borstrøm and Petersen, submitted). When differences in the quality of phonological representations were taken into account, no other variable explained further variance in gains in phoneme awareness.

A similar pattern was found in the untrained, not-at-risk children ($N = 48$) with the exception that general cognitive factors and pre-reading skills also contributed to the prediction of gains in phoneme awareness. These additional factors were expected to be of importance since the lack of explicit instruction left it up to the children to develop phonemic awareness from the more general activities in their kindergarten and home surroundings. So the more reflective of the children, and those children with some letter knowledge, would be likely to pick up more knowledge about phonemes from their environment than would less reflective children and children with little letter knowledge.

In sum, the findings support the general idea that the quality of the phonological representations set the stage for development of phoneme awareness. Children who started kindergarten with relatively *well-specified phonological representations of spoken words* profited the most from phoneme awareness training – and were those who later had the fewest problems in learning to read (Elbro et al., 1998). Awareness of larger linguistic units, such as syllables or morphemes, did *not* predict gains in phoneme awareness. Consequently, what matters for the development of phoneme awareness may simply be the amount of phonetic information stored with each phonological representation rather than, for instance, the internal structure of the representation.

In any case, if quality of phonological representation matters, training phoneme awareness will only take care of a part of the dyslexia problem. We don't yet know how to help children develop the quality of their phonological representations. How this could be accomplished is just one of many difficult tasks that future research is facing in this area.

One Step Ahead: Prediction of Superior Reading

So far this chapter has focused on the description, prediction, and prevention of poor reading. The practical need for research-based insights into reading difficulties is strong, and for obvious reasons. It is much less obvious why one should want to predict the development of superior reading. There is, however, one important theoretical reason. If it can be shown that superior reading is not *just* the mirror image of poor reading, it should at least provide a warning against making false inferences from one group to the other, and it should warn against the use of statistical procedures, such as multiple regression analyses, that analyse the whole of the continuum as one, from the poorest reader to the very best.

In the Copenhagen dyslexia study, an attempt was made to predict superior reading in the second grade (Elbro, 1997). The 25 per cent best readers were selected as 'superior readers' and compared with the rest of the children. Sixteen measures of linguistic abilities at the beginning of the kindergarten grade were then used to predict the reading outcome ('superior' versus 'poor or average'). The independent variables were the same as those in the analyses mentioned above. The results were very much the same for letter knowledge and phoneme awareness as in the prediction of poor reading, but there was a noticeable difference with respect to phonological representations. The accuracy and distinctiveness of the phonological representations were less predictive of superior reading; rather, single *picture naming speed* was a strong predictor. This means that children who entered the kindergarten grade with *rapid access* to the phonological representations of well-known words were more likely than others to become superior readers in the second grade.

This change of importance from accuracy to speed of access to phonological representations fits well with the increasing importance of reading speed once basic decoding accuracy has been attained. It seems immediately understandable that quick access to the sound representation of words would be one of the underpinnings of reading speed. This explanation is also in accordance with findings from studies of reading development in regular orthographies like German, Dutch, and Finnish. Since the grapheme–phoneme mappings are quite transparent in these languages, the task of mastering them is easier than mastering those of deep orthographies, such as Danish and English. Consequently, reading speed becomes relatively more important from an early stage in reading development (Wimmer, 1996; Wimmer, Landerl and Schneider, 1994). Correspondingly, naming speed of individual pictures has been shown to be a very important predictor of early reading development in regular orthographies (Schneider and Näslund, 1993).

Conclusion

Much of the 100-year history of dyslexia research is a sad story. Many researchers have attempted to define dyslexia in ways that reflected a particular view of the causes of dyslexia, and this view has later been shown to be wrong. As the underlying hypotheses have been proved wrong, most of the research based on them has been rendered irrelevant or otherwise useless. This chapter has focused on what I believe to be the results of the more fruitful approach that has gained increasing popularity over the last few decades. This modern approach is based on a broad operational definition of dyslexia and on converging evidence from several independent studies carried out in different alphabetic orthographies (see also Stanovich, 1998, especially pp. 123–7).

The first step following this approach was the detailed study of the particular reading and spelling patterns of (fairly unselected) children who have great difficulties in learning to read and write. From a large number of studies it is now well known that the majority of poor readers have difficulties with the acquisition of the alphabetic nature of written language. They fail to acquire the fundamental correspondences between letters and sounds, and between letter patterns and sound patterns. This failure is long lasting and in many cases clearly detectable well into adulthood, and it shows up most markedly in tasks involving reading of new words (pronounceable nonwords).

The next step was to search for causes for the problems with the acquisition of the alphabetic principle. There is now little doubt that awareness of sound segments of words is a central factor in reading development. Normally this awareness develops in parallel with the acquisition of decoding skills – or as a response to a special preschool training programme. But sometimes it does not. This is when the child is most obviously at risk of dyslexia.

Difficulties in the development of awareness of small segments of spoken words appears to be part of a more general phonological processing problem that seems to stem from poor abilities to encode phonological material (see Brady, 1997). Indeed, they often occur in combination with problems in repetition of long, unfamiliar words, in naming pictured objects, and in retrieval of words based on a part of the sound of the word (e.g., the initial sound).

Fortunately, the consequences of these encoding problems may be to some extent overcome by early intervention. Programmes that combine initial reading instruction with a well-structured programme designed to enhance segmental awareness have been shown to be successful.

However, not all children respond to even the best of such programmes. There is now *some* evidence that unresponsive children may possess phonological representations of words which are too *underspecified* to allow for access to and manipulation of segments of spoken words (Elbro, 1996; Elbro et al., submitted; Reitsma and Wesseling, 1998). The research in this area is only in its infancy, and not a single study has yet been carried out on the causal direction.

Finally, a point was made of the possible differences between factors that predict poor reading and factors that predict superior reading. It was suggested that reading speed becomes more important with the development of reading ability, and with it the nature of the predictors change. One consequence is that researchers should stop looking at the whole range of variation and concentrate on ability differences that are of practical or theoretical relevance. Practitioners have done so as long as there has been a concern for children who fail to learn to read.

References

Adams, M. J., Foorman, B. R., Lundberg, I., and Beeler, T. (1998) *Phonemic Awareness in Young Children: A Classroom Curriculum*. Baltimore, MD: Paul Brookes.

Blachman, B. A. (ed.) (1997) *Foundations of Reading Acquisition and Dyslexia: Implications for Early Intervention* (Mahwah, NJ: Lawrence Erlbaum).

Boder, E. (1971) Developmental dyslexia: A diagnostic screening procedure based on three characteristic patterns of reading and spelling. In B. Bateman (ed.), *Learning Disorders*, vol. 4: *Reading*, Seattle, Washington: Special Child Publications, pp. 297–347.

Borstrøm, I., and Elbro, C. (1997) Prevention of dyslexia in kindergarten: Effects of phoneme awareness training with children of dyslexic parents. In C. Hulme and M. Snowling (eds), *Dyslexia: Biology, Cognition and Intervention*, London: Whurr, pp. 235–53.

Bradley, L., and Bryant, P. E. (1983) Categorizing sounds and learning to read – a causal connection. *Nature, 301*, 419–21.

Brady, S. A. (1997) Ability to encode phonological representations: An underlying difficulty in poor readers. In B. Blachman (ed.), *Foundations of Reading Acquisition and Dyslexia: Implications for Early Intervention*, Mahwah, NJ: Erlbaum, pp. 21–48.

Bruck, M. (1990) Word recognition skills of adults with childhood diagnoses of dyslexia. *Developmental Psychology, 26*, 439–54.

Bryant, P., and Goswami, U. (1986) Strengths and weaknesses of the reading level design: A comment on Backman, Mamen, and Ferguson. *Psychological Bulletin, 100*, 101–3.

Bryant, P., and Impey, L. (1986) The similarities between normal readers and developmental and acquired dyslexics. *Cognition, 24*, 121–37.

Byrne, B., and Fielding-Barnsley, R. (1995) Evaluation of a program to teach phonemic awareness to young children: A 2- and 3-year follow-up and a new preschool trial. *Journal of Educational Psychology, 87*, 488–503.

Cary, L., and Verhaeghe, A. (1994) Promoting phonemic analysis ability among kindergartners. *Reading and Writing: An Interdisciplinary Journal, 6*, 251–78.

Castles, A., and Coltheart, M. (1993) Varieties of developmental dyslexia. *Cognition, 47*, 149–80.

Downing, J., and Leong, C. K. (1978) *Psychology of Reading.* New York: Macmillan.

Elbro, C. (1990) *Differences in Dyslexia: A Study of Reading Strategies and Deficits in a Linguistic Perspective.* Copenhagen: Munksgaard.

Elbro, C. (1993) Dyslexic reading strategies and lexical access: A comparison and validation of reading strategy distributions in dyslexic adolescents and younger, normal readers. In R. M. Joshi and C. K. Leong (eds), *Reading Disabilities: Diagnosis and Component Processes*, Dordrecht: Kluwer, pp. 239–51.

Elbro, C. (1996) Early linguistic abilities and reading development: A review and a hypothesis. *Reading and Writing: An Interdisciplinary Journal, 8*, 453–85.

Elbro, C. (1997) Different language abilities predict poor and good reading in the early grades. Paper presented at the AERA meeting, Chicago, May 1997.

Elbro, C., and Arnbak, E. (1996) The role of morpheme recognition and morphological awareness in dyslexia. *Annals of Dyslexia, 46*, 209–40.

Elbro, C., Borstrøm, I., and Petersen, D. K. (1998) Predicting dyslexia from kindergarten: The importance of distinctness of phonological representations of lexical items. *Reading Research Quarterly, 33*, 36–60.

Elbro, C., Borstrøm, I. B., and Petersen, D. K. (submitted) Causes and consequences of the development of phoneme awareness: A longitudinal and intervention study of normal and at-risk children. *Journal of Experimental Child Psychology.*

Elbro, C., Haven, D., and Jandorf, B. D. (1997) Gode og dårlige læsere efter 9. klasse. Første del af en efterundersøgelse. *Psykologisk Pædagogisk Rådgivning, 34*, 19–42.

Elbro, C., Nielsen, I., and Petersen, D. K. (1994) Dyslexia in adults: Evidence for deficits in non-word reading and in the phonological representation of lexical items. *Annals of Dyslexia, 44*, 205–26.

Fletcher, J. M., Morris, R., Lyon, G. R., Stuebing, K. K., Shaywitz, S. E., Shankweiler, D. P., Katz, L., and Shaywitz, B. A. (1997) Subtypes of dyslexia: An old problem revisited. In B. A. Blachman (ed.), *Foundations of Reading Acquisition and Dyslexia: Implications for Early Intervention*, Mahwah, NJ: Lawrence Erlbaum, pp. 95–141.

Foorman, B. R., Francis, D. J., Shaywitz, S. E., Shaywitz, B. A., and Fletcher, J. M. (1997) The case for early reading intervention. In B. A. Blachman (ed.), *Foundations of Reading Acquisition and Dyslexia: Implications for Early Intervention*, Mahwah, NJ: Lawrence Erlbaum, pp. 243–64.

Fowler, A. E. (1991) How early phonological development might set the stage for phoneme awareness. In S. Brady and D. Shankweiler (eds), *Phonological Processes in Literacy: A Tribute to Isabelle Y. Liberman*, Hillsdale, NJ: Lawrence Erlbaum, pp. 97–118.

Francis, D. J., Shaywitz, S. E., Stuebing, K. K., Shaywitz, B. A., and Fletcher, J. M. (1994) Measurement of change: Assessing behavior over time and within a developmental context. In G. R. Lyon (ed.), *Frames of Reference for the Assessment of Learning Disabilities. New Views on Measurement Issues*, Baltimore: Paul H. Brookes, pp. 29–58.

Frith, U. (1985) Beneath the surface of developmental dyslexia. In K. E. Patterson, J. C. Marshall, and M. Coltheart (eds), *Surface Dyslexia. Neuropsychological and Cognitive Studies in Phonological Reading*, London: Lawrence Erlbaum, pp. 301–30.

Gallagher, A. M., Laxon, V., Armstrong, E., and Frith, U. (1996) Phonological difficulties in high-functioning dyslexics. *Reading and Writing: An Interdisciplinary Journal*, 8, 499–509.

Gilger, J. W., Pennington, B. F., and DeFries, J. C. (1991) Risk for reading disability as a function of parental history in three family studies. *Reading and Writing: An Interdisciplinary Journal*, 3, 205–17.

Gjessing, H.-J. (1980) Function analysis of reading and writing behavior. In R. M. Knights and D. J. Bakker (eds), *Treatment of Hyperactive and Learning Disordered Children: Current Research*, Baltimore: University Book Press.

Jacobson, C., and Lundberg, I. (in press) Early prediction of individual growth in reading. *Reading and Writing: An Interdisciplinary Journal*.

Juel, C. (1988) Learning to read and write: A longitudinal study of 54 children from first through fourth grades. *Journal of Educational Psychology*, 80, 437–47.

Katz, R. B. (1986) Phonological deficiencies in children with reading disability: Evidence from an object-naming task. *Cognition*, 22, 225–57.

Katz, R. B. (1996) Phonological and semantic factors in the object-naming errors of skilled and less skilled readers. *Annals of Dyslexia*, 46, 189–208.

Lundberg, I., Frost, J., and Petersen, O.-P. (1988) Effects of an extensive program for stimulating phonological awareness in preschool children. *Reading Research Quarterly*, 23, 263–84.

Nicolson, R. I., and Fawcett, A. J. (1994) Reaction times and dyslexia. *Quarterly Journal of Experimental Psychology*, 47A, 29–48.

Olofsson, Å., and Lundberg, I. (1985) Evaluation of long term effects of phonemic awareness training in kindergarten: Illustrations of some methodological problems in evaluation research. *Scandinavian Journal of Psychology*, 26, 21–34.

Olson, R. K., Wise, B., Johnson, M. C., and Ring, J. (1997) The etiology and remediation of phonologically based word recognition and spelling disabilities: Are phonological deficits the 'hole' study? In B. A. Blachman (ed.), *Foundations of Reading Acquisition and Dyslexia: Implications for Early Intervention*, Mahwah, NJ: Lawrence Erlbaum, pp. 305–28.

Pennington, B. F., Van Orden, G. C., Smith, S. D., Green, P. A., and Haith, M. M. (1990) Phonological processing skills and deficits in adult dyslexics. *Child Development*, 61, 1753–78.

Petersen, D. K., and Elbro, C. (in press) Pre-school prediction and prevention of dyslexia: A longitudinal study with children of dyslexic parents. In T. Nunes (ed.), *Reading Research and the Teaching of Reading*, Hove: Psychology Press.

Rack, J. P., Snowling, M. J., and Olson, R. K. (1992) The nonword reading deficit in developmental dyslexia: A review. *Reading Research Quarterly*, 27, 28–53.

Reitsma, P., and Wesseling, R. (1998) Precursors to phonological awareness. Paper presented at the Fifth Annual Meeting of SSSR in San Diego, CA, 17–19 April 1998.

Scarborough, H. S. (1998) Early identification of children at risk for reading disabilities. In B. K. Shapiro, P. J. Accardo, and A. J. Capute (eds), *Specific Reading Disability: A View of the Spectrum*, Timonium, ML: York Press, pp. 75–119.

Scarborough, H. S., and Domgaard, R. M. (1998) An exploration of the relationship between reading and serial rapid naming. Paper presented at the Fifth Annual Meeting of SSSR in San Diego, CA, 17–19 April 1998.

Schneider, W., Küspert, P., Roth, E., Visé, M., and Marx, H. (1997) Short- and long-term effects of training phonological awareness in kindergarten: Evidence from two German studies. *Journal of Experimental Child Psychology*, 66, 311–40.

Schneider, W., and Näslund, J. C. (1993) The impact of early metalinguistic competencies and memory capacity on reading and spelling in elementary school: Results of the Munich longitudinal study on the genesis of individual competencies (LOGIC). *European Journal of Psychology of Education*, 8, 273–87.

Seymour, P. H. K. (1986) *Cognitive Analysis of Dyslexia*. London: Routledge & Kegan Paul.

Seymour, P. H. K., and Evans, H. M. (1996) Foundation level dyslexias. Paper presented at the COST workshop in Stavanger, 1996.

Singleton, C. (1997) Screening early literacy. In J. R. Beech and C. Singleton (eds), *The Psychological Assessment of Reading*, London: Routledge, pp. 67–101.

Snowling, M., Wagtendonk, B., and Stafford, C. (1988) Object-naming deficits in developmental dyslexia. *Journal of Research in Reading*, 11, 67–85.

Stanovich, K. E. (1993) Does reading make you smarter? Literacy and the development of verbal intelligence. In H. Reese (ed.), *Advances in Child Development and Behaviour*, Orlando, FL: Academic Press, vol. 24, pp. 133–80.

Stanovich, K. E. (1998) *How to Think Straight about Psychology* (5th edn). New York: Longman.

Stanovich, K. E., Siegel, L., Gottardo, A., Chiappe, P., and Sidhu, R. (1997) Subtypes of developmental dyslexia: Differences in phonological and orthographic coding. In B. A. Blachman (ed.), *Foundations of Reading Acquisition and Dyslexia: Implications for Early Intervention*, Mahwah, NJ: Lawrence Erlbaum, pp. 115–41.

Torgesen, J. K., Wagner, R. K., and Rashotte, C. A. (1994) Longitudinal studies of phonological processing and reading. *Journal of Learning Disabilities*, 27, 276–86.

Turner, M. (1998) *Psychological Assessment of Dyslexia*. London: Whurr.

Wimmer, H. (1996) The early manifestation of developmental dyslexia: Evidence from German children. *Reading and Writing: An Interdisciplinary Journal*, 8, 171–88.

Wimmer, H., Landerl, K., and Schneider, W. (1994) The role of rhyme awareness in learning to read a regular orthography. *British Journal of Developmental Psychology*, 12, 469–84.

Wimmer, H., Mayringer, H., Raberger, T., and Stadler, B. (1998) Reading and balancing: Evidence against the automatization deficit explanation of developmental dyslexia. Paper presented at the Fifth Annual Meeting of SSSR in San Diego, CA, 17–19 April 1998.

Wolf, M. (1986) Rapid alternating stimulus naming in the developmental dyslexias. *Brain and Language*, 27, 360–79.

Wolf, M. (1997) A provisional, integrative account of phonological and naming-speed deficits in dyslexia: Implications for diagnosis and intervention. In B. A. Blachman (ed.), *Foundations of Reading Acquisition and Dyslexia: Implications for Early Intervention*, Mahwah, NJ: Lawrence Erlbaum, pp. 67–92.

Wolff, P. H., Michel, G. F., Ovrut, M., and Drake, C. (1990) Rate and timing precision of motor coordination in developmental dyslexia. *Developmental Psychology*, 26, 349–59.

Chapter Eight

Meaninglessness, Productivity and Reading: Some Observations about the Relation between the Alphabet and Speech

BRIAN BYRNE AND ALVIN M. LIBERMAN

The observant reading teacher will have noticed that children who are impaired in identifying printed words manifest their difficulties in several ways. Some, for example, learn a stock of printed words 'by sight' but fail to fathom the rules relating print to speech, remaining incapable of reading new words independently. Others may know how to 'sound out' individual letters, like *l*, *a*, and *d*, yet not be able to 'blend' them to produce the word 'lad'. At the same time, the observant teacher has noted, these children are perfectly capable of speaking and listening, exhibiting a command of speech that far outstrips their command of print. We believe that at the heart of this mix

We thank Susan Brady for helpful comments on a draft of this chapter, and also extend our thanks to Michael Studdert-Kennedy and Donald Shankweiler for sharpening some of the ideas that we have promoted in this chapter. Liberman's research has been supported by grants from the NIH to Haskins Laboratories, and Byrne's has been supported by grants from the Australian Research Council. Preparation of the chapter was aided by a grant from the University of New England. The authors made equal contributions to this chapter. The order of authorship is alphabetical.

of abilities and disabilities stand certain facts about the relation of the alphabet to speech, and our aim is to amplify and justify this belief. We hold the view that teachers and teacher educators who appreciate how the alphabet relates to speech will be better placed to further appreciate why learning to read may be hard.

We start our analysis from the seemingly obvious notion that being aware of the meaningless phonologic constituents of words – the *phonemes*, so called – that the letters *l*, *a*, and *d* stand in for is essential to the proper use of the alphabetic cipher that represents these constituents. (A *cipher* is a code which systematically encodes a message – the letter *l* stands in for the phoneme /l/ whenever the phoneme occurs.) The awareness we refer to would be present in the child who could indicate that 'lad' is composed of three phonemes, or that 'lad' and 'log' begin with the same phoneme. We note that researchers have arrived at three important conclusions: The requisite awareness is poorly developed in pre-literate children; the degree to which it is present is one of the best predictors of success in learning to read; and procedures calculated to establish it increase the likelihood that the would-be reader will make good progress (for reviews of this extensive literature, see Adams, 1990; Brady and Shankweiler, 1991; Byrne, 1998; Goswami and Bryant, 1990; Gough, Ehri and Treiman, 1992; Share, 1995). Those conclusions are now well established, widely recognized, and strongly emphasized in scientific accounts of how children learn to read and why some don't. Rarely considered, however, are four questions that must, in our view, be answered if the aforementioned conclusions are to be properly understood.

1   What is the importance to language of the meaninglessness of its basic constituents?
2   Why is awareness of those constituents not necessary for speech, nor a normal consequence of having mastered it?
3   How might development of such awareness be made harder by the language habits the pre-literate child brings to the task of learing to read?
4   What does all this imply for instruction?

Our aim is to ventilate those questions by bringing together such facts about language and the child's conception of it as seem relevant.

What is the Importance to Language of the Meaninglessness of its Basic Constituents?

All nonhuman creatures communicate, appropriating for the purpose one or more of every conceivable medium. Thus, some use acoustic signals, some optical, some chemical, some mechanical, and, not to be outdone, electric fish do it electrically. But however various the media, all these systems have a critical characteristic in common: There is always a direct link between signal and meaning; meaningless signals are never re-arranged to form intermediate structures that convey different meanings. This simple design has two serious consequences: (1) the number of meanings that can be communicated is small, being limited to the number of distinctively different signals the creature can readily make and identify; and (2) the system is closed, which is to say that, short of calling a convention to get agreement on a proposed addition, there is no way to create a new signal that will be immediately recognized as having communicative significance.

With the foregoing considerations in mind, one sees the point of Studdert-Kennedy's (in press) incisive observation that a critical step in the evolution of language was taken when 'the component signals were bleached . . . of meaning'. That was critical, because it made possible the use of the *particulate principle of self-diversifying systems* (Abler, 1989), realized in the all-important combinatorial strategy that produces an indefinitely large number of meaningful morphemes by variously combining and permuting a very small number of meaningless phonemes. (*Morphemes* are units of meaning, like *lad*, or *walk* and *-ing* of *walking*.) If each basic unit were meaningful, the combinatorial strategy would have required that all conceivable elements of meaning be identified, an obviously impossible task; and even if such an inventory could have been assembled, the combinations of meaningful elements required to transmit even the simplest messages would have been prohibitively elaborate. But with units that take on meaning only in their various combinations and permutations, all who command the system assign meanings as needed, with the result that the lexicon can be both large and flexible, though the number of particles is small and fixed. And it is surely just such a large and flexible lexicon that is basic to the unbounded generativity of language; it is hard to imagine biologically plausible systems that would have allowed morphology and syntax to take language very far if they had been restricted to the small and fixed vocabularies that the non-combinatorial strategy allows.

So it was that, paradoxical though it might seem, meaninglessness played a critical role in the evolution of a uniquely productive system for conveying meanings. And meaninglessness has proved to be equally important in the development of transcriptions that preserve the productivity of the system. To see that productivity at work in speech consider the moment when some English speaker first said 'nerd' or 'wonk'. No matter that no listener had ever heard those utterances before, all knew immediately that they belonged to a class holding special communicative privileges – more specifically, that they were phonologically legal structures, hence perfectly able to convey whatever meanings came their way. Accordingly, listeners were fully prepared to infer the intended meanings on hearing such sentences as, 'All work and no play makes Jack a nerd,' or 'President Clinton is a policy wonk.' Exactly that happens just as readily when a writing system is substituted for speech, provided the writing transcribes the meaningless elements of speech, and provided, too, that those elements can be brought to the attention of the reader. Those requirements having been met, there remains only the seemingly trivial task of connecting the elements to the alphabetic characters that have been arbitrarily chosen to represent them.

Why is Awareness of those Constituents Not Necessary for Speech, Nor Yet a Normal Consequence of Having Mastered it?

While it is widely accepted that phonological awareness is important for children learning to read, few have asked why it matters not at all for speaking and listening (but see Liberman, 1992; 1996, chapter 1; 1997; and 1998, for relevant discussion). The question is none the less important, because the answer takes us to the heart of the profound biological difference between speech and reading/writing, deepening our appreciation of the task the teacher faces in helping the child to develop from one who speaks to one who also reads and writes. Unfortunately for the purposes of this chapter, one does not find the answer in the surface manifestations of speech or in the conventional theories that deal with them; rather, one must look to processes that lie deeper and are comprehended by a theory that runs counter to the received view. That theory is likely, therefore, not to be the one that is assumed, if only tacitly, by students of reading/writing, so it is appropriate to describe it here. Given constraints of length, however, we cannot offer a full account, only a brief summary designed to convey the flavour of the arguments. Reasonably comprehensive presentations are to be found elsewhere (Liberman, 1996; Liberman and Mattingly, 1985; 1989).

The conventional view of speech – the one held by almost all students of language and, *a fortiori*, by students of reading/writing – holds that the meaningless elements of speech are sounds, and that the primary processes by which they are produced and perceived are not specific to language, but rather depend on capacities of an ordinary motor and auditory sort (Diehl and Kluender, 1989; Kuhl, 1981; Lindblom, 1991; Stevens and Blumstein, 1978). Thus, on the listener's side of the exchange, the sounds of speech produce auditory percepts no different in kind from those evoked by squeaking doors or wailing sirens. However, even the most conventional theorists recognize, though usually without being explicit about it, that the combinatorial processes of language do not work on such auditory representations, only on elements that belong to a distinctly linguistic mode. At the most fundamental level of that mode, where our concern lies, those elements are phonetic in character. Accordingly, the conventional speech theorists assume a second stage, beyond primary perception, where the ordinary auditory representations are, by some secondary cognitive process, given phonetic status.

To see how that aspect of the conventional view ill serves our understanding of reading and writing, one has only to develop its most obvious implications. Putting attention on just the reading side of the process, one sees that the auditory percepts that are assumed on the conventional view to be the primary representations of the listener are as nonphonetic in nature as the visual percepts that must be assumed on any view to be the primary representations of the reader; accordingly, the two representations are equally remote from language, hence equally in need of the cognitive exertions required to make them part of it. Analogous considerations apply to the relation between speaking and writing. It follows, then, that the conventional view cannot explain why listening and speaking are so much easier and more natural than reading and writing. Indeed, such a view implies, to the contrary, that reading/writing ought to have the advantage; after all, print is a clearer signal than speech, the hand a more versatile effector than the tongue, and the eye a more capable receptor than the ear.

The problem becomes the worse confounded when one sees that if the development of language had been as it is made to appear on the conventional view, the requirements of particulate communication would have forced speech into a form that would have made phonological awareness immediately available to all who had managed to produce and perceive it. The most relevant requirement is that the meaningless elements of the phonology be commutable – that is, discrete, invariant, and categorical. That is an absolute requirement of a particulate system, not to be compromised in any way. It means for the perceptual side of the process that if the elements had been sounds and their auditory consequences, then the particulate nature of speech would have had to be manifest at the acoustic surface. As a consequence, speech would have become an acoustic alphabet. In that case, one would have uttered the word 'lad' by producing each of its three phonetic units as a discrete, invariant, and categorical sould – [l] [a] [d] – which is to say that speaking would have been no different from spelling, hence everyone who was able to speak would, *ipso facto*, have been able to spell. Listeners, for their part, could hardly have been unaware of the three sounds the speaker spelled, and so would almost certainly have developed phonological awareness as a by-product of perceiving speech. Learning to read and write would then have been trivially easy conversions from one alphabet to another. Unfortunately for literacy, however, there would have been no language to read or write. Spelled speech would have been tediously time-consuming, and would, in addition, have delivered the meaningless elements so slowly that listeners would have found it virtually impossible to organize them into the larger units (morphemes, words, phrases, sentences) that the hierarchical aspect of the particulate system requires. Speech perception would also have been problematic, for delivering the alphabetic sounds at the rates that speakers normally attain would have overreached the temporal resolving power of the ear, making it impossible to apprehend the discrete elements and correctly perceive the order of their occurrence.

Given the obvious shortcomings of the conventional assumptions about speech, the reading researcher may wish to look for help to a view that is much less conventional. On that view, one sees that the elements of speech are not sounds, but gestures of the articulator organs. Those gestures are discrete, invariant, and categorical motor processes that control changes in the cavities of the vocal tract, and so produce the sounds of speech. Having evolved with speech, the gestures are specifically adapted to the needs of particulate communication; accordingly, they are distinctly phonetic particles by their very nature, requiring no cognitive translation to make them so. Selection pressure in evolution was for gestures that took advantage of the independence of the several parts of the articulatory apparatus, gestures that could therefore be overlapped, interleaved, and merged – that is, co-articulated. Control of these uniquely phonetic gestures, and especially of the co-articulatory manoeuvres for which they were specialized, fell to a correspondingly specialized device – some have called it a *phonetic module*. The consequence of those evolutionary developments was a way to produce strings of the elemental phonetic gestures at the rates of 10 to 15 segments per second that humans do, in fact, readily achieve. Moreover, by co-articulating the gestures, speakers produce the word 'lad' as a coherent syllable, a short, single, and seamless piece of sound; they don't 'spell' it by uttering three sounds. In that connection, we know, of course, that people can speak without being able to spell – indeed, without even being aware that such a thing as spelling is possible. That is so, we might now suppose, because the phonetic module requires only that the speaker think of the word, whatever that entails; the module then spells it, automatically selecting and coordinating the appropriate gestures.

The module also packages the phonetic message very efficiently for the ear. That efficiency is owing in part to the way co-articulation folds information about several successive phonetic elements into a single piece of sound, thereby circumventing the limitation on rate of perception that is set by the temporal resolving power of the ear. Perceptual efficiency is also increased by the fact that co-articulation marks the order of the segments by variations in the shape of the acoustic signal, thus relieving the ear of the need to judge the order of sounds that follow each other in close temporal succession. But these critically important gains come at a cost, for co-articulation destroys all correspondence in segmentation between the sounds of speech and the particulated phonetic message they convey. A result is that speech is not an acoustic alphabet or simple substitution cipher, but a code that is complex in specifically phonetic ways. However, the special, and especially thorny, characteristics of the code result from the way the component phonetic gestures are co-articulated, so the key to the code must lie in the phonetic module. It is, after all, the device that governs co-articulation; therefore, it commands all the constraints necessary to process the speech sounds so as to recover the co-articulated gestures that caused them. Accordingly, perception of the meaningless elements of speech is immediate and effortless, not because the process is simple, but because the phonetic module is so well adapted to its complex task.

We have now a basis for answering the questions about speech and reading/writing that were raised earlier on. Speech is easier and more natural than reading/writing, because, given the specialized module, listener and speaker are dealing at the most primary level with representations that are distinctly phonetic by their very nature, needing no cognitive effort to translate them into appropriately phonetic form. It follows that the productive potential of the particulate system is available precognitively – that is, in the most fundamental representations of the meaningless acts and percepts it takes as its building blocks. Lacking direct access to the phonetic module, the reader/writer, on the other hand, cannot arrive at those appropriately particulated elements except by translation from the nonphonetic acts that produce the alphabetic letters and the equally nonphonetic visual percepts that are their consequences. It is, of course, just such a translation that requires an explicit awareness of the particulate structures it must match. Thus, evolution put the listener/speaker on the most intimate terms with language, leaving the reader/writer to cultivate its acquaintance deliberately and through arbitrarily chosen optical intermediaries. One sees, then, that the difference in biological status between listening/speaking and reading/writing rests ultimately in the phonetic module and what it does for the former processes but not the latter.

As for why awareness of the meaningless phonological constituents is not normally a consequence of mastering speech, there are at least two reasons that should now be apparent. One is that, as we have seen, the representations of the listener/speaker are immediately appropriate for all further language processing. Requiring no attention, therefore, they get none; the would-be reader must learn to attend, and that takes some doing. The other reason is that, given the utter lack of correspondence in segmentation between sound and phonetic structure, the true 'alphabetic' nature of speech is not so apparent as it would be if, as the conventional view would have required, speech were alphabetic at the acoustic surface. Therefore, 'sounding out' a word in order to reveal its internal alphabetic structure misrepresents the way that structure is conveyed by the sound, and is likely, therefore, to be less effective that the teacher might hope. In spite of those difficulties, listener/speakers *can* become aware of the meaningless segments that the word comprises; indeed, if they could not, alphabetic reading and writing would be impossible. But achieving the degree of awareness that beginning reading requires is effortful; it does not come naturally, nor does it always come easily.

How Might Development of Such Awareness be Made Harder by the Language Habits the Pre-literate Child Brings to the Task of Learning to Read?

Having seen why the would-be reader will have mastered speech while ignoring the meaningless phonologic structures on which its words depend, we understand the absence of phonologic awareness. We also understand that this lack of awareness has cost nothing in the ability to communicate by speech, for the outputs of the phonetic module, being pieces of language by their very nature, do not require the kind of attention that would be needed if, like the letters of the alphabet, they were only arbitrary stand-ins. In speech, therefore, the would-be reader has been able, with good effect, to devote full attention to the meanings that the phonologic structures communicate. We might suppose, therefore, that first contacts with print will not find the child starting from a neutral position. We might suppose, in other words, that the child will find it most natural to follow the cognitively less demanding route that is available to a listener/speaker but not, unfortunately, to a reader/writer. That route bypasses phonologic awareness in favour of attention to the meaningful products of language. Unfortunately, the child whose attention is fully focused on meaning is likely to fail to understand how to use the alphabet productively to represent any combination of phonemes the language allows.

But how is it possible that a child with an orientation to ignore phonology can make anything at all of a cipher whose very basis rests there? For an obvious answer, consider, yet again, that speech forms words by combining and permuting meaningless phonologic segments. As a consequence, any transcription that adopts the phonemes as its currency will necessarily accept words as well. It follows, then, that just as there is a particular alphabetic character for every phoneme, so there is a particular combination of characters for every morpheme.[1] This is to say that a writing system that systematically represents phonemes will just as systematically represent morphemes. The individual letters of *lad* are transcriptions of the individual phonemes that the word comprises, and the letter group as a whole is a transcription of the morpheme as a whole. More generally, as Van Orden et al. (1990) recognized, a writing system of a certain 'grain size' will also be a writing system for all larger grain sizes. This allows a child learning to use an alphabetic transcription to assume, correctly, that the system records the meaningful morphemes, while simultaneously failing to notice that it also records the meaningless phonemes. In listening to speech, the child has, presumably, done precisely that, as if the sounds represented morphemes

[1]   We refer here to an ideal alphabet. English falls short of the ideal, as is well recognized. There are fewer letters than phonemes, and as a consequence, patterns of letters have to do the work of the missing letters. Other, historical influences have further distanced English spelling from a unique mapping of spelling onto pronunciation, although it needs to be acknowledged that many of the regularities in English spelling are morphophonological rather than phonologic, exemplified by the single letter *s* for a single morpheme, *plural*, despite two phonetic renditions, /s/ and /z/, as in *cats* and *dogs*. While these factors doubtless complicate the process of learning to read, our concerns are not with these complications. We think that our theses would apply even if English happened to be the ideal alphabet. For recent evidence that reading difficulties in a 'transparent' orthography, Spanish, derive from problems of phonological awareness, see Jiménez González (1997).

directly, and not the phonemes of which those morphemes are formed.

Evidence to the effect that children are indifferent to phonology in their early contacts with print has existed for some time. It consists, for the most part, of observations of children's spontaneous and evoked attempts to specify relations between language and print. Ferreiro (1986), for example, reported on a child who, at two-and-a-half, was happy to allow that ELEFANTE (elephant) said 'elephant' when placed next to a picture of an elephant, but that it said 'lion' when placed near a picture of a lion (and 'horse' and 'donkey' appropriately). Also indicating the tendency for the child to go directly from print to meaning, are the observations of Levin and Korat (1993), who, for example, noted that young children tended to use more letters to represent 'coop', which has just one syllable in Hebrew, than 'chicken', which has four. It was as if the children were assuming a direct relation between the visual characteristics of the print and the meaning.

That children are to some degree aware of the morphological but not the phonological structure of words was also indicated, albeit indirectly, in a study of the correlates of progress in reading (Fowler and Liberman, 1995). There it was found that morphological awareness did correlate with reading, but only for those derivations that required also a phonological change (e.g., *courage, courageous*), not for those in which the morphological structure was perfectly transparent (e.g., *danger, dangerous*). Apparently, it was only the phonologic awareness, so necessary for reading, that the children had not achieved.

One of us (B.B.), together with his colleagues, approached this matter directly by determining experimentally whether the child would carry over to his early encounters with alphabetic transcriptions the 'listening' habit of attending, at the first level of language processing, only to the meaningful morphemes. If so, then, as we have implied, the task of bringing the meaningless phonemes into focus would be significantly complicated by a tendency on the child's part to begin by attending to the wrong units. To find out whether or not that is, in fact, a complication required of the investigators that they contrive experimental situations that would, in effect, put them into the mind of the child negotiating the earliest stages of reading acquisition. Accordingly, we devised experiments designed to present to the child equivocal evidence about the phonologic or morphologic interpretation of the letters, thus allowing the experimenters to see which interpretation the child would choose.

In one experiment by Byrne (1996), preschool children with very limited letter knowledge were taught to read the pairs of words *book* and *books*, and *hat* and *hats*. Even though these were the first systematically arranged words that the children had been asked to learn, they did so with relative ease. Clearly, within each pair, successful discrimination must have been based on the letter *s*, because that is all that distinguishes the members of the pairs. But what had the children learned about that letter? Its role in representing an aspect of meaning, plurality; its role in representing an aspect of phonology, /s/; or both? We inquired about this by presenting the children with new pairs of words. They could not, and were not asked to, read the new words, but instead to match the words to spoken alternatives. The alternatives, like the words that the children had learned, were distinguished by the letter *s*. Some, like *cap* and *caps*, recaptured the essential feature of the learning set, a pair of words contrasting in number (singular and plural) and in the presence of a final voiceless /s/. Others, like *dog* and *dogs*, embodied the number contrast but not the precise final phoneme (in *dogs* it is the voiced /z/). Yet others, like *bus* and *bug*, or in another experiment, *pur* (which we said was 'purr') and *purs* ('purse'), maintained the phonetic contrast /s/ but not the number contrast. A typical test item consisted of the child being shown the pair, *cap* and *caps*, say, being told that one said 'cap' and one said 'caps', and being invited to point to the one which said 'caps'.

Characteristically, the children succeeded in the first two cases, *cap* and *caps*, and *dog* and *dogs*, i.e., those in which *s* represented an aspect of meaning, plurality, as well as a phonological element. But they did not typically succeed in the third type of case, *bus* and *bug*, or *pur* and *purs*, in which the role of *s* was to mark a purely phonological contrast – performance was at chance level. Nor, in another experiment, did most children detect the phonological role of letter groups like -*er* when they were present a distinguishing components of pairs like *small* and *smaller*. After learning to read such pairs, the children could successfully decide between test items like *mean* and *meaner*, where -*er* maintained its function of representing an aspect of meaning as well as of sound, but not between test items like *corn* and *corner*, where *-er* played only a phonological role.[2] The results of these experiments imply that children expect to find that print does what speech does, which is to carry meaning, and miss the point that both do what they do by encoding the meaningless elements of the phonology.

At this point we can cash in the observation made earlier that alphabets code meaningful as well as meaningless elements of language. Recall that they do this because alphabets do everything that phonemes do, including combining into larger sequences corresponding to morphemes. The point is that children will have their initial, meaning-oriented hunches about print confirmed if it is confirmation that they are seeking. They *will* find a neat correspondence between print sequences and morphological structures, because it exists. This being so, some may not even begin the next, hard part of learning to read, namely detecting the internal phonologic structure of words. They may remain convinced that they have discovered the basic currency with which the writing system conducts its business.

That this is more than a theoretical possibility is demonstrated by the existence of sizeable numbers of children who can learn to read words by rote but fail to discover the key to pronouncing words that they have not seen in print before (Byrne, 1998; Byrne, Freebody and Gates, 1992; Freebody and Byrne, 1988). This is exactly the pattern of reading that we would expect of children who think that print records, say, morphemes, but nothing more elemental in language. For it is only when children notice that print obeys the very particulate principle that makes spoken language possible that they can be

---

[2]   In a recent attempt to replicate this particular result by B. B. and P. E. Bryant, children did appear to detect the phonological role of *-er*, as evidenced by successful transfer to items like *corner*. Further research is needed to reconcile these findings. Note that there have been several successful replications of the study employing the letter, and phoneme, *s*, so the reconciliation may reside in the contrast between phonemes and syllables as detectable phonological objects. It is perhaps worth noting, however, that in another experiment reported in Byrne (1996), children who did not know either the name or the sound of the letter *s* failed to make anything of the syllable *-est* in words like *forest* and *harvest* after learning to reliably distinguish pairs like *small* and *smallest*.

as productive in dialing with new written words as they are in dealing
with new spoken words.

What does All this Imply for Instruction?

Trying to adopt the child's point of view, which was a purpose of the
experiments we've described, signalled a commitment to a particular
way of studying the growth of knowledge, one that we believe to be
especially apt when decisions about educational practices are at stake.
In particular, it enlightens us about the knowledge and habits of mind
that the child brings to learning how to substitute an alphabetic transcription of speech for speech itself. Obviously, educators charged
with designing teaching practices need to be aware of what the child
already knows, and is able effortlessly to do, so they can identify, by
subtraction as it were, what remains to be taught. It makes little
sense to teach that which is already known and well established in
behaviour. Indeed, in the case of reading acquisition, such teaching
can be downright harmful if, as is sometimes the case, it serves merely
to reinforce that which is appropriate to speech but inimical to
progress in reading. Thus, in speech it is perfectly normal and
nicely expedient for the child to arrive at the goal of meaning while
remaining innocently unaware of the phonologic route used to get
there.

Small wonder then that pre-literate children are biased in favour
of the units that bear meaning, at the expense of those that do not.
Yet it is precisely the latter that the child must also learn to appreciate if the particulate principle, together with the productivity it under-
lies, is to be transferred from the speech the child already commands
to the transcription of speech which needs to be mastered. We should,
therefore, be concerned about certain widely accepted assumptions
about speech and reading that would seem to head the teacher in the
wrong direction. Chief among these is a basic premise of so-called
Whole Language, which is that children should learn to read and
write 'the same way they learned oral language, by using it in authentic literacy events that meet their needs' (Goodman, 1986, p. 24).
Of course, children cannot do that, biology being what it is. But if
the teacher is nevertheless misled into believing that they can, the
teacher's attention, and therefore that of the beginning reader, will be
directed towards exactly the wrong parts of the process. Not far

behind in the potential for misleading the teacher is the corollary injunction not to break 'whole (natural) language up into bite-size, but abstract little pieces' (Goodman, 1986, p. 7). That is part of the larger Whole Language plea that the teacher not try to turn the child into a linguist, lest the child's attempts at linguistic analysis convert the naturally easy process of reading into something unnaturally hard. But, as we have seen in the studies reported here, the pre-literate child has already acquired the analytic approach of the linguist, as shown by the predisposition to segment some words into their morphological units during attempts to read those words for the first time. That tendency to analyse words into their meaningful constituents is surely not to be deplored, for morphology is productive in its own way, and developing a conscious awareness of it promotes a more effective use of the language and fosters a better understanding of its spelling patterns. What remains to be done, therefore, is not to encourage the child to abandon morphology, but rather to encourage linguistic analysis downward to the phonologic particles of which the morphemes, whether spoken or written, are composed. Surely, we will do that most effectively if we understand exactly what has to be learned and why that might be hard.

References

Abler, W. (1989) On the particulate principle of self-diversifying systems. *Journal of Social and Biological Structures*, 12, 1–13.

Adams, M. J. (1990) *Beginning to Read: Thinking and Learning about Print*. Cambridge, MA: MIT Press.

Brady, S., and Shankweiler, D. (eds) (1991) *Phonological Processes in Literacy: A Tribute to Isabelle Y. Liberman*. Hillsdale, NJ: Erlbaum.

Byrne, B. (1996) The learnability of the alphabetic principle: Children's initial hypotheses about how print represents spoken language. *Applied Psycholinguistics*, 17, 401–26.

Byrne, B. (1998) *The Foundation of Literacy: The Child's Acquisition of the Alphabetic Principle*. Hove: Psychology Press.

Byrne, B., Freebody, P., and Gates, A. (1992) Longitudinal data on the relations of word-reading strategies to comprehension, reading time, and phonemic awareness. *Reading Research Quarterly*, 27, 141–51.

Diehl, R. L., and Kluender, K. R. (1989) On the objects of speech perception. *Ecological Psychology*, 1, 121–44.

Ferreiro, E. (1986) The interplay between information and assimilation in beginning literacy. In W. H. Teale and E. Sulzby (eds), *Emergent Literacy: Writing and Reading*, Norwood, NJ: Ablex, pp. 15–49.

Fowler, A., and Liberman, I. Y. (1995) The role of phonology and orthography in morphological awareness. In L. B. Feldman (ed.), *Morphological Aspects of Language Processing*. Hillsdale, NJ: Erlbaum.

Freebody, P., and Byrne, B. (1988) Word-reading strategies in elementary school children: Relations to comprehension, reading time, and phonemic awareness. *Reading Research Quarterly*, 23, 441–53.

Goodman, K. (1986) *What's Whole in Whole Language?* Portsmouth, NH: Heinemann.

Goswami, U., and Bryant, P. E. (1990) *Phonological Skills and Learning to Read*. Hillsdale, NJ: Erlbaum.

Gough, P. B., Ehri, L. C., and Treiman, R. (eds) (1992) *Reading Acquisition*. Hillsdale, NJ: Erlbaum.

Jiménez González, J. E. (1997) A reading-level match study of phonemic processes underlying reading disabilities in a transparent orthography. *Reading and Writing*, 9, 32–40.

Kuhl, P. K. (1981) Discrimination of speech by nonhuman animals: Basic auditory sensitivities conducive to the perception of speech-sound categories. *Journal of the Acoustical Society of America*, 70, 340–9.

Levin, I., and Korat, O. (1993) Sensitivity to phonological, morphological, and semantic cues in early reading and writing in Hebrew. *Merrill-Palmer Quarterly*, 39, 213–32.

Liberman, A. M. (1992) The relation of speech to reading and writing. In R. Frost and L. Katz (eds), *Orthography, Phonology, Morphology, and Meaning*, Amsterdam: Elsevier, pp. 167–78.

Liberman, A. M. (1996) *Speech: A Special Code*. Cambridge, MA: MIT Press.

Liberman, A. M. (1997) How theories of speech affect research in reading and writing. In B. Blachman (ed.), *Foundations of Reading Acquisition and Dyslexia: Implications for Early Intervention*, Hillsdale, NJ: Erlbaum, pp. 3–19.

Liberman, A. M. (1998) When theories of speech meet the real world. *Journal of Psycholinguistic Research*, 27.

Liberman, A. M., and Mattingly, I. G. (1985) The motor theory of speech perception revised. *Cognition*, 21, 1–36.

Liberman, A. M., and Mattingly, I. G. (1989) A specialization for speech perception. *Science*, 243, 489–94.

Lindblom, B. (1991) The status of phonetic gestures. In I. G. Mattingly and M. Studdert-Kennedy (eds), *Modularity and the Motor Theory of Speech Perception*, Hillsdale, NJ: Erlbaum, pp. 7–24.

Share, D. L. (1995) Phonological recoding and self-teaching: Sine qua non of reading acquisition. *Cognition*, *55*, 151–218.

Stevens, K. N., and Blumstein, S. E. (1978) Invariant cues for place of articulation in stop consonants. *Journal of the Acoustical Society of America*, *64*, 1358–68.

Studdert-Kennedy, M. (in press) The particulate origins of language productivity: From syllable to gesture. In J. Hurford, M. Studdert-Kennedy, and C. Knight (eds), *Approaches to the Evolution of Language: Social and Cognitive Bases*. Cambridge: Cambridge University Press.

Van Orden, G. C., Pennington, B. F., and Stone, G. O. (1990) Word identification in reading and the promise of subsymbolic psycholinguistics. *Psychological Review*, *97*, 488–522.

Chapter Nine

Phonological Development and Reading by Analogy: Epilinguistic and Metalinguistic Issues

USHA GOSWAMI

The importance of phonological skills for reading and spelling development is now widely recognized by both researchers and educators. Further, the need to develop phonological skills in all children as part of literacy acquisition is stressed in *National Literacy Strategy Framework for Teaching* and in *English in the National Curriculum*. Both of these publications highlight the importance of giving children explicit tuition in rhyme and analogy skills as well as explicit tuition in grapheme–phoneme correspondences. These are welcome developments, reflecting the most recent empirical research on reading acquisition. This chapter will review recent research evidence that explains why it is important to include tuition at both of these levels of phonological structure in order to develop reading and spelling skills in English-speaking children. Gombert's (1992) theory of metalinguistic development will be used as a framework for thinking about the different ways in which children *represent* phonological knowledge. It will be shown that most children begin learning to read using implicit phonological knowledge, which represents the syllable and the rime. Following direct tuition, explicit phonological knowl-

This chapter is based on a paper entitled 'Phonological Development and Reading by Analogy: What is Analogy, and What is it Not?', published in *Journal of Research in Reading*, 18, 139–45.

edge develops. This either represents the phoneme or the rime, depending on the level of spelling–sound correspondence which the child is being taught. It will be suggested that the early (epilinguistic) availability of rime structures and the structure of the English orthography (which reflects the rime) mean that it is important to include rime-level tuition alongside tuition in grapheme–phoneme correspondences from the beginning of learning to read. Recent publications that have questioned whether tuition in rhyme and analogy has a place in early literacy teaching are discussed in the light of this new framework.

Background: Research Evidence for the Importance of Rhyme and Analogy in Reading Development in English

Orthographic analogies in reading

Analogical reasoning is a fundamental cognitive skill (e.g., Brown, 1989; Gentner, 1989; Goswami, 1991a; 1992; 1996a; Halford, 1987; 1993). Cognitive-developmental studies of analogical reasoning in children have shown that analogies are used by children as young as 1, 2 and 3 years of age in domains as different as physical reasoning, causal reasoning and grammatical development (see Goswami, 1998, for a review). This research has also shown that a critical factor governing the use of analogy is *relational knowledge*. If children have represented certain relations, they can make analogies on the basis of those relations. For example, 3- and 4-year-old children who understand physical causal relations like *melting* and *wetting* can complete analogies of the form *chocolate is to melting chocolate as snowman is to puddle* (Goswami and Brown, 1989). Factors that have been found to promote the use of analogy across different domains include the provision of hints to use analogies, the provision of direct teaching in an analogy strategy, the provision of multiple exemplars, and the existence of perceptual similarities between the entities being compared in the analogy (see Goswami, 1992, for a summary). Analogical reasoning strategies are clearly available long before children begin learning to read, and quite a lot is known about how to promote the use of analogies in learning.

Analogies in reading involve using the spelling–sound pattern of one word, such as *beak*, as a basis for working out the spelling–sound correspondence of a new word, such as *peak*. This kind of analogy is supported by perceptual similarity, as the two words look similar because of the shared spelling segment (which is *eak* in this example). The relations that a child needs to have represented in order to use analogies in reading are the sound relations or phonological relations that operate in the language that they are learning to read. The child has already represented some of these phonological relations, as language is used every day when speaking and comprehending, and is largely used accurately. However, the beginning reader has typically only represented phonological structure at an implicit level. One of the main tasks in learning to read is for the child to relate this phonological structure to the spelling system of their language – its orthographic structure (which, after all, reflects phonological structure). One way of doing this is to use analogies.

Early analogy research in the field of reading development set out to investigate whether an analogy mechanism was available to beginning readers. This research compared 6-year-old children's analogies between words like *beak* and new words like *bean* (which shares the initial 3 letters with *beak*) and *peak* (which shares the final 3 letters with *beak*, e.g., Goswami, 1986; 1988). The paradigm used was the 'clue' word task, in which children were shown a spelling pattern (such as *beak*) and were asked to use it to read new words such as *bean* and *peak*. Two strong findings emerged from this early research. The first was that analogies between the ends of words (*beak–peak*) were much easier for young children to draw than analogies between the beginnings of words (*beak–bean*), despite the fact that the perceptual similarity (3 shared letters) in each case was equivalent. The second was that end analogies (*beak–peak*) emerged first developmentally. Analogy effects were also found in studies of prose reading (Goswami, 1988). Given the importance of relational (phonological) knowledge for successful analogizing, this pattern of analogy use seemed likely to reflect children's implicit knowledge about phonological structure.

The sequence of phonological development

Indeed, in discussing this pattern of analogy use, Goswami and Bryant (1990) suggested that the relative ease with which beginning readers used 'end' analogies might be linked to phonological development. A large number of research studies have shown that there is a developmental progression in the units of sound that young children can identify within spoken words (see Goswami and Bryant, 1990, for a review).

The first phonological distinction that emerges is at the level of the *syllable*. Even 4-year-olds can tell you that a word like *valentine* or *telephone* has three syllables, while a word like *birthday* or *dinner* has two. The next phonological distinction that emerges is between *onsets* and *rimes*. The terms onset and rime derive from linguistic theory, and denote units of sound (see Treiman, 1988). The onset is the spoken sound that corresponds to any consonants at the beginning of each written syllable, and the rime corresponds to the sound of the rest of the syllable. For example, the spoken word *valentine* consists of the syllables *val*, *en* and *tine*.[1] The onsets in *valentine* are the phonemes /v/ in *val*, and /t/ in *tine*, and the rimes are the sounds corresponding to the *al* in *val*, the *en*, and the *ine* in *tine*.[2] For single-syllable words, rimes and rhymes are equivalent. The rime in *beak* is *eak*, the rime in *light* is *ight*, the rime in *cold* is *old*, and the rime in *swing* is *ing*. Onset–rime awareness is present in most 4- to 5-year-olds, and is usually measured by tasks requiring rhyme judgements.

The final level of phonological awareness that emerges with development is the phonemic level. *Phonemes* are the smallest units of sound that change the meaning of spoken words. *Cat* and *cap* differ by a single phoneme at the end, and *ship* and *lip* differ by a single phoneme at the beginning. Phonemes usually correspond to single alphabetic letters, as in the examples *t* and *p* in *cat* and *cap*. However, they can also correspond to digraphs (pairs of letters with a single sound). *Sh* is a digraph, and so are *ea* in *beak* and both occurrences of *ph* in *photograph*. Phonemic awareness does not usually emerge until children have been learning to read for about a year, and is

---

[1]   Linguists are divided about where to place syllable divisions in different words, and consequently there are no universally accepted rules that one can follow when judging syllable divisions. An alternative parsing could be *va-len-tine*.

[2]   As noted above, the terms onset and rime strictly refer to units of *sound*. However, they will be used in the rest of this chapter as a shorthand for referring to the spelling units that reflect those units of sound as well.

Table 9.1   Levels of phonological development

Spoken word:	'valentine'		
Phonological segments:			
1. Syllabic	(val) +	(en) +	(tine)
2. Onset–rime	(v + al) +	(en) +	(t + ine)
3. Phonemes	(v) + (a) + (l) + (e) + (n) + (t) + (*i*) + (n)		

absent in illiterate adults (e.g., Morais, Cary, Alegria and Bertelson, 1979).

Phonological awareness described in terms of an awareness of *all* of the constituent phonemes in words appears to depend critically on learning to read an alphabetic script. Adults who have never learned to read, Japanese children who are learning a non-alphabetic script, and young children who have not yet learned to read, seem to lack phonemic awareness. This developmental progression in the awareness of subword phonology is depicted in table 9.1. More recent research has supported this sequence of phonological development (e.g., Bowey and Hansen, 1994; Treiman and Zukowski, 1996), and has shown that the same developmental sequence is found in children who are learning other languages (see Goswami, in press, a, for a review).

The relatively late emergence of phonemic awareness does not mean, however, that children lack *any* knowledge about phonemes until they have been learning to read for about a year. Even pre-readers can hear individual phonemes at the *beginnings* of words, when these initial phonemes often constitute single-phoneme onsets. Many English words have single-phoneme onsets. Simple examples are the /c/ in *cat*, the /d/ in *dog*, and the /s/ in *sun*. When onsets correspond to single phonemes, then most children can learn the corresponding letter–sound relations without difficulty. This facility does not extend to the isolation of an initial sound within a consonant cluster. If you tell a young child that *c* is for *crab*, or *s* is for *snail*, then they will have difficulty in relating the alphabetic letter to the correct phoneme. Their difficulty lies in segmenting the onset.

Gombert (1992) has described this sequence of phonological development in terms of the *representational changes* occurring in the child's mental lexicon. His theory makes an important distinction between *epilinguistic* knowledge and *metalinguistic control* over phonological structures. Epilinguistic knowledge is linguistic knowledge that is used as a basis for linguistic behaviour but is not yet accessible to conscious inspection. On the basis of research evidence in many languages, Gombert argues that epilinguistic knowledge represents syllables and rimes. Phonological awareness tasks that do not require the child to manipulate phonology, such as recognition tasks, can be performed using epilinguistic knowledge. Most phonological awareness tasks, however, require the child to manipulate phonology in some way (for example, to delete a sound in a word, or to segment a word). Gombert argues that these tasks require a degree of metalinguistic control over phonological structures. The acquisition of metalinguistic control over phonological structures is driven by external factors, such as tuition in literacy. If literacy tuition focuses on phonemes, then children may become able to manipulate phonemes before they can manipulate onsets and rimes in certain phonological awareness tasks. The distinction between epilinguistic and metalinguistic knowledge means that we must be wary of assuming that all phonological awareness tasks are comparable.

Phonological awareness and the use of analogies

With respect to reading, Gombert suggests that the precociously developing ('epilinguistic') sensitivity to rimes at the implicit level is used by the cognitive system as soon as reading begins. One way in which such knowledge might be used is in reading by analogy. Gombert's theory would lead us to expect analogies based on rimes to emerge before analogies based on single phonemes, as rimes are represented in the mental lexicon before the child receives formal literacy teaching. Analogies based on rimes are indeed found before analogies based on phonemes, and individual differences in rime awareness are related to individual differences in analogy use (e.g., Goswami, 1990a; 1991b; Goswami and Mead, 1992). However, analogies based on phonemes such as vowel digraphs emerge relatively quickly once reading instruction has commenced, at a reading age of around 6 years 10 months (e.g., Goswami, 1993). Recently, Savage and Stuart (1998, Experiment 2) have reported vowel digraph analogies in even younger children with a mean reading age of 6 years 6 months. The range of reading ages was rather large in this experiment (from 5 years 9 months to 7 years 4 months), however, and so the older readers may have contributed more vowel analogies than the younger readers.

The availability of the rime as a phonological structure could mean that rime analogies are not based on orthographic similarities. Children may be as likely to make an appropriate rime analogy (such as *head–bread*) as an inappropriate rime analogy (such as *head–said*). Obviously, inappropriate analogies would not help the child to learn about spelling–sound relations. This potential problem has been studied by estimating whether 'phonological priming' is occurring when children use analogies in reading. If reading analogies were entirely due to phonological priming, we would expect inappropriate analogies such as *head–said* to be as frequent as appropriate analogies such as *head–bread*. This does not occur (Goswami, 1990b). Although a few inappropriate analogies are made in the clue word task, no phonological priming is found in prose reading. Children are also less likely to use inappropriate analogies based on spelling similarities (such as *speak–steak*) in the clue word task than appropriate analogies (such as *speak–leak*; Goswami, 1988). Such experiments suggest that analogies are used largely productively in early reading.

Rhyme and the alphabetic code in English

A number of longitudinal studies have shown a clear-cut connection between early rhyming skills and later reading progress (e.g., Bradley and Bryant, 1983; Bryant, Maclean, Bradley and Crossland, 1990; Ellis and Large, 1987; Maclean, Bryant and Bradley, 1987). Children who are good at recognizing shared rhyme when they are 3 and 4 years old become better readers and spellers. So good rhyming skills seem to help children to crack the 'alphabetic code'. Why should this be? One reason seems to be that learning the spelling patterns for rimes is a very good way of organizing the English spelling system. English spelling is often criticized for being highly ambiguous. The sounds of words like *light, through* and *people* bear little resemblance to the individual letter–sound correspondence that make up the spelling patterns of these words. On closer inspection, however, most spelling–sound ambiguity derives from changes in vowel pronunciation. Most vowels change their pronunciation with the consonants that follow them. For example, the 'a' sound in *cat, hat,* and *mat* is consistent, but different from the 'a' sound in *car, far* and *star*. The 'a' sound in *ball, hall* and *tall* is different again. In each case, however, the 'a' sound is largely consistent within its rime group.

These observations have been confirmed by research. A recent statistical analysis of the English orthography carried out by Treiman, Mullennix, Bijeljac-Babic and Richmond-Welty (1995) showed that one of the spelling units that offers the most consistent mappings to phonology in English reflects the rime. Treiman et al. calculated how many times individual letters had the same pronunciations when they occurred in the same positions across different words for all of the consonant–vowel–consonant (CVC) monosyllabic words of English (e.g., 'h' in *hen, hope, hour* etc., 'p' in *hop, sip, help* etc.). The CVC words in this analysis included words spelled with vowel digraphs, like *bean* and *peak*, and words with 'rule of e' spellings, like *make* and *pale*. Treiman et al. found that the pronunciation of vowels was very inconsistent across different words (51 per cent), whereas the pronunciation of initial and final consonants was reasonably consistent (C_1 = 96 per cent, C_2 = 91 per cent). An analysis of the spelling–sound consistency of the larger spelling units in the words, namely the onset–vowel (C_1V) and rime (VC_2) units, showed a clear advantage for the rime. Whereas only 52 per cent of CVC words sharing a C_1V spelling had a consistent pronunciation (for example, *bea* in *beak* and *bean*), 77 per cent of CVC words sharing a VC_2 spelling had a consistent pronunciation (for example, *eak* in *peak* and *weak*). This statistical analysis of the properties of the English orthography shows very clearly that the spelling–sound consistency of written English is greatest for initial consonants (onsets), final consonants, and rimes.

Converging evidence for the importance of rimes in English comes from statistical analyses of other word sets. Stanback (1992) has found that 824 different rimes make up the 43,041 syllables of the

17,602 words in the Carroll, Davies and Richman (1971) children's word frequency index, 616 of which are in rime families. Wylie and Durrell (1970) found that knowledge of just 37 rimes enabled children to read 500 of the most frequently occurring words in primary grade texts. These analyses suggest that explicit tuition at the level of onsets and rimes should be very useful for young readers of English. It is certainly beneficial for older dyslexic readers (see Gaskins, Downer and Gaskins, 1986; Greaney and Tunmer, 1996; Greaney, Tunmer and Chapman, 1997).

Clearly, however, these analyses are peculiar to the English language. Onset–rime units would not be expected to be useful for beginning readers of *any* alphabetic orthography. In orthographies which are extremely regular in their letter–sound correspondences, such as German and Norwegian or Spanish and Greek, rime units would not be expected to confer a particular advantage on beginning readers since a focus on rime does not increase the consistency of spelling–sound relations. Early analogies in such orthographies would be expected to depend on phonemes. Current research suggests that this is the case (see Goswami, Gombert and de Barrera, 1998; Goswami, Porpodas and Wheelwright, 1997). Furthermore, there would be no reason to expect a special relationship between rhyming and reading in these more regular orthographies. Accordingly, it is misleading to use studies in other languages to question the existence of a link between rhyming and reading in English (e.g., Nation and Hulme, 1997). Although rhyme awareness might be weakly related to reading development in regular orthographies because of the status of the rime as an epilinguistic unit, the strong and specific relationship found in English between rhyming and reading is unlikely to be found, as the orthographic structure of regular orthographies does not give salience to the rime. Indeed, recent studies in orthographies like German and Norwegian have found only weak relationships between rhyming and reading (e.g., Hoien, Lundberg, Stanovich and Bjaalid, 1995; Wimmer, Landerl and Schneider, 1994).

Goswami and Bryant's 1990 theory

To develop a theoretical framework to describe these research findings on the role of rhyme and analogy in beginning reading,

Goswami and Bryant (1990) suggested that the process of learning to read could be characterized as a series of causal connections. Three causal connections were proposed, a connection between preschool awareness of rime and alliteration and later progress in reading and spelling, a connection between tuition at the level of the phoneme and the development of phonemic awareness (which was suggested to be rapid following such tuition), and a connection between progress in spelling and progress in reading (and vice versa). Gombert's (1992) theory allows us to be more specific about how these causal connections work. The first connection, between preschool awareness of rime and alliteration and later progress in reading, can be seen as a connection between epilinguistic knowledge and reading development. The second connection, between tuition at the level of the phoneme and the development of phonemic awareness, can be seen as a general connection between tuition in literacy and the emergence of metalinguistic control over phonological structures. As the need to spell also requires the achievement of metalinguistic control over phonological structures, the third connection, between spelling and reading, can be explained as a connection between metalinguistic development and further reading and spelling progress.

In expanding the first connection, Goswami and Bryant suggested that the link between early rhyme awareness and later progress in reading and spelling could be at least partly explained by children's use of analogies in reading: 'Our evidence suggests that right from the start, and perhaps with very little explicit instruction to do so, children learn to associate onsets and rimes with strings of letters' (1990, p. 147). The role of development in children's ability to learn these associations was also emphasized: 'Our data suggest that they [children] make [analogical] inferences at the beginning but not often and not all that successfully . . . we think that a great deal of development takes the form of children just getting better at strategies which they use right from the start' (p. 147). Thus early analogies depend on epilinguistic knowledge. With the development of metalinguistic control over phonological structures, analogies are used more frequently and more successfully. As metalinguistic control develops partly through tuition in literacy, this highlights the importance of the role that teachers need to play in developing children's analogy strategies. In thinking about this role, it is important to remember that analogy is not the *only* strategy that children use in early reading, and that not all children will successfully use rime analogies as soon as they encounter print.

Which skills should teachers foster in order to encourage the development of analogy strategies? One is good sight word knowledge, as children will use more analogies as the size of their reading vocabulary increases (see Goswami, 1986). Another is metalinguistic control over onset–rime structures. Children get better at making analogies as their phonological skills improve, and this probably reflects the increasingly explicit representation of phonological knowledge at the level of the rime. Early epilinguistic knowledge of rime will to some extent become metalinguistic as a consequence of exposure to the orthographic structure of English (see Goswami and East, 1998). However, teachers can facilitate the acquisition of metalinguistic control over onset–rime structures by teaching children to group words on the basis of onsets and rimes at both a phonological and an orthographic level, and by teaching them how to use an analogy strategy (e.g., Goswami, 1994; 1995; 1998; in press, b; Goswami and East, 1998).

Many studies have now confirmed Goswami's (1986) suggestion that rime units are used more frequently by children as reading vocabulary expands (the *rime frequency* effect: Bowey and Hansen, 1994; Bowey and Underwood, 1996; Leslie and Calhoon, 1995; Treiman, Goswami and Bruck, 1990). Studies have also confirmed that an analogy strategy is available to beginning readers, whether the clue word task is used or not (e.g., Ehri and Robbins, 1992; Moustafa, 1995; Walton, 1995), although some studies report a reduction in analogizing in the absence of clue words, as would be expected (e.g., Bruck and Treiman, 1992; Muter, Snowling and Taylor, 1994; Savage and Stuart, 1998). Further, recent connectionist simulation models of reading have shown that the rime plays an important role in reading acquisition in English, with networks 'discovering' onset–rime mappings at an early stage of learning associations between print and sound. This holds even when models are trained with relatively few real words in order to mirror the earliest stage of reading (e.g., Zorzi, Houghton and Butterworth, 1998). There is thus an impressive amount of convergent evidence showing the importance of rhyme and analogy in early reading. However, a few recent studies appear discrepant with Goswami and Bryant's

(1990) theory, or have at least been interpreted as such by their authors. These studies will now be discussed.

Recent Debate about the Importance of Rhyme and Analogy in Reading Development in English

Recent studies that have led to debate about the role of rhyme and analogy in reading development in English can be organized into three areas. These are studies that query the importance of rhyme for reading development in English, studies that query the early availability of rime structures, and studies that attempt to re-open the 'phonological priming' debate.

Studies querying the importance of rhyme for reading development in English

Two recent studies by Hulme and his colleagues (Muter, Hulme, Snowling and Taylor, 1997; Nation and Hulme, 1997) have been used to question the earlier work of Bryant and his colleagues on the importance of rhyme for reading development in English (Bradley and Bryant, 1983; Bryant et al., 1990; Ellis and Large, 1987; Maclean et al., 1987). Muter et al.'s study was most similar to Bryant's work, as it used a longitudinal design. Muter et al. followed 38 4-year-olds for a period of two years. Tests of onset–rime awareness and phoneme awareness were given at 4 years, and reading was measured at 5 and 6 years. Muter et al. reported that a factor analysis showed two independent phonological factors, a 'phoneme' factor which was a significant predictor of reading in their sample, and a 'rhyme' factor which was not. Muter et al. concluded that early rhyming skills were not a determinant of early reading skills, and that teachers should no longer be encouraged to develop rhyming skills as part of the early reading curriculum (p. 391).

More recently, however, Muter et al. have become aware of a number of scoring errors in their data set, and have published an Erratum (Muter et al., in press). Bryant has re-analysed their data without these errors and using a different procedure for scoring onset–rime awareness, and has found that phonological awareness is described by a single factor encompassing *both* their onset–rime and phonemic measures (Bryant, in press). This single factor is highly predictive of reading in their sample.

Nation and Hulme (1997) used a cross-sectional design to query Bryant's findings about the predictive importance of rhyme for reading. They set out to examine whether tests of onset–rime awareness and tests of phoneme awareness would account for significant variance in reading when multiple regression equations were used. This statistical technique allows one to examine whether phonological measures at the two levels account for *independent* portions of the variability in reading, and in this sense allows an estimate of the 'predictive strength' of the two kinds of measure (Nation and Hulme did not use multiple regression as a test of prediction in the longitudinal sense, in which a variable measured at time 1, such as onset–rime awareness, uniquely predicts a second variable measured at time 2, such as reading; see Bryant et al., 1990). Three small groups of 6-year-olds, 8-year-olds and 9-year-olds took part in their study. None of their phonological measures (onset–rime or phoneme) correlated significantly with reading in their sample of beginning readers (6-year-olds), which is an extremely unusual finding and suggests a lack of power in their design. When correlations were derived for the total group of children aged from 6 to 9 years, then all of their phonological measures correlated with reading except for one measure of onset–rime segmentation. This measure also (unsurprisingly, given the lack of correlation) did not account for significant variance in reading in a multiple regression equation. Nation and Hulme argued that the failure of onset–rime segmentation to 'predict' reading in the multiple regression equation across this large age range was "a clear contradiction of the predictions made by Goswami and Bryant (1990)" (p. 165). They also pointed out that each year-group performed at around the same level in the onset–rime segmentation task, with the 6-year-olds segmenting 55 per cent of the (mainly complex nonsense-word) stimuli successfully, the 8-year-olds 58 per cent, and the 9-year-olds, 60 per cent. These performance levels were taken as evidence that onset–rime segmentation is difficult: 'This finding seriously questions Goswami and Bryant's (1990) suggestion that awareness of onset–rime develops early and naturally' (p. 164). Yet at the same time, Nation and Hulme reported that the youngest children in their study found onset–rime segmentation easier than phonemic segmentation (55% correct versus 24% correct).

In fact, Nation and Hulme's findings are entirely consistent with the distinction between epilinguistic knowledge about rime and the acquisition of metalinguistic control over phonological structures noted by Gombert (1992). Nation and Hulme report that the children in their study were being taught to read by methods that emphasized the phoneme. This leads us to expect that, as the children experienced more teaching, performance in a task requiring metalinguistic control (such as a segmentation task) should improve at the level of the phoneme, which is exactly what Nation and Hulme found. This demonstrates the importance of the teaching method for the development of metalinguistic control over phonological structures. If explicit literacy teaching at the onset–rime level had been given, then we can predict that onset–rime segmentation skills would also have improved. This prediction was tested in a recent study by Goswami and East (1998). They gave an onset–rime segmentation task to a group of 32 5-year-old children. Half of their sample were unable to perform the segmentation task at all prior to instruction, scoring 0. Following a short period of reading instruction based on rhyme and analogy methods, all of the children became able to segment words into onsets and rimes. Initial onset–rime segmentation ability and improvement in onset–rime segmentation were not correlated with reading ability. Goswami and East suggested that onset–rime segmentation is not correlated with reading ability because *all* children can learn to segment words into onsets and rimes, irrespective of the level of their reading skills.

Studies querying the availability of rime structures

Two recent studies by Seymour and his colleagues have questioned whether rime structures are available from the beginning of reading, and have consequently questioned the existence of a pathway from 'large' (onset–rime) units to 'small' (phonemic) units in reading development (Duncan, Seymour and Hill, 1997; Seymour and Evans, 1994). Seymour and Evans (1994) used a task in which 4-, 5- and 6-year-old Scottish children were asked to 'speak like a robot' in order to segment words into 2, 3 or many parts. The stimuli that they were asked to segment comprised a mixture of simple and complex monosyllabic words. The children were given no guidance concerning which 2, 3 and many parts were expected as responses. Seymour and

Evans found that the 4- and 5-year-old children were unable to perform the task at any level, and the 6-year-olds were more successful in segmenting the words into many parts (scored as correct when the many parts corresponded to phonemes – 60 per cent correct) than into 2 parts (scored as correct when the 2 parts corresponded to onset–rime units – 33 per cent correct). In a synthesis (blending) task given at the same time, the 5- and 6-year-olds showed more success with onset–rime units than with phonemes. Seymour and Evans focused on the segmentation results. As the children in their study were receiving a systematic phonics reading programme based on the phoneme, they concluded that, where early letter–sound teaching was in force, reading development followed a 'small unit to large unit' pathway.

Again, this result is entirely predictable from Gombert's (1992) theory. Seymour and Evans are discussing an effect that reflects the literacy teaching experienced by their sample, rather than an effect that reveals the 'natural' path of reading development. The fact that the children studied by Seymour and Evans were receiving intensive tuition at the phonemic level explains why 'many-part' responses were easier than '2-part' responses. The lack of explicit task instructions also explains children's difficulty in deciding which '2 parts' to segment. Although 70 per cent of the responses made by the children studied by Seymour and Evans consisted of 2 parts, only a minority of these 2-part responses conformed to an onset–rime division.

To test the 'small unit to large unit' notion further, Duncan et al. devised the 'common unit' tasks. In the phonological common unit task, children were required to identify the phonological unit shared between two words spoken by the experimenter. For example, if the experimenter said 'home–gnome', the child was meant to respond 'ome', whereas if the experimenter said 'home-sum', the child was meant to respond '/m/'. In the orthographic common unit task, children were meant to circle the letters that corresponded to a sound spoken by the experimenter. For example, if the child was given the written word 'home' and the experimenter said 'ome', the child was meant to circle the letters OME. As in Seymour and Evans (1994), the children were not explicitly told the kind of responses that were required in these tasks. Responses corresponding to the onset, rime, peak (vowel), body (onset–vowel) and coda (final phoneme/s) were

measured. Duncan et al. found that the identification of units corresponding to rimes was most difficult in both 'common unit' tasks.
Performance in each task was strongest with onsets, followed by
codas (final consonants) and peaks (vowels). Duncan et al. drew
the conclusion that 'large unit theories may not be capable of
predicting the *preferred* course of initial reading acquisition' (p. 198,
my emphasis).

Once more, we can see that these results are exactly as would be
expected given Gombert's (1992) framework. The children studied
by Duncan et al. were receiving systematic phoneme-based tuition in
reading, and the common unit tasks are metalinguistic tasks. Duncan
et al.'s sample had learned to produce single phonemes and to think
about grapheme–phoneme relations rather than to produce phonological segments like 'ome' and to think about rime spellings, and this
was reflected in their common unit task performance. Furthermore,
again the children were not given any explicit task instructions.
Although they were told in the phonological common unit task
that the shared sound was either at the beginning or at the end of
the words, these instructions seem more likely to make children
think about the very end sound in words – the final consonant
(coda) – rather than the rime. Curiously, although Duncan et al.
acknowledge that Gombert's (1992) theory may be important
for interpreting their results, they set up Gombert's framework
in opposition to Goswami and Bryant's (1990) theory (see Duncan
et al., 1997). Gombert's theory actually extends that of Goswami
and Bryant (see Gombert, 1992; Gombert, Bryant and Warrick,
1997).

If Duncan et al.'s results in the common unit tasks indeed reflect
a lack of explicit tuition in reading at the level of the rime, then children who receive such explicit tuition should perform much better
with rimes in the common unit tasks. This prediction was tested by
Goswami and East (1998). They gave the same common unit tasks
using the same stimuli to a group of English 5-year-olds both prior
to and following a short period of instruction with a 'rhyme and
analogy' reading programme (Goswami, 1996b). At pre-test, namely
before the children received the rhyme and analogy instruction, patterns of performance in the common unit tasks mirrored those
reported by Duncan et al. (1997). Following the short intervention
(approximately 5 hours spread over 8 weeks), selective and significant

improvements in the rime versions of the task were found. These gains were *larger* than the improvements that were found to occur naturally in the Scottish sample during two years of reading tuition at the phonemic level (these children are followed up in Duncan et al., 1998). Two conclusions can be drawn. The first is that methods of reading instruction have a strong impact on performance in metalinguistic tasks, as predicted by Gombert. The second is that, for rimes, relatively brief periods of literacy tuition result in the achievement of markedly improved levels of metalinguistic control. It seems likely that 'rhyme and analogy' tuition has relatively rapid effects because it builds on the child's epilinguistic knowledge about rime.

Studies re-opening the 'phonological priming' debate

Two recent studies have argued that orthographic analogy effects in beginning reading should be understood in terms of phonological priming (Bowey, Vaughan and Hansen; 1998; Savage and Stuart, 1998, Experiment 1), although for rather different reasons. The study by Bowey et al. set out to re-investigate whether the advantage reported for rime analogies in beginning readers was reliable once phonological priming effects were taken into account. This was felt to be important on the basis of the mistaken assumption that Goswami and Bryant claimed that 'orthographic rimes serve as functional units of word identification from the outset of reading, even before new readers have a reading vocabulary large enough to be readily measurable' (Bowey et al., 1998, p. 109). Goswami and Bryant actually said 'beginning readers are ready to make analogies even though they know so few written words and therefore have such a small basis for using any analogies at all' (p. 77).

Bowey et al. devised a new experimental technique based on 'analogy booklets' to re-investigate phonological priming effects. Three booklets, each containing 72 words, were given to 6- and 7-year-old children with reading ages at levels of around 6 years 9 months and 7 years, to be read as quickly as possible. Each booklet had 12 pages with 6 words per page. One of these was a clue word, one was an analogy word, one was a phonological prime, and three were control words. One booklet contained rime analogies and rhyme primes, one contained beginning (*beak–bean*) analogies and beginning primes, and one contained vowel analogies (*beak–heap*) and vowel primes. Bowey et al. found that the children could make all three kinds of analogies (as would be expected given their reading ages, see Goswami, 1993). However, they reported that only the beginning analogy effect remained after controlling for phonological priming.

The main difficulty lies in how to interpret this finding, which depends on the reliability of the adjustments made for phonological priming. In fact, these adjustments only considered one kind of phonological priming, the kind intentionally put into the experiment by the experimenters. Closer inspection of the design of the 'analogy booklets' reveals two additional and unintended sources of phonological priming in Bowey et al.'s experiment (see also Goswami, in press, c). One is intra-list vowel priming. As Bowey et al. used only 4 vowel phonemes to derive their experimental word lists, the same vowels kept repeating across the 72 words in each booklet. The second is unintended intra-list rime priming. Some of the clue and test words that Bowey et al. included in their 'beginning analogy' and 'middle analogy' booklets were actually rime analogy words or rhyme primes for some of the other test words. There were at least 12 unintentional rime analogy words and rhyme primes of this type in the beginning analogy booklet (e.g., *beat–seat–heat, rail–bail–mail–pale*), and at least 15 unintentional rime analogy words and rhyme primes in the middle analogy booklet (e.g., *deep–peep–leap, weed–deed–feed–reed*). Recall that there were only 12 *intentional* rime analogy words and rhyme primes in the rime analogy booklet. The unintended intra-list priming and rime analogy effects were thus of a comparable magnitude to the experimental effects that the authors were looking for. These problems render Bowey et al.'s data on phonological priming effectively uninterpretable.

Savage and Stuart (1998, Experiment 1) used a version of the clue word technique in their study of phonological priming, which was carried out with 6-year-olds. However, rather than using non-analogous words that rhymed with the clue word to test for phonological priming (e.g., *bread–said*), they gave children the pronunciation of clue words that were analogous to the test words (e.g., *beak–peak*) but *without* showing the children the spelling patterns of these words. The critical comparison was between a group of children who were both shown the clue word *beak* and given its pronunciation prior to presentation of test words like *peak* (the analogy group), and a group who were told 'Your clue word says "beak", what does this word say?' without actually seeing the spelling pattern of *beak* prior to receiving test words like *peak* (the phonological priming group). Savage and Stuart argued that, if analogy effects in early reading depend on phonological priming, equivalent levels of test word reading should occur in these two conditions. This was what they found. They then stated 'present results strongly suggest that the use of orthographic analogies from a single source of lexical knowledge is not an acquisition strategy available to children in the earliest stages of learning to read' (p. 96).

This paradigm does not provide an adequate test of phonological priming, however, because Savage and Stuart's critical manipulation induced the children to guess words with similar pronunciations to the clue word. Savage and Stuart told the children that their clue words were 'a clue to the mystery of how to read some new words'. The experimenter then said 'Your clue word says beak' prior to presenting the first two test words, and repeated this after every subsequent two words. As the children only heard the sounds of the clue words, the most rational assumption was that these clue words helped them with the mystery of reading by being a clue to pronunciation. This interpretation is supported by the fact that Savage and Stuart found equivalent levels of 'transfer' to beginning analogy words (e.g., *beak–bean*) *in the phonological prompt condition only*. In addition, the children may already have had some knowledge of some of the clue words, and the experimenter saying 'Your clue word says beak' may have brought the spelling patterns of these words to mind, enabling the use of orthographic analogies in the phonological priming condition. Again, this interpretation is supported by additional data reported by Savage and Stuart. They found that the children in the analogy group could read 55 per cent of the clue words correctly when this was checked at the end of the experiment, and that the children in the phonological priming group could read 40 per cent of the clue words correctly. Some of the clue-word spelling patterns were thus clearly known to the critical group of children who were not shown the clue words during the experiment.

Finally, it is important to note that a degree of phonological priming would be expected to occur in analogy tasks. A key point is that it is the salience of the rime unit in *spoken* language that contributes to its functional importance in the orthography (Kessler and Treiman, in press; Treiman et al., 1995). Phonological priming effects are familiar in word naming tasks with adults, where rhyme priming effects are particularly strong (e.g., Grainger and Ferrand, 1996). Given the salience of the rime in the phonology of the English language and its effects in adult reading, it would be surprising if no rhyme priming effects at all were found with children. This salience is one of the factors that can be exploited by teachers who use analogy methods in the classroom.

Non-research-based critiques

Finally, a number of recent publications aimed at teachers and parents have questioned whether tuition in rhyme and analogy has a place in early literacy teaching (e.g., Chew, 1994; McGuiness, 1998). These publications are either intended to promote a particular method of teaching reading (e.g., McGuiness, 1998), or appear to regard the so-called 'new phonics' of rhyme and analogy as an attempt to undermine the proper teaching of reading in the classroom. Chew, for example, states that 'Researchers like Goswami . . . believe that teachers should build on children's understanding of rhyme *rather than* use approaches based on an understanding of the way in which letters of the alphabet relate to individual speech sounds' (p. 4, my emphasis). McGuiness states 'the notion that "rhyme" = "phonological awareness" = "phoneme awareness" has permeated the National Curriculum guidelines. Teachers are led to believe that teaching rhyming games and segmenting by onset and rime will have a direct impact on learning to read and spell' (p. 148).

There are of course many opinions about how reading should best be taught, and in order to distinguish between these opinions we need empirical research. The continual development of our knowledge about the factors that affect reading acquisition through well-designed experimental studies is preferable to the expression of opinions that are not empirically based. Some of the statements made in these publications are simply wrong. Goswami and Bryant did not counsel teachers against using 'approaches based on an understanding of the way in which letters of the alphabet relate to individual speech sounds', as claimed by Chew. Instead, they pointed out that one important way in which letters of the alphabet relate to speech sounds in English is through rime units. McGuiness misunderstands Bryant's use of multiple regression equations, leading her to state quite wrongly that 'sensitivity to rhyme has not been shown to be a strong predictor of reading skill' (p. 148). This leads her to reject evidence that teaching rhyming games and segmenting by onset and rime have a direct impact on learning to read and spell. She is also wrong in stating that the National Curriculum has got phonological awareness confused with phonemic awareness. The new National Literacy Framework in particular is very clear about the sequence of phonological development, and gives justified prominence to the need to teach grapheme–phoneme relations as well as onsets and rimes.

Conclusion: Epilinguistic and Metalinguistic Factors in Rhyme and Analogy in Early Reading Development

This chapter began by reviewing the research base that established the importance of rhyme and analogy as one of the key factors in early reading development in English. It also highlighted common principles that guide the use of analogies in reading and the use of analogies in other areas of cognition. It was noted that children use analogies successfully when they have represented the relevant relational knowledge, when they have a basis for using an analogy, when they have multiple exemplars available, and when they are taught to use an analogy strategy. In reading, this means that analogies will be used when children have represented the relevant phonological knowledge (for example, knowledge about rime as a phonological unit), and when they have a relevant clue word in their reading vocabulary. It also means that more analogies will be made by children with larger reading vocabularies or who know more than one clue word (multiple exemplars), and that more analogies will be made by children who receive explicit tuition in orthographic and phonological connections at the level of the rhyme. These factors also mean that not all children will use analogies spontaneously. An individual child's use of analogy will depend partly on the level of his or her phonological skills and on the size of the reading vocabulary. It was also emphasized that the availability of an analogy strategy does not necessarily mean that it will be used. For some children, analogy as a strategy has to be taught if it is to be used efficiently.

Gombert's (1992) distinction between epilinguistic skills and metalinguistic control over phonological structures was then introduced. It was suggested that this framework enables a deeper understanding of how the three causal connections in early reading proposed by Goswami and Bryant (1990) exert their causal influences. The connection between preschool awareness of rime and alliteration and later progress in reading and spelling can be understood as a connection between phonological awareness at the epilinguistic level and reading development. The connection between tuition at the level of the phoneme and the development of phonemic awareness can be understood as part of a more general connection between the teaching methods employed in the classroom and the emergence of metalinguistic control over phonological structures at the level of both onset–rime and phoneme. The connection between spelling and reading can also be understood in terms of metalinguistic control, as learning to spell also requires the explicit representation of phonological knowledge. Recent research on the role of rhyme and analogy in early reading was then interpreted within this framework.

The journal article upon which this chapter is based concluded with a checklist of what analogy was 'not'. Analogy is not an approach to reading that wishes to exclude teaching about letters and sounds. It does not exclude teaching about blending, or teaching about the alphabet. It is not an approach to reading that enables most children to learn spelling–sound correspondences spontaneously, without explicit tuition, and it is not an approach to reading that attempts to displace the teaching of grapheme–phoneme relations. Rather, analogy is a basic cognitive strategy that is available to all children. It has a role to play in reading, as it does in the acquisition of many other skills. This role is intimately connected to the fact that one important way in which letters of the alphabet relate to speech sounds in English is through rime units. Analogies in reading will be used spontaneously by children who have good phonological skills at the onset–rime level, and who build up large reading vocabularies. However, explicit instruction is important for the use of analogies in reading for most children, and this is why teachers *should* be encouraged to develop rhyming and analogy skills as part of the early reading curriculum.

References

Bowey, J. A., and Hansen, J. (1994) The development of orthographic rimes as units of word recognition. *Journal of Experimental Child Psychology*, *58*, 465–88.

Bowey, J. A., and Underwood, N. (1996) Further evidence that orthographic rime usage in nonword reading increases with word-level reading proficiency. *Journal of Experimental Child Psychology*, *63*, 526–62.

Bowey, J. A., Vaughan, L., and Hansen, J. (1998) Beginning readers' use of orthographic analogies in word reading. *Journal of Experimental Child Psychology*, *68*, 108–33.

Bradley, L., and Bryant, P. E. (1978) Difficulties in auditory organisation as a possible cause of reading backwardness. *Nature*, *271*, 746–7.

Bradley, L., and Bryant, P. E. (1983) Categorising sounds and learning to read: A causal connection. *Nature*, *310*, 419–21.

Brown, A. L. (1989) Analogical learning and transfer: What develops? In S. Vosniadou and A. Ortony (eds), *Similarity and Analogical Reasoning*, Cambridge, UK: Cambridge University Press, pp. 369–412.

Bruck, M., and Treiman, R. (1992) Learning to pronounce words: The limitations of analogies. *Reading Research Quarterly*, *27* (4), 374–89.

Bryant, P. E. (in press) Sensitivity to onset and rime does predict young children's reading: A comment on Muter, Hulme, Snowling and Taylor (1997). *Journal of Experimental Child Psychology*.

Bryant, P. E., Maclean, M., Bradley, L., and Crossland, J. (1990) Rhyme, alliteration, phoneme detection, and learning to read. *Developmental Psychology*, *26*, 429–38.

Carroll, J. B., Davies, P., and Richman, B. (1971) *Word Frequency Book*. New York: American Heritage.

Chew, J. (1994) *Professional Expertise and Parental Experience in the Teaching of Reading, or Mother Often Knows Best*. York: Campaign for Real Education.

Cunningham, A. E. (1990) Implicit vs explicit instruction in phonemic awareness. *Journal of Experimental Child Psychology*, *50*, 429–44.

Duncan, L. G., Seymour, P. H. K., and Hill, S. (1997) How important are rhyme and analogy in beginning reading? *Cognition*, *63*, 171–208.

Duncan, L. G., Seymour, P. H. K., and Hill, S. (1998) *Small-to-Large Unit Progression in Metaphonological Awareness and Reading*. Manuscript submitted for publication.

Ehri, L. C., and Robbins, C. (1992) Beginners need some decoding skill to read words by analogy. *Reading Research Quarterly, 27* (1), 12–28.

Ellis, N. C., and Large, B. (1987) The development of reading: As you seek, so shall ye find. *British Journal of Psychology, 78*, 1–28.

Gaskins, I. W., Downer, M. A., and Gaskins, R. W. (1986) *Introduction to the Benchmark School Word Identification/Vocabulary Development Program*. Media, PA: Benchmark Press.

Gentner, D. (1989) The mechanisms of analogical learning. In S. Vosniadou and A. Ortony (eds), *Similarity and Analogical Reasoning*, London: Cambridge University Press, pp. 199–241.

Gombert, J. E. (1992) *Metalinguistic Development*. Hemel Hempstead, Herts: Havester Wheatsheaf.

Gombert, J. E., Bryant, P., and Warrick, N. (1997) Children's use of analogy in learning to read and to spell. In C. A. Perfetti, M. Fayol, and L. Rieben (eds), *Learning to Spell*, New Jersey: Erlbaum, pp. 221–35.

Goswami, U. (1986) Children's use of analogy in learning to read: A developmental study. *Journal of Experimental Child Psychology, 42*, 73–83.

Goswami, U. (1988) Orthographic analogies and reading development. *Quarterly Journal of Experimental Psychology, 40A*, 239–68.

Goswami, U. (1990a) A special link between rhyming skills and the use of orthographic analogies by beginning readers. *Journal of Child Psychology and Psychiatry, 31*, 301–11.

Goswami, U. (1990b) Phonological priming and orthographic analogies in reading. *Journal of Experimental Child Psychology, 49*, 323–40.

Goswami, U. (1991a) Analogical reasoning: What develops? A review of research and theory. *Child Development, 62*, 1–22.

Goswami, U. (1991b) Learning about spelling sequences: The role of onsets and rimes in analogies in reading. *Child Development, 62*, 1110–23.

Goswami, U. (1992) *Analogical Reasoning in Children*. Hillsdale, NJ: Erlbaum.

Goswami, U. (1993) Toward an interactive analogy model of reading development: Decoding vowel graphemes in beginning reading. *Journal of Experimental Child Psychology, 56*, 443–75.

Goswami, U. (1994) Phonological skills, analogies and reading development. *Reading, 28* (2), 32–7.

Goswami, U. (1995) Phonological development and reading by analogy: What is analogy, and What is it not? *Journal of Research in Reading, 18*, 139–45.

Goswami, U. (1996a) Analogical reasoning and cognitive development. In H. Reese (ed.), *Advances in Child Development and Behaviour*, 26, 91–138.

Goswami, U. (1996b) *The Oxford Reading Tree Rhyme and Analogy Programme*. Oxford, UK: Oxford University Press.

Goswami, U. (1998) *Cognition in Children*. Hove: Psychology Press.

Goswami, U. (in press, a) Orthographic representations in different orthographies. To appear in M. Harris and G. Hatano (eds), *A Cross-Linguistic Perspective on Learning to Read*. Cambridge: Cambridge University Press.

Goswami, U. (in press, b) Phonological and lexical processes. To appear in M. L. Kamil, P. B. Mosenthal, P. D. Pearson and R. Barr (eds), *Handbook of Reading Research*, vol. III (1998).

Goswami, U. (in press, c) Orthographic analogies and phonological priming: A comment on Bowey, Vaughan and Hansen (1998). *Journal of Experimental Child Psychology*.

Goswami, U., and Brown, A. L. (1989) Melting chocolate and melting snowmen: Analogical reasoning and causal relations. *Cognition*, 35, 69–95.

Goswami, U., and Bryant, P. E. (1990) *Phonological Skills and Learning to Read*. Hillsdale, NJ: Lawrence Erlbaum.

Goswami, U., and East, M. (1998) *Epilinguistic and Metalinguistic Factors in Rhyme and Analogy in Beginning Reading: The Importance of Teaching*. Manuscript submitted for publication.

Goswami, U., Gombert, J., and de Barrera, F. (1998) Children's orthographic representations and linguistic transparency: Nonsense word reading in English, French and Spanish. *Applied Psycholinguistics*, 19, 19–52.

Goswami, U., and Mead, F. (1992) Onset and rime awareness and analogies in reading. *Reading Research Quarterly*, 27 (2), 152–62.

Goswami, U., Porpodas, C., and Wheelwright, S. (1997) Children's orthographic representations in English and Greek. *European Journal of Psychology of Education*, 12 (3), 273–92.

Grainger, J., and Ferrand, L. (1996) Masked orthographic and phonological priming in visual word recognition and naming: Cross-task comparisons. *Journal of Memory and Language*, 35, 623–47.

Greaney, K. T., and Tunmer, W. E. (1996) Onset/rime sensitivity and orthographic analogies in normal and poor readers. *Applied Psycholinguistics*, 17, 15–40.

Greaney, K. T., Tunmer, W. E., and Chapman, J. W. (1997) Effects of rime-based orthographic analogy training on the word recognition skills of children with reading disability. *Journal of Educational Psychology*, 89, 645–51.

Halford, G. S. (1987) A structure-mapping approach to cognitive development. *International Journal of Psychology*, 22, 609–42.

Halford, G. S. (1993) *Children's Understanding: The Development of Mental Models*. Hillsdale, NJ: Erlbaum.

Hansen, J., and Bowey, J. A. (1994) Phonological analysis skills, verbal working memory and reading ability in second grade children. *Child Development*, 65, 938–50.

Hoien, T., Lundberg, L., Stanovich, K. E., and Bjaalid, I. K. (1995) Components of phonological awareness. *Reading and Writing*, 7, 171–88.

Kessler, B., and Treiman, R. (in press) Syllable structure and phoneme distribution. *Journal of Memory and Language*.

Kirtley, C., Bryant, P., Maclean, M., and Bradley, L. (1989) Rhyme, rime and the onset of reading. *Journal of Experimental Child Psychology*, 48, 224–45.

Leslie, L., and Calhoon, A. (1995) Factors affecting children's reading of rimes: Reading ability, word frequency and rime neighbourhood size. *Journal of Educational Psychology*, 87, 576–86.

Lundberg, I., Olofsson, A., and Wall, S. (1980) Reading and spelling skills in the first school years predicted from phonemic awareness skills in kindergarten. *Scandinavian Journal of Psychology*, 21, 159–73.

Maclean, M., Bryant, P. E., and Bradley, L. (1987) Rhymes, nursery rhymes and reading in early childhood. *Merrill-Palmer Quarterly*, 33, 255–82.

McGuinness, D. (1998) *Why Children Can't Read*. London: Penguin.

Morais, J., Cary, L., Alegria, J., and Bertelson, P. (1979) Does awareness of speech as a sequence of phones arise spontaneously? *Cognition*, 7, 323–31.

Moustafa, M. (1995) Children's productive phonological recoding. *Reading Research Quarterly*, 30, 464–75.

Muter, V., Hulme, C., Snowling, M., and Taylor, S. (1997) Segmentation, not rhyming, predicts early progress in learning to read. *Journal of Experimental Child Psychology*, 65, 370–96.

Muter, V., Hulme, C., Snowling, M., and Taylor, S. (in press) 'Segmentation, not rhyming, predicts early progress in learning to read: Erratum'. *Journal of Experimental Child Psychology*.

Muter, V., Snowling, M., and Taylor, S. (1994) Orthographic analogies and phonological awareness: Their role and significance in early reading development. *Journal of Child Psychology and Psychiatry*, 35, 293–310.

Nation, K., and Hulme, C. (1997) Phonemic segmentation, not onset–rime segmentation, predicts early reading and spelling skills. *Reading Research Quarterly*, 32, 154–67.

Savage, R., and Stuart, M. (1998) Sublexical inferences in beginning reading: Medial vowel digraphs as functional units of transfer. *Journal of Experimental Child Psychology*, 69, 85–108.

Seymour, P. H. K., and Evans, H. M. (1994) Levels of phonological awareness and learning to read. *Reading and Writing*, 6, 221–50.

Stanback, M. L. (1992) Syllable and rime patterns for teaching reading: Analysis of a frequency-based vocabulary of 17,602 words. *Annals of Dyslexia*, 42, 196–221.

Treiman, R. (1988) The internal structure of the syllable. In G. Carlson and M. Tanenhaus (eds), *Linguistic Structure in Language Processing*, Dordrecht, Netherlands: Kluger, pp. 27–52.

Treiman, R., Goswami, U., and Bruck, M. (1990) Not all nonwords are alike: Implications for reading development and theory. *Memory and Cognition*, 18, 559–67.

Treiman, R., Mullennix, J., Bijeljac-Babic, R., and Richmond-Welty, E. D. (1995) The special role of rimes in the description, use and acquisition of English orthography. *Journal of Experimental Psychology, General*, 124, 107–36.

Treiman, R., and Zukowski, A. (1991) Levels of phonological awareness. In S. Brady and D. Shankweiler (eds), *Phonological Processes in Literacy*. Hillsdale, NJ: Erlbaum.

Treiman, R., and Zukowski, A. (1996) Children's sensitivity to syllables, onsets, rimes and phonemes. *Journal of Experimental Child Psychology*, 61, 193–215.

Wagstaff, J. M. (1994) *Phonics that Work! New Strategies for the Reading/Writing Classroom*. Jefferson City, MO: Scholastic.

Walton, P. D. (1995) Rhyming ability, phoneme identity, letter–sound knowledge and the use of orthographic analogy by prereaders. *Journal of Educational Psychology*, 87, 587–97.

Wimmer, H., Landerl, K., and Schneider, W. (1994) The role of rhyme awareness in learning to read a regular orthography. *British Journal of Developmental Psychology*, 12, 469–84.

Wylie, R. E., and Durrell, D. D. (1970) *Elementary English*, 47, 787–91.

Zorzi, M., Houghton, G., and Butterworth, B. (1998) The development of spelling–sound relationships in a model of phonological reading. *Language and Cognitive Processes*, 13, 337–71.

Chapter Ten

The Messenger may be Wrong, but the Message may be Right

CONNIE JUEL

There has been a fierce debate in the last few decades between those reading theorists who insist upon the criticality of efficient word recognition and those who believe just the opposite: that visual information contained within words is only occasionally sampled by the reader to construct meaning from text. Smith (1971) expresses this latter view:

> The more difficulty a reader has with reading, the more he relies on the visual information; this statement applies to both the fluent reader and the beginner. In each case, the cause of the difficulty is inability to make full use of syntactic and semantic redundancy, of nonvisual sources of information. (p. 221)

From this view, the reader is seen as selectively sampling visual information only when the *context* forces the reader to do so (Goodman, 1970/1976; Smith, 1973). (See Juel, 1991a; Stanovich, 1991a; 1991b, for further discussion of this debate.)

The reason this debate became so intense is that it is often theoretically tied to methods of reading instruction – a topic which has seldom been devoid of emotion. Those who believe the reader samples his or her way through text and infrequently and incompletely processes individual words see little reason to require young children to engage in activities which dwell upon words or word parts (as is done in phonics instruction). The basic reading process is viewed as the same process whether the reader is a beginner or a skilled reader (Goodman and Goodman, 1979, p. 148). The Goodmans believe the difference between the two readers is the amount of world knowledge and language which they bring to the reading task. With increased world knowledge the skilled reader is able to make better use of context to generate hypotheses about upcoming content and to sample less and less of the visual information from the actual words in the text. The type of text the young reader should see, then, is one replete with rich vocabulary.

The above view of reading as a 'psycholinguistic guessing game' (Goodman, 1970/1976) has largely been disproved, however. There is now a large body of studies indicating that poor readers primarily differ from good readers in context-free word recognition, and not in deficiencies in ability to use context to form predictions. In fact, poor readers often rely *more* on context to try to derive meaning than do good readers, because poor readers lack efficient word recognition (see reviews in Gough, 1983; Juel, 1991a; Perfetti, 1985; Stanovich, 1980; 1986; 1991a; Stanovich and Stanovich, this volume).

Eye-movement studies, together with computer simulations of reading, further suggest that the word recognition processes of the skilled reader operate with all or nearly all of the visual data (i.e., the letters in every word), and do so in a highly efficient, modular fashion. Word recognition is not informed by the reader's hypotheses but instead operates exclusively by the connection strengths of orthographic patterns (Foorman, in press; Seidenberg and McClelland, 1989; Stanovich, 1991a).

While models of reading as a top-down, hypothesis-driven process are largely disproven, it does not follow that the views held by such theorists about reading instruction are necessarily invalid. Models of the reading process should inform those who construct models of instruction, but they do not directly translate into models of how to teach reading. That the skilled reader looks at almost every word and letter in text does not necessarily imply that the way to teach children to read is to have them spell out every letter in text.

Children learn about printed language in partly the same way they learn about spoken language: they are active hypothesis-makers and take in information (whether it be oral or print), ponder it, and form increasingly sophisticated hypotheses about its nature (Clark and

Clark, 1977). Such hypotheses lead to predictable patterns, including: overgeneralizations (e.g., 'go*ed*' and 'brok*ed*' in oral language, and 'deskes' instead of 'desks' and 'lefes' instead of 'leafs/leaves' in spelling) and apparent regressions (such as saying 'broked' after earlier use of 'broke' in oral language, or laboriously 'sounding out' words that were formerly effortlessly read) (Bissex, 1980; Söderbergh, 1977).

Written language is not, however, a biologically driven process like oral language (Liberman and Liberman, 1992). Human cultures exist without written language and written language has evolved as a cultural, and not a biological, phenomenon. It is virtually inevitable that any child with the ability to hear will learn to speak. On the other hand, if we were to provide vast quantities of print to a child there is no guarantee that that child would learn to read. The child's task in learning to read is much more difficult and unnatural, requiring more knowledge about the 'mechanics' of the system than is required by the biologically driven process of learning to speak (Gough and Hillinger, 1980; Liberman and Liberman, 1992). While approaching learning to read as an active hypothesis-maker, the child is much more likely to stumble, to fixate on unproductive hypotheses, and to require explicit guidance in the task of learning to read. One child in my longitudinal study of reading development continued to write words with only the letters in his own name well into second grade (Juel, 1994a).

The reader may be sensing an apparent paradox. The skilled reader's word recognition has been portrayed as a fast-acting, modular process, devoid of conscious hypothesis-testing. Yet the child learning to read has been described as an active 'hypothesis-tester'. The child uses whatever works to derive meaning from the page. Often story context is used, prior to well-developed decoding processes. As the child is able to connect some letters to phonemes, she can more successfully get the words through combining this information with what makes sense in the context of what she is reading. Active use of context to supplement orthographic information decreases as knowledge of orthographic patterns increases. Indeed, the longer the child continues to rely on context and does not increase in the use of orthographic information to identify words, the poorer the reader she is at the end of first grade (Biemiller, 1970).

The qualitative shifts in information used to identify unknown words (e.g., story context versus orthographic information) has led most current reading researchers to portray the process of learning to read as one that occurs in stages (see Ehri, this volume). With each new stage there is a qualitative shift in the type of information the child uses to identify unknown words. These differences in word identification are related to growth in knowledge about orthography. Each stage reflects additional, and ultimately more efficient, knowledge about orthography which can be used to recognize words. Early in the process a child may correctly read a word because he recalls all or some of its letters. Later, the child may correctly read a word because he knows the relationships between letters and phonemes, and eventually the child may correctly read a word because the connections among its letters have forged strong orthographic patterns. When the child misreads or misspells, the way the child did so is revealed by qualitatively different and predictable errors. A child spelling a word by visually remembering all its letters may misspell 'rain' as 'rian' (without using sound as a placeholder it is easy to reverse letters), but this would be a very unusual spelling error for a child using letters and phonemes (Juel, 1991a).

'Psycholinguistic' models, with their emphasis on improved oral language skills as the primary vehicle for improving early reading, necessarily must de-emphasize the importance of decoding skills. Proponents of such models want early reading materials that are rich in vocabulary and meaning. Those who have emphasized the importance of early learning of spelling–sound correspondences, on the other hand, tend to favour reading materials with vocabulary which lays bare the alphabetic principle. Resnick (1979) described the ensuing conflict:

> It lies in part in a fundamental competition between code and language demands in early reading. Learning the code requires a controlled vocabulary but language processing requires a rich language with which to work. This conflict cannot be wished away.   (p. 330)

At least that has been the conventional thought. Yet traditional phonics has rarely pleased even those who believe that fostering word recognition ability is at the heart of early reading instruction. First, the texts traditionally used in phonics approaches were dreadful (e.g.,

'Nan and Dan got in the tan van'). Second, most phonics approaches did not do enough to help children perceive words as sequences of phonemes, so that connecting letters to sounds through phonics instruction made little sense (Juel, 1994a; 1994b). In other words, telling children that the letter 'f' makes the sound they hear at the beginning of 'fish' makes no sense to the child who does not perceive a /f/ at the beginning of 'fish'. Third, most phonics came in the form of drill and skill worksheets and workbooks. It was 'add-on' phonics in the sense that it was independent from the stories children were reading in their basals (Beck, 1981). Most basal reading series in the United States from the late 1920s until 1993 have used a high frequency word approach – with high frequency words repeated numerous times. Words in the reading textbooks often had no relation to what was covered in the week's phonics lessons. Children might be taught the sound of the short 'o', for example, in the phonics lesson, and practise filling in a short 'o' workbook page – but read stories with few, if any, short 'o' words and even words that contained other patterns (e.g., *come, to, for, home*). In this common situation, many first-grade children ceased trying to use letter-sounds to decode words (Juel and Roper-Schneider, 1985).

In the 1980s children saw approximately 1000 different words in first grade (Hoffman et al., 1994). Most early reading texts continued to contain controlled vocabulary of the sort:

I am not happy.
I do not like this.
I will get off here.
I will look around.   (Silver, Burdett, and Ginn, 1989, pp. 44–5)

Phonics instruction occurred primarily in the workbooks. While the disassociation of phonics from text reading made little sense, in some ways the use of high frequency vocabulary did – if one considers the structure of printed English. In grades 3–8, 50 per cent of the words in school books (e.g., in textbooks, tradebooks, magazines) are accounted for by only 109 different words, 75 per cent of words in running text are accounted for by 1000 words, and fully 90 per cent of the words in texts are accounted for by 5000 words (Adams, 1990, p. 160). These percentages are not that different from what adults see in print. So, teach these words and you've covered a lot –

though the plot-lines in stories will be severely restricted by the vocabulary choices and the need to repeat the same words.

At any rate, what we essentially had for approximately the last 70 years in the United States was reading instruction in first grade that would please neither those who were interested in presenting children with real literature nor those who were interested in coordinating phonics instruction with beginning reading materials. By 1993, however, a radical change took place. Responding to cries for authentic children's literature, written by real children's literature authors, strict vocabulary controls disappeared nearly overnight. Basal textbooks turned into anthologies of children's literature. Stories written by a variety of well-known authors were simply bound together. In Silver, Burdett, and Ginn's 1993 series, for example, *Rosie's Walk* by well-known author Pat Hutchins is typical of the fare that beginning first-grade children now see in their earliest readers. In this children's favourite, Rosie the hen takes a walk:

> ... around the pond
> over the haystack
> past the mill
> through the fence
> under the beehives. . . .   (pp. 81–97)

Rosie is not walking through the most common words of English. There are lots of pictures to help the reader (assuming the youngster knows the vocabulary). The text has a rhythmical cadence that may help. The increased use of pictures and repetition of patterns, rhymes, and structures are in fact hallmarks of the new textbooks. In order to support the beginning reader through text written without vocabulary control, anthologies used during first grade are full of this type of predictable text: 50 per cent of the texts in the five most popular 1993 first-grade reading series in the United States were based on rhyme or predictable elements; only 15 per cent of the texts were realistic stories (Hoffman et al., 1994). The predictable story-lines and picture support are necessary props to enable children to get through text that presents upwards of 1600 unique words to children in first grade in text that lacks much repetition of the content words.

There has been a fundamental change in early reading instruction: no longer are children held accountable for the majority of words in the texts (e.g., pond, haystack, beehives). Instead, strategies are fostered. So, for example, children might be instructed to try to figure out a not instantly recognized word in *Rosie's Walk* by looking at the pictures, considering the first letter-sound, and monitoring for sense. The teacher might say upon reaching 'pond': 'Look, where is Rosie? What is the name for water like that that starts with a /p/?' After reading this story, children are not expected to recognize the word 'pond', but after frequent such encounters the child is expected to grasp the /p/ and connect it to the letter 'p'. Depending on the philosophy of a programme or teacher, additional 'phonics' instruction may follow. The word 'hen', for example, might lead to a discussion of the 'en' phonogram, with a link being made to other 'en' words.

Is such strategy-based instruction effective? Such strategies appear to be successful in one-to-one instruction like Reading Recovery. A typical Reading Recovery lesson includes the rereading of familiar little books (often predictable text) and the introduction of a new book. In both instances the teacher provides just enough scaffolding to facilitate the child's own reading. In the teacher's orientation to a new book, for example, the teacher may purposely refer to vocabulary that may be new or difficult for the child as she flips through the pages (e.g., 'Look at what Santa brought the child – a skateboard'). Such scaffolding sets up the child's eventual reading (i.e., of the word 'skateboard' when the child comes to that page). If the child pauses upon reaching the word 'skateboard', the teacher might refer back to previous conversations ('What did we say Santa brought?'), the picture cue on the page, or the initial phoneme in 'skateboard'. Reference to the initial phoneme is often made with the statement, 'Get your mouth ready'. If the child misreads 'skateboard' as 'rollerblades' the teacher might prompt the child to consider what letter 'rollerblades' begins with and whether that letter is seen at the beginning of 'skateboard'. If the child self-corrects without teacher support (e.g., initially reads 'skateboard' as 'rollerblades' and then says 'skateboard'), the teacher will encourage the child to state how she 'fixed' it – to verbalize her strategy so it will later be recalled (e.g., 'How did you know that said "skateboard"?').

What this type of dialogue promotes is the use of productive hypotheses/strategies and the disuse of nonproductive ones. Reading Recovery also includes substantial amounts of phonemic awareness training as well as writing which emphasizes perceiving phonemes in spoken words and connecting those phonemes to letters. In fact, writing is the primary vehicle in Reading Recovery through which letter-sounds are taught. This makes sense, as the phonemes in spoken words can be elongated or stressed, and connected to a letter in a most transparent way.

As helpful as Reading Recovery is to a struggling reader, the addition of direct code instruction might make it even stronger. Iversen and Tunmer (1993) found that the addition of explicit code instruction involving phonograms to the standard Reading Recovery tutorial lesson significantly increased the speed at which children learned to read.

Recently I analysed extensive data collected from a tutoring project where university student-athletes (many of whom were themselves poor readers) tutored 'at-risk' first-grade children. The programme had been shown to be effective overall (Juel, 1991b), but I was interested in examining what made it effective. Video-tapes and/or tape-recordings were made of each tutoring session. Two major analyses were done. First, a quantitative analysis was done on minutes spent on various tutoring activities. Second, a qualitative analysis was made of the video-tapes of those tutors who were especially successful. The qualitative analysis revealed three features that the most successful dyads shared: (1) obvious affection, bonding and verbal and non-verbal reinforcement of children's progress; (2) lots of scaffolded reading and writing experiences; and (3) considerable explicit cognitive modelling of reading and writing processes by the tutor (Juel, in preparation).

Scaffolded reading and writing requires that the tutor provide just enough information for the child so that the child can do the task with the tutor's assistance. In spelling the word 'fat', for example, the tutor might help the child who pauses after writing 'f' to elongate the /a/ and connect it to the letter 'a', or remind the child of an 'at' word she knows, 'cat'. In many respects, I think the type of scaffolding the tutors did was similar to that fostered in Reading Recovery (Clay and Cazden, 1992).

Closely related to scaffolding, the most effective tutors frequently informed their children about how reading and writing work. The tutors 'walked' the children through the processes of word recognition and spelling, so that the tasks were clearer, more accessible, and less mysterious. One of the most effective techniques for modelling reading processes was role-reversals. The tutors pretended to be the child; the child pretended to be the teacher. Through this role-reversal, the tutor could model thought-processes of, for example, how to approach a difficult word.

Quantitative analysis showed that the most successful tutors spent significantly more time in two activities than did the less successful tutors. First, they spent more time in direct letter-sound instruction. They might, for example, use letter-cards to make words (e.g., changing 'cat' to 'hat' to 'fat' to 'fan'). Secondly, they made more use of the 'build-up' readers we had made (Guszak, 1985). Build-up readers slowly introduce high frequency vocabulary, as well as new words which contain common phonogram patterns. The first page in the first build-up reader had only one word, 'run', which was repeated many times in different formats (e.g., 'Run, ——, run. Run, run, run, ——.'). There were blanks where the child could tell the tutor, or could write on their own, what would 'run'. Each subsequent page in the build-up added another word.

Some children may simply need more direct instruction and even some controlled vocabulary text to grasp the alphabetic principle. This may be even more necessary in regular classroom situations where dialogue cannot be as personalized as it is in one-to-one tutoring. The use of children's literature in place of controlled vocabulary texts (of either the high-frequency word or the phonics type) has not been widespread for long enough to accumulate much evidence. What research we do have, however, suggests that while such instruction in regular classrooms is effective in getting across basic print concepts, it is not as effective in helping children recognize words as is more traditional instruction (see, *Educational Psychologist*, vol. 29, 1994). Hiebert's research in whole-language classrooms provides strong evidence that systematic guidance in word patterns, in addition to the reading of predictable books, may be especially helpful to children who depend upon schools to become literate (Hiebert, 1994).

I think that it was wrong to abandon controlled vocabulary texts on the assumption that reading is a psycholinguistic guessing game. The current emphasis on strategy instruction, scaffolded reading experiences including the use of predictable text, and the use of writing to foster letter-sounds, however, may provide good outcomes for those teachers and children who dreaded reading instruction in dull texts and even duller workbooks. It may help semi-skilled readers as well. Direct instruction and controlled vocabulary texts with beginning readers (perhaps some of the time) might still be helpful. We need more research.

References

Adams, M. J. (1990) *Beginning to Read: Thinking and Learning about Print*. Cambridge, MA: MIT Press.

Beck, I. L. (1981) Reading problems and instructional practices. In G. E. MacKinnon and T. G. Waller (eds), *Reading Research: Advances in Theory and Practice*, New York: Academic Press, vol. 2, pp. 53–95.

Biemiller, A. (1970) The development of the use of graphic and contextual information as children learn to read. *Reading Research Quarterly*, *13*, 223–53.

Bissex, G. L. (1980) *Gnys at Wrk*. Cambridge: MA: Harvard University Press.

Clark, H. H., and Clark, E. V. (1977) *Psychology and Language*. New York: Harcourt Brace Jovanovich.

Clay, M. M., and Cazden, C. B. (1992) A Vygotskian interpretation of reading recovery. In C. B. Cazden, *Whole Language Plus*, New York: Teachers College Press, pp. 114–35.

Educational Psychologist (1994) Special issue: The scientific evaluation of the whole-language approach to literacy development. *Educational Psychologist*, *29*, 173–222.

Foorman, B. R. (in press) The relevance of a connectionist model of reading for 'The Great Debate'. *Educational Psychology Review*.

Goodman, K. S. (1970/1976) Reading: A psycholinguistic guessing game. In H. Singer and R. Ruddell (eds), *Theoretical Models and Processes of Reading*, Newark, DE: International Reading Association, pp. 497–508.

Goodman, K. S., and Goodman, Y. M. (1979) Learning to read is natural. In L. B. Resnick and P. A. Weaver (eds), *Theory and Practice of Early Reading*, Hillsdale, NJ: Erlbaum, vol. 1, pp. 137–54.

Gough, P. B. (1983) Context, form, and interaction. In R. Rayner (ed.), *Eye Movements in Reading*, New York: Academic Press, pp. 203–11.

Gough, P. B., and Hillinger, M. L. (1980) Learning to read: An unnatural act. *Bulletin of the Orton Society*, *30*, 179–96.

Guszak, F. J. (1985) *Diagnostic Reading Instruction in the Elementary School* (3rd edn). New York: Harper and Row.

Hiebert, E. H. (1994) Becoming literate through authentic tasks: Evidence and adaptations. In R. B. Ruddell, M. R. Ruddell, and H. Singer (eds), *Theoretical Models and Processes of Reading* (4th edn), Newark, DE: International Reading Association, pp. 391–413.

Hoffman, J. V., McCarthey, S. J., Abbott, J., Christian, C., Corman, L., Curry, C., Dressman, M., Elliott, B., Matherne, D., and Stahle, D. (1994) So what's new in the new basals? A focus on first grade. *Journal of Reading Behavior*, 26, 47–74.

Iversen, S., and Tunmer, W. E. (1993) Phonological processing skills and the Reading Recovery program. *Journal of Educational Psychology*, 85, 112–26.

Juel, C. (1991a) Beginning reading. In R. Barr, M. L. Kamil, P. D. Pearson, and P. Mosenthal (eds), *Handbook of Reading Research*, New York, NY: Longman, vol. 2, pp. 759–88.

Juel, C. (1991b) Cross-age tutoring between student athletes and at-risk children. *The Reading Teacher*, 45, 178–86.

Juel, C. (1994a) *Learning to Read and Write in One Elementary School*. New York: Springer-Verlag.

Juel, C. (1994b) The role of phonics in the integrated language arts. In L. M. Morrow, J. K. Smith, and L. C. Wilkinson (eds), *The Integrated Language Arts: Controversy to Consensus*, Needham, MA: Allyn and Bacon, pp. 133–54.

Juel, C. (in preparation). *What Is It about One-on-one Tutoring that Most Helps a Poor Reader?*

Juel, C., and Roper/Schneider, D. (1985) The influence of basal readers on first-grade reading. *Reading Research Quarterly*, 20, 134–52.

Liberman, I. Y., and Liberman, A. M. (1992) Whole language versus code emphasis: Underlying assumptions and their implications for reading instruction. In P. B. Gough, L. C. Ehri, and R. Treiman (eds), *Reading Acquisition*, Hillsdale, NJ: Erlbaum, pp. 343–66.

Perfetti, C. A. (1985) *Reading Ability.* New York: Oxford University Press.

Resnick, L. B. (1979) Theories and prescriptions for early reading instruction. In L. B. Resnick and P. A. Weaver (eds), *Theory and Practice of Early Reading*, Hillsdale, NJ: Erlbaum, vol. 2, pp. 321–38.

Seidenberg, M. S., and McClelland, J. L. (1989) A distributed, developmental model of word recognition and naming. *Psychological Review*, 96, 523–68.

Silver, Burdett and Ginn (1989) *All Through the Town.* Needham, MA: Silver Burdett and Ginn.

Silver, Burdett and Ginn (1993) *Here Comes the Band!* Needham, MA: Silver Burdett and Ginn.

Smith, F. (1971) *Understanding Reading.* New York: Holt, Rinehart and Winston.

Smith, F. (ed.) (1973) *Psycholinguistics and Reading*. New York: Holt, Rinehart and Winston.

Söderbergh, R. (1977) *Reading in Early Childhood: A Linguistic Study of a Preschool Child's Gradual Acquisition of Reading Ability*. Washington, DC: Georgetown University Press.

Stanovich, K. E. (1980) Toward an interactive–compensatory model of individual differences in the development of reading fluency. *Reading Research Quarterly, 16*, 32–71.

Stanovich, K. E. (1986) Matthew effects in reading: Some consequences of individual differences in the acquisition of literacy. *Reading Research Quarterly, 21*, 360–406.

Stanovich, K. E. (1991a) Changing models of reading and reading acquisition. In L. Rieben and C. A. Perfetti (eds), *Learning to Read*, Hillsdale, NJ: Erlbaum, pp. 19–31.

Stanovich, K. E. (1991b) Word recognition: Changing perspectives. In R. Barr, M. L. Kamil, P. B. Mosenthal, and P. D. Pearson (eds), *Handbook of Reading Research*, New York: Longman, vol. 2, pp. 418–52.

Chapter Eleven

Afterword: The Science and Politics of Beginning Reading Practices

MARILYN JAGER ADAMS

The so-called Great Debate (Chall, 1967) about the value of phonics instruction has been a battle of cross-talk between two positions – each strongly felt and strongly justified in argument, both less than compelling in implementation. Yet, as you have now read across the chapters in this book, recent scientific research has made enormous progress in understanding the knowledge and processes involved in learning to read. More heartening still, this information has served not only to strengthen and refine each case, but to strengthen and refine each as the complement rather than alternative to the other.

Surely no one involved in literacy education is unaware of the Great Debate over the teaching of phonics. Nevertheless, it is nearly impossible for the spectator to fathom its passion or to appreciate its real obstructiveness to our educational system at large, or its progress. In this closing chapter, I will therefore step back from the issues that have gained the immediate spotlight to try to elucidate the debate in terms of the beliefs and tensions that have underlain it.

Science and Politics

My own direct involvement in this controversy began rather abruptly in the late 1980s. At the time, it had come to the attention of the US Congress that the diagnosed incidence of specific reading disability in US schools was mushrooming. Whereas in the mid-1970s, only 2–3 per cent of US school children were so diagnosed, the rate approaches 20 per cent today. In response to this alarm, the Congress passed two measures. Through the Health Research Extension Act, they authorized the National Institute of Child Health and Human Development (NICHD), a branch of the National Institute of Health, 'to gain a better understanding of the nature, causes, and cures of reading difficulties in children and adults through long-term, prospective, longitudinal, and multidisciplinary study'. Through the Human Services Reauthorization Act, they required the US Secretary of Education to review the scientific literature informing the role of phonics in beginning reading instruction. The latter task was passed to the Center for the Study of Reading at the University of Illinois, and, through the Center, to me.

The product of my assignment was the book *Beginning to Read: Thinking and Learning about Print* (Adams, 1990) and its *Summary* (Stahl, Osborn and Lehr, 1990). I am aware that *Beginning to Read* was a difficult book for many to read. It was also a difficult book for me to write, and that was true not just socially but also cognitively.

The principal reason why this book was cognitively difficult to write was that, at the time, the relevant information was scattered across at least a dozen different disciplines and subdisciplines. As is the way in our fields, each of these subdisciplines is supported by its own separate sets of journals and books, and each had accrued its own perspective on the issues along with its own relatively distinct terminology and knowledge base. Furthermore, both within and across these disciplines, the bulk of information was available only bitwise, distributed piece by underwhelming piece across myriad chapters and journal articles. In and of themselves, so many of these papers seemed so dismissably specific – so many, the kinds of papers that, given to even your best graduate students, the response is a disgruntled 'So?'

Yet the overlap was there. Collectively, these papers told a story that was rich in empirical breadth and depth and undeniably compelling in message and force. Key issues had been recognized again and again, both within and across the different fields. Within fields, as researchers scrutinized, challenged, and reassessed each others' hypotheses and findings, they peeled away mistaken notions even while gradually defining, affirming, and refining their successors. Across fields, meanwhile, approaching the issues from different perspectives and through different methods of inquiry, the various literatures tended, not merely to replicate, but also to complement, extend, and validate each other.

Cognitively speaking, then, part of the difficulty of writing this book was that it was like working on a 50,000 piece jigsaw puzzle – in poor light and without the box cover. Even so, that was not the greatest difficulty. Nor was it that these different fields and perspectives were wholly new to me. To the contrary, my problem was that they were familiar. My problem was that as I had studied these different bodies of research and theory over the years, I had organized and understood them in different compartments in my own head. My challenge was to figure out how to make them fit together as part of the same puzzle, and that was the hardest part: the exertion involved in restructuring my own knowledge, in moving in and backing off, in turning the pieces this way and that to figure out how they might interlock across my own mental boundaries.

Due to the profession's deeply divided attitudes as to whether a code- or meaning-oriented curriculum was most appropriate for beginners, writing this book was also socially difficult. At the outset, I was told that if I wrote this book, I would lose old friends and gain new enemies. It was true. As I wrote, I was contacted repeatedly by both 'sides'. I was reminded that I knew what I had to say and cautioned to filter the literature accordingly. Even before I began, I was told I would be shot. Afterwards, at the IRA [International Reading Association] Reading Hall of Fame, it was announced that I should be shot – with a silver bullet, no less. For having written this book, I have variously been accused of being a nazi, a behaviourist, a right-wing religious fanatic, a child abuser, and a phonicator. On release, the book was dismissed as far too political to be co-distributed by the International Reading Association or to be reviewed by certain journals. It has been described as government-subsidized propaganda, and even as the work of the devil.

This book, in short, was politically incorrect and evidently profoundly so, in topic, in content, and in message. What is in this shockingly political book? Again, it is science. The book is a review of the results of scientific research on reading. In the remainder of this chapter, what I wish to examine is that science. I wish to examine it both cognitively and socially, in terms of the challenges, responsibilities, and perils of our profession.

Political Incorrectness and Epistemology

In fact, *Beginning to Read* was not the first politically incorrect project on which I've worked. There was also a project that we undertook for the Republic of Venezuela, just a few years earlier.

Our project for Venezuela began in 1979, with a visit from a gentleman named Luis Alberto Machado. On winning the election, the then-President of Venezuela had invited Dr Machado to choose among existing Ministries. Dr Machado refused them all; none of them was what he wanted. What he wanted was to be Minister for the Development of Human Intelligence. What he wanted was a chance to do what he believed education should, but – for reasons of institutional entrenchment – could not do. He wanted to teach students to think.

Beyond incorrect, Dr Machado's mission was politically heretical.

'Ridiculous!' shrieked the rich, 'You can't make those people smart. They are stupid. If they were smart, they'd be rich like us!'

'Foul!' cried the guardians of the poor, 'This is diversionary. The real issue is economics. He is trying to co-opt the masses!'

Nevertheless, Dr Machado persevered. Yes, he agreed, it is the nature of the human beast to get as much as he can for his own and, yes, the best control on this tendency is to make the weak more powerful. However, he insisted, the ultimate human power is not money, it is intelligence. And, as a commodity, the beauty of intelligence is that it does not conserve: For one person to have more, it is not necessary that anyone else have less. As he saw it, moreover, the most intelligent society possible would be the most varied, productive, and compatible society imaginable.

With this in mind, Dr Machado eventually approached Harvard University, asking for help. Harvard, in turn, came to Bolt Beranek and Newman Inc. for help (BBN is the Cambridge, MA, research and development company for which I worked at the time). A combination of people from Harvard and BBN eventually agreed to consider the feasibility of the project.

We began with a literature review. What it told us was not encouraging. We reported honestly to Dr Machado that across a number of similarly intended efforts – none had produced what struck us as robust, generalizable, or transferable improvements in cognitive abilities.

Dr Machado was unflappable. 'Did their IQ scores go down?' he asked. Well no, of course not. 'Ah, then their IQ scores stayed exactly the same!' he inferred. Well, not really, we explained. 'Then their IQ scores must have gone up!' he exclaimed. Well, maybe a little on average, we conceded, but. . . . 'What is a little?' he demanded. 'Ten points? Five points? One point? One point times 20,000,000 people is 20,000,000 IQ points for my country! This is good.'

Dr Machado won. We agreed to try.

As we moved into this project, I watched my smartest colleagues flip-flop erratically from euphoria ('What a wonderful project!') to panic and despair ('I don't have any idea what to do!'). Our anxiety about how to do a good job was constantly inflamed by the more and less devastating misunderstandings that unavoidably arise when working cross-culturally and by the tensions within our own group created by the ever-tight delivery schedule. Very often, the only thing that kept us going was the heartfelt conviction that Dr Machado's dream was potentially as uplifting as it was vulnerable to social and political dismissal and derision. If we failed to produce, we would feel liable for risking its viability. We *had* to succeed to the best of our abilities.

We frequently travelled to Venezuela to work with Venezuelans, in class and out. We found Venezuela to be a happy country with full, whole-hearted revere for learning. It committed itself to learning for learning's sake with remarkable zeal. Even so, the kind of learning we most often saw was strictly rote learning, even where the value of rote learning made little sense to us. Imagine, for example, a classroom full of children trying to learn pages full of 3- and 4-digit multiplication problems by rote recitation of the digits.

What was missing? As nearly as we could put a finger on it, it was the basic operating principle that it is generally possible to *understand* things. What was missing was the conviction that one can understand things. More, what was missing seemed to be the very inclination even to *try* to understand things. What might we do to help that?

What we finally settled on was, with hindsight, remarkably unoriginal. Better said, it was classically unoriginal. It was, as I now see, just plain Aristotelian. We taught our Venezuelan students how conceptually to pick apart the objects and events in their lives. We taught them how to analyse everything, from pencils and brainteasers to history and complex decisions, into their distinctive features and the dimensions to which those features belonged. We showed them explicitly how the basic processes of reasoning structured themselves on the dimensions and features of their terms. And we taught them how to use this way of viewing their world over and over, methodically, reflectively, and evaluatively, to initiate and inspect their own inferences and reasoning in every kind of problem and problem domain we could concoct and squeeze into the curriculum (Adams, 1989).

Our objective was to induce transfer, and, to our gratification if surprise, we evidently succeeded in some significantly measurable ways. In a controlled evaluation involving 500 seventh-grade students in the barrio schools of Barquisimeto, Venezuela, the curriculum was shown to yield strong positive results (Herrnstein, Nickerson, deSanchez and Swets, 1986). Even so, what I wish to focus on is not the results, but the nature of the growth that I believe underlay them.

Our starting assumption in designing the Venezuelan curriculum was that one does not and, indeed, cannot teach people to think. Instead, our belief was that, no matter how old or young and no matter how schooled or unschooled they may be, *all* people think. To think is an irrepressible, natural part of being human.

What then was our goal? Our goal was to help make the processes and materials of thought available to our students to use at their own will and for their own purposes. It was not to teach them something new. It was to help them learn how to examine the inner parts and the structural relations that were necessarily deeply and inherently embedded in things that they already knew full well. Our goal was to help give our students conscious, reflective access to their own knowledge and processes of thought.

What we were doing, in other words, was banking our effort on a categorical distinction between learning and understanding. Within this view, *learning* consists in the establishment of internal representations of the materials or phenomena to be learned about. Learning, in other words, is the more or less direct record of one's experience.

Understanding, in contrast, is derivative. Understanding corresponds to the discovery of erstwhile tacit relations both within and between subsets of such knowledge; its first and often most elusive requirement is the very noticing of such relations. In designing the Venezuelan curriculum as we did, it was the inclination toward reflection and understanding that we were trying to support.

Learning versus Understanding

When did you first notice the 'busy' in 'business' or the 'probe' in 'probability'? When did you first notice that 'Twinkle, Twinkle Little Star' and the 'ABC Song' have almost the same tune? When did you first notice that the little symbol for 'short' division looks just like a little fraction, just as it should?

The mental representations of such separately familiar phenomena may overlap substantially. How could they not, after all? Yet, the point is that unless the corresponding relations have been functional in your experience, such overlap – however rich – is very likely to elude your notice.

Occasionally, you do notice such overlap by yourself. Other times, somebody points it out to you. Either way, such relations are generally affirmed and appreciated with relative ease – if only they are brought to your attention. This seems right, for it *should* be easy to notice something that you already know full well.

Many such noticings fall into the category of 'not particularly consequential'. Yet, consequential or inconsequential, they tend also to be 'interesting' – which strikes me as interesting all by itself. Think about it. Arousal of such latent overlap is the core stuff of mental play. Jokes make us laugh. Mysteries are a recreational genre. It is precisely the tension in a movie that sucks us in. Our own newest theories and insights tend to be so exciting to us that we can hardly keep them to ourselves; then, a moment later, the good ones seem so obvious and mundane that it's hard to write the paper.

The capacity to gain conscious, reflective access to commonalties, distinctions, and relations that are embedded in the meshwork of experience must be critical to the ability to restructure memory. Similarly, this capacity must be essential for active generalization, transfer, wonder, and the ability to build productive and comprehensive knowledge from the contextually bound and sloppy records of learning and experience. It seems clear that if such cross-conceptual merging of information occurred easily or without notice, the organizational structure of our minds would dissolve. On the other hand, toward promoting the newer learning and thought that such discovery affords, how very adaptive that there seems to be something about the very notice of such embedded relations that pleases the psyche and captures its attention.

Understanding versus Phonics in Learning to Read

There are two salient dimensions of text. It has form and it has meaning. As educators, the reifying reason that we teach students to read, is for meaning. It is for the knowledge, perspective, and understanding that texts invite. And therewith arises the rhetorical contrast that lies at the core of the Great Debate: How should we, as educators, conceive the young learner? Should we see children as active, thinking beings – ready and able to discover structure, to learn and grow through their own human interest and curiosity about the world around them? Or should we see them as passive and indifferent, as empty vessels to be filled with the procedures and facts that we mete out? The precedence of meaning is closely tied to the very meaningfulness and romance of the educator's profession.

In this spirit, the teaching of rank skills, such as phonics, seems unenlightened. Such instruction forces children's attention to the micro-form of text – to individual letters and their connections to meaningless speech sounds, to precise spellings and their mappings to semantically moot pronunciation. And in all this detail, it forces children's attention away from meaning – the single reason for reading in the first place. Thus it is that, over the years, teaching students to concern themselves with phonics came to be seen as a misguided diversion from helping them to appreciate and respond to meaning.

Indeed, why might one even consider teaching phonics? The reason, very simply, is that our written language is fundamentally alphabetic. Among the ironies here is that, while teaching phonics is oft held as the regressively unenlightened obsession of the boorish right, the invention of the alphabet has, in contrast, been hailed as the most intellectually liberating invention in the social history of the world. Historian David Diringer (1968, p. 161) described it as 'the creation of a "revolutionary writing", a script which we can perhaps term "democratic" (or, rather, a "people's script"), as against the "theocratic" scripts that preceded it'.

After all, though a language may express limitless numbers of ideas and embrace thousands upon thousands of words, no language admits more than a few dozen phonemes. The number of symbols in an alphabetic system are thus few enough to be memorized by almost anyone and, once memorized, adequate for reading and writing any speakable expression in the language, with one proviso: One must also understand the logic of the system; the symbols represent phonemes.

It is, of course, this very alphabetic logic that phonics instruction is intended to instil. How then can it be that one is so very right while the other is so horridly wrong?

In fact, for thousands of years, the alphabetic foundations of literacy were taken for granted. Reading instruction was simple and straightforward. People were taught the letters and forthwith given the texts that they were expected to read (Mathews, 1966). The trick, of course, was that what they were meant to read was precious little, generally consisting of only the Lord's Prayer, the Creed, and perhaps the Ten Commandments or a few Psalms – all of which were hand-printed or carved into a little slab of wood or metal for handy reference.

Beginning in the fifteenth century, and increasingly as technology made paper and print more available, all of this began to change. Suddenly, the reader was faced with so many words! Not surprisingly, with hindsight, even having learned the letters and their sounds, many people found that the task of reading all those words was just too hard.

The solution was phonics with a vengeance. Lists of simple syllables – such as *ba, be, bi, bo, bu* and *ab, eb, ib, ob, ub* – were devised to illustrate and exercise the alphabetic principle. As hornbooks gave way to folios, these lists were extended first to tables and then to pages and pages of syllables and words, organized by their lengths and phonetic similarities. As an example, Noah Webster's blue-back speller – which is said to have sold more copies in its time than even the Bible – contained 74 pages of these lists, with typically hundreds of words or syllables on each page. The student was to learn to spell and pronounce all of these before moving into the reading of meaningful text for its own sake (Smith, 1974).

If such practice sounds painfully boring to your contemporary ears, you may be soothed to know that it was berated as painfully boring back then, too. In Europe, Samuel Heinecke (1727–90) (cited in Mathews, 1966, p. 35) derided it as a 'senseless playing with sounds', a 'babble-factory', a 'pim-pel-pam-pel'. In America, the method was condemned as 'irksome and vexatious to both teacher and scholar' (Bumstead, 1840; cited in Smith, 1974, p. 87). Horace Mann, the first Secretary of Education in Massachusetts, protested that 'Not a single faculty of the mind is exercised excepting that of imitating sounds. . . . A parrot or an idiot could do the same thing' (1844, p. 17; cited in Smith, 1974, p. 78).

Nevertheless, people did learn to read. And that was true not merely of those whose parents before them had not read, but of an entire people whose culture before them had not read.

In colonial America, public reading instruction was initially legislated so that people could read (and better yet, memorize) the Bible. Further, because Bibles were still scarce and literacy even scarcer, the premium was on learning to read aloud for the benefit of others. After the Revolutionary War, the religious texts were generally displaced by nationalistic and moralistic material. Still, recognizing that a person's sway in participatory government was not independent of his elocution, the emphasis on pronunciation and oral delivery was maintained. During those early years, in other words, careful attention to phonics and oral reading was compatible with the prevailing goals of literacy instruction.

Across the nineteenth century, as the number of available books, periodicals, and pamphlets increased rapidly, the touted values of reading became those of increasing one's knowledge and intellectual powers (Kaestle, 1991). Alongside, the abundance of books that were published in that blossoming era of universal literacy were what we might call content-area books – books of history, science, and facts. By and large, children's readers were devoid of fiction.

Then increasingly, toward the end of the nineteenth century, literature too became available. And as it did, something interesting happened. As though at once, informational texts were dropped from the schoolbooks. As though in one voice, prominent scholars agreed that the highest purpose in teaching children to read was to develop in them an appreciation of literature for the sake of literature (Smith, 1974).

Was this enthralment with the newly available literature just one more example of the same phenomenon we've been mulling? Note that, except incidentally, stories do not contain new information. Instead, what they do is lead their readers to rearrange, reconstrue, and reflect on the already familiar pieces of life and thought. Arguably, literature – at its best – is nothing more or less than an invitation to what I have called understanding. The literati appeared wholly captivated by its newly found pleasures and stimulation.

Coincidentally or not, it was at just this point that educators began to ask whether didacticism might disrupt the very goal of the literacy endeavour. Herbart wrote: 'The intent to teach spoils children's books at once; it is forgotten that everyone, the child included, selects what suits him from what he reads' (1895, p. 73; cited in Smith, 1974, p. 118). Francis Parker, chief reading advisor on John Dewey's team, proposed that if properly motivated and freed to think, children would 'learn to read as they learn to talk – and we know they talk when they have something to say' (1900, p. 13; cited in Mathews, 1966, p. 130). These attitudes were extended to the materials offered to young readers, as well. Thus, Charles W. Eliot, then President of Harvard University, wrote,

> It would be for the advancement of the whole public school system if every reader were hereafter to be absolutely excluded from the school. I object to them because they are not real literature; they are but mere scraps of literature, even when the single lessons or materials of which they are composed are taken from literature. But there are a great many readers that seem to have been composed especially for the use of children. They are not made up of selections from recognized literature, and as a rule this class is simply ineffable trash. . . . I believe that we should substitute in all our schools real literature for readers.   (Eliot, 1891, p. 497)

By the turn of the century, reading pedagogues were urging that children should not be asked to dwell on the words, not even at the outset. Oral reading was discouraged because it was seen to divert attention from thought to pronunciations and expression. Instead, children were to be taught to read silently and, in so doing, to transcend the words. From the start, they were to be focused on and guided by meaning and understanding – for this, after all, was the goal and dynamic of true literacy. I am repeatedly struck by the similarities, in argument and even in wording, between what was written at that time and those writings that more recently catalysed the Whole Language movement.

But here's the problem: The issue of understanding. If what can be understood depends on what one already knows, then learning cannot start with understanding. Nor can learning be finessed by understanding. If one's prior knowledge constitutes the mental medium for understanding, then understanding cannot be achieved without it.

Understanding and Research on Beginning Reading

After 100 years of refining this meaning-first point of view, no wonder that the message of *Beginning to Read* was disruptive. As reviewed again in the present volume, scientific research objectively, meticulously, repeatedly, and incontrovertibly documents, first, that to read with fluency and reflective comprehension, students *must* acquire deep and ready working knowledge of the spellings of words and their mappings to speech, and second, that poorly developed knowledge of spellings and spelling–sound correspondences is the most pervasive cause of reading delay or disability (Rack, Snowling and Olson, 1992; Stanovich, 1986). Moreover, toward helping students acquire such knowledge, instruction is invaluable. Indeed, a recent study among those sponsored by NICHD suggests that with the exception of no more than 1–3 per cent of children, reading disability can be prevented through well-designed early instruction (Vellutino et al., 1996). Research shows further that such instruction is most effective when it includes explicit, systematic instruction on the alphabetic principle as well as activities and materials designed to engage children in practising and using their growing knowledge of spellings and spelling–speech correspondences both in isolation and in the context of meaningful reading and writing (Bond and Dykstra, 1967; Brown and Felton, 1990; Chall, 1967; Foorman et al., 1998).

In the present context, the research on reading has also given us a poetic recap. As it turns out, the reason conventional phonics is often so tedious and unproductive is that, without proper guidance, many children very simply fail to notice the overlap between the patterns of the letters that comprise written words and the phonological patterns of their own overlearned speech. Therein lies the critical importance of the research on developing children's phonemic awareness. Its lesson can be boiled down to exactly one point: To learn to read an alphabetic script, one must *understand* its logic, one must gain reflective awareness of the already overlearned phonological relations that the system represents.

The Importance of Science

There is one more set of issues that I wish to address before closing. The revulsion toward *Beginning to Read* was due not only to its message but equally to the medium through which that message was built. What was that objectionable medium? It was scientific research. Thus, even among educators and educational researchers, science is under fire even as the scientific method is being questioned and marginalized.

What is the scientific method? I quote from Karl Popper's (Popper, 1976) autobiography:

> We start our investigation with problems . . . and we choose a problem which we hope we may solve. The solution, always tentative, consists in a theory, an hypothesis, a conjecture. The various competing theories are compared and critically discussed in order to find their shortcomings. . . .

The scientific method, he explains, let us 'speak of better and of worse theories in an objective sense. The better theories are those with the greater content and the greater explanatory power.' The reason they are better is because they are more vulnerable to disproof. The greater their content and reach, the greater their chance of clashing with descriptions of observable facts. The method of science, he explains, is 'to expose our theories to the severest criticism possible, in order to detect where we have erred'.

Of special note, Popper also bothers to point out that his theory of science is basically one and the same as his theory of human knowledge or understanding. The only difference being that science is understanding that is pursued specifically for purposes of problem-solving. Both are distinct from learning *per se*. As he put it, both are *conjectural*; both are *products* of our intellectual activities. They are produced, in other words, only by lending one's mind to reflective, critical exploration of one's knowledge.

There is nothing wicked about science. It is only a method. Yet it is an invaluable method. It is a method for evaluating truth without deferring to precedence, authority, power, or prior belief. We need science. Without some impartial means of arbitrating truth, we are at the mercy of our emotions and fancies. Without some impartial standard for validating truth, we relinquish our choices to power-politics and bias. Without some communally accepted body of truth, we have no community and we can have no confidence. Science provides just such an impartial and consensual means. Moreover, where science is applied to problems in real need of address and provided its outcomes are shared with those who can use them to make a difference, there is no surer path toward progress. We need science: Not just scientists, but everybody.

References

Adams, M. J. (1989) Thinking skills curricula: Their promise and progress. *Educational Psychologist*, 24, 25–77.

Adams, M. J. (1990) *Beginning to Read: Thinking and Learning about Print*. Cambridge, MA: MIT Press.

Bond, G. L., and Dykstra, R. (1967) The cooperative research program in first-grade reading instruction. *Reading Research Quarterly*, 2, 5–142.

Brown, I. W., and Felton, R. H. (1990) Effects of instruction on beginning reading skills in children at risk for reading disability. *Reading and Writing: An Interdisciplinary Journal*, 2, 223–41.

Bumstead, J. F. (1840) *My Little Primer*. Boston: Perkins and Marwin.

Chall, J. S. (1967) *Learning to Read: The Great Debate*. New York: McGraw-Hill.

Diringer, D. (1968) *The Alphabet*. London: Hutchinson.

Eliot, C. W. (1891) Literature in the school. *Educational Review*, 2.

Foorman, B., Francis, D. J., Fletcher, J. M., Schatschneider, C., and Mehta, P. (1998) The role of instruction in learning to read: Preventing reading failure in at-risk children. *Journal of Educational Psychology*, 90, 37–55.

Herbart, J. F. (1895) *Science of Education and Aesthetic Revelation of the World*. Boston: D. C. Heath.

Herrnstein, R. J., Nickerson, R. S., deSanchez, M., and Swets, J. A. (1986) Teaching thinking skills. *American Psychologist*, 41, 1279–89.

Kaestle, C. F. (1991) *Literacy in the United States*. New Haven, CT: Yale University Press.

Mann, H. (1844) Method of teaching young children on their first entering school. *The Common School Journal*, 6. Boston: W. B. Fowle and N. Capen.

Mathews, M. M. (1966) *Teaching to Read: Historically Considered*. Chicago: University of Chicago.

Parker, F. W. (1900) *Course of Study*, 1. Chicago: University of Chicago.

Popper, K. (1976) *Unended Quest: An Intellectual Autobiography*. LaSalle, IL: Open Court.

Rack, J. P., Snowling, M. J., and Olson, R. K. (1992) The nonword reading deficit in developmental dyslexia: A review. *Reading Research Quarterly*, 26, 28–53.

Smith, N. B. (1974) *American Reading Instruction*. Newark, DE: International Reading Association.

Stahl, S. A., Osborn, J., and Lehr, F. (1990) *Beginning to Read: Thinking and Learning about Print: A Summary*. Champaign, IL: Center for the Study of Reading, University of Illinois.

Stanovich, K. E. (1986) Matthew effects in reading: Some consequences of individual differences in the acquisition of literacy. *Reading Research Quarterly*, 21, 360–406.

Vellutino, F. R., Scanlon, D. M., Sipay, E., Small, S., Pratt, A., Chen, R., and Denckla, M. (1996) Cognitive profiles of difficult-to-remediate and readily remediated poor readers: Early intervention as a vehicle for distinguishing between cognitive and experiential deficits as basic causes of specific reading disability. *Journal of Educational Psychology*, 88, 601–38.

Webster, N. (1798) *The American Spelling Book*. Boston: Isaiah Thomas and Ebenezer Andrews.

Subject Index

alphabetic principle, the, 23, 50, 54, 75, 204, 209, 221, 224
analogical reasoning, 175
analogy,
  in word reading, 80–1, 90, 95–6, 174–96
  orthographic, 175–6, 190, 192
  phoneme, 179–80
  rime, 179–80, 184, 191
  vowel, 191
articulatory gestures, 163
at-risk children, 140–1

BAS single word reading test, 117

Chinese, 48, 54, 83, 86
cipher, 74–5, 158
co-articulation, 163–4
comprehension, listening, *see* listening comprehension
comprehension monitoring, 44, 53
comprehension, reading, *see* reading comprehension
connectionist models of reading, 184
context,
  in comprehension, 17, 46
  in word recognition, 15–19, 43–6, 54, 65, 101, 202–3
Copenhagen dyslexia study, 139–40, 143, 148–9

decoding, 59–76, 80, 94–5
developmental delay, 131
developmental phases, in learning to read, 79–102
Dual Route Theory, of word recognition, 47
dyslexia, 131–51
  acquired, 119, 135
  adult, 133
  correlational studies of, 138–9
  definition of, 134
  developmental, 131
  'double deficit' hypothesis, 137
  'dyseidetic', 136
  intervention studies of, 144–6
  language problems and, 146–8
  'phonological', 136
  prediction of, 132, 139–46
  prevention of, 132
  proximal causes of, 138
  'surface', 135
  variability in, 134–8

emergent literacy, 53
environmental print, 85
Epilinguistic knowledge, 179, 183–4, 187, 190, 195
eye movements in reading, 44–5, 72, 202

fingerpoint reading, 86

grapheme, 80
grapheme–phoneme correspondence rules, inferring of, 113–16

inferences in reading, 44, 45, 53

learning *vs* understanding, 217–20
letter-by-letter recoding strategy, 135
letter name knowledge, 87, 88, 101–2, 141
letter sound knowledge, 121
listening comprehension, 111
literacy, autonomous model of, 1, 3, 5–6, 8

meaning, construction of, 43, 48, 53, 59–76
metalinguistic awareness, 174–5
metalinguistic control, 179, 183–4, 187, 190, 195
miscue analysis, 59–76, 81
morpheme, 137, 159, 166–7, 171
morphological awareness, 167–9
morphological decomposition, 137–8

Neale Analysis of Reading Ability, 111
New Literacy, 1–11
nonword reading, 133

onset-rime, 177–9
    awareness, 185–7
    segmentation, 188
oral language, and reading, 20, 109–10
orthographic representations, 136
orthography, 149–50
    deep, 145, 149
    regular, 149, 182
    transparent, 166
    see also writing system

particulate principle of self-diversifying systems, 159
phase models of reading development, *see* reading development, phases of
phoneme/phonemic awareness, 75, 144–8
    and learning to read, 51–2, 158, 225
    training in, 144–8, 207–8
    see also phonological/phonological awareness

phoneme segmentation, 23, 114–18, 122–7, 188
phonetic cue reading, 88, 90, 92
phonetic module, 163–4
phonics, 12–14, 19, 29–30, 73–5, 188, 201, 204–7, 213–14, 220–4
phonologic/phonological awareness, 50–4, 87, 141, 150, 162, 165, 167
    and learning to read, 51–2, 110–12, 118–28, 160, 174–96
    training in, 25–6, 28, 52
    see also phoneme/phonemic awareness
phonological analysis task, 50–1, 133–4
phonological development, 176–9
phonological priming, 180, 185, 190–3
phonological processing, 23–6, 132–4
phonological recoding, 80, 116, 118, 120–1, 133; *see also* decoding
phonological representations, quality of, 141, 146–8, 150
phonology, use in reading, 43, 46–8, 54–5
    pre-lexical, 47
    post-lexical, 47
picture naming, 136, 149
prediction, in word reading, 65–7, 72–3, 80–1
psycholinguistic models of reading, 204

rapid automatized naming, 137
reading acquisition,
    analytic *vs* holistic, 24–7
    phonics *vs* whole-language, 12–30
reading-age-match design, 138–9
reading comprehension, 17, 28–9, 44, 53–4, 70–2, 111, 133
reading development, phases of, 79–102, 204
    alphabetic, 83
    consolidated alphabetic, 83–4, 96–8, 100
    full alphabetic, 83, 92–6, 100
    logographic, 83–4
    orthographic, 83–4
    partial alphabetic, 83, 87–91, 94, 99
    pre-alphabetic, 83–7, 99
reading instruction, 52–3, 96, 127–8, 170–1, 204–10
    history of, 221–4

Reading Recovery, 207–8
reading speed, 60, 149
rhyme and analogy training programme,
    187, 189–90
rhyme awareness, 51, 174, 177
    training in, 187, 189–90
rime, 174–5, 181–4

scientific method, 213–26
self-teaching mechanism, 23, 121
sight vocabulary, 113
    learning of, 118–27
sight-word reading, 79–82, 94–5, 101
    and use of analogy, 184
Simple View of reading, 70–1, 73
speech,
    and reading, 21, 157–71, 202–3; see
        also oral language
    conventional theory of, 161–3
spelling, 95, 195
stage models of reading development, 83;
        see also reading development, phases
        of
superior reading, prediction of, 87, 148–9

syllabic awareness, 51

teaching method, 187, 193–4

Venezuela project, 216–19
visual cue reading, 85, 90
visual memory, 119–22, 126–7
visual word form memory, 136
vocabulary, 87

whole language, 12–15, 19, 20, 25–7,
        29–30, 53, 59–60, 63, 67, 72–3,
        75–6, 170–1, 209, 224
word-by-word strategy in reading, 134–5
writing system, 48–53, 54, 160, 166
    alphabetic, 49–50, 54–5, 74, 112, 178,
        182
    Chinese, 48, 54, 83, 86
    German, 91, 182
    logographic, 49, 83–4
    partial alphabetic, 49
    syllabic, 49
    see also orthography

Author Index

Abbott, J., 211
Abler, W., 159, 171
Aborn, M., 16, 30, 37
Accardo, P.J., 154
Ackerman, B., 17, 37
Adams, M.J., xiv, xv, 14, 20, 21, 24, 26, 30, 67, 72, 76, 79, 94, 102, 120, 128, 144, 151, 158, 171, 205, 210, 214, 218, 226
Adler, A., 18, 37
Alegria, J., 51, 56, 178, 199
Alford, J., 16, 30, 64, 76
Allington, R.L., 18, 30
Altwerger, B., 85, 105
Anderson, R.C., 14, 30
Anderson, R.I., 53, 55, 105
Armstrong, E., 139, 153
Armstrong, W., 61, 62
Arnbak, E., 137, 138, 152
Atkins, P., 118, 128
Austin, S., 17, 31

Baker, L., 17, 30, 53, 55
Bakker, D.J., 153
Balota, D., 36
Ball, E.W., 24, 25, 30, 31, 110, 128
Barker, T., 84, 108
Barnes, M.A., 37, 47, 57
Baron, J., 25, 40, 51, 58

Barr, R., 39, 78, 104, 106, 198, 211, 212
Barron, R.W., 79, 102
Bateman, B., 151
Bear, D., 88, 106, 107
Beard, R., xiv, xv, xvi, 12, 30, 42
Beck, I.L., 51, 57, 205, 210
Becker, C.A., 17, 31
Beech, J.R., 155
Beeler, T., 144, 151
Bell, L., 47, 51, 57
Ben-Dror, I., 17, 31
Bentin, S., 24, 31
Berent, I., 23, 31, 47, 48, 55, 57
Berlin, B., 7, 10
Berninger, V., 108
Bertelson, P., 51, 56, 178, 199
Besner, D., 31, 34
Bialer, I., 37
Biemiller, A., 18, 31, 203, 210
Bijeljac-Babic, R., 181, 200
Birdwhistell, R.L., 7, 10
Bjaalid, I.K., 182, 199
Bissex, G.L., 203, 210
Blachman, B.A., 25, 26, 30, 31, 110, 128, 132, 151, 153, 154, 155, 156, 172
Black, R.S., 25, 31
Blanchard, J., 103
Bloom, P.A., 73, 76
Blumstein, S.E., 161, 173

Boas, F., 7, 10
Boder, E., 135, 136, 151
Bond, G.L., 75, 76, 224, 226
Borstrøm, I.B., 141, 145, 147, 151, 152
Bowey, J.A., 24, 31, 95, 97, 98, 102, 110,
   128, 178, 184, 190, 191, 196, 198, 199
Boyarin, J., 4, 10
Bradley, L., 24, 25, 26, 28, 31, 32, 35, 51,
   53, 55, 110, 128, 144, 151, 180, 185,
   196, 199
Brady, S.A., 51, 55, 77, 146, 150, 151,
   153, 157, 158, 171, 200
Bressman, B., 50, 57
Briggs, P., 17, 31
Brown, A.L., 17, 30, 175, 196, 198
Brown, D.E., 7, 10
Brown, I.S., 26, 28, 32
Brown, I.W., 224, 226
Bruce, D., 23, 32
Bruck, M., 14, 17, 20, 24, 25, 26, 30, 32,
   97, 108, 133, 151, 184, 196, 200
Bryant, P.E., 6, 23–6, 28, 31–3, 35, 51,
   53, 55, 80, 105, 110, 128, 136, 139,
   144, 151, 152, 158, 172, 176, 177,
   180, 183–6, 189, 190, 193–9
Bumstead, J.F., 222, 226
Burke, C.L., 59, 76, 85, 106
Butterworth, B., 184, 200
Byrne, B., xiii, 14, 21, 25, 32, 84, 88, 89,
   103, 110, 128, 144, 145, 152, 157,
   158, 168, 169, 171, 172

Cain, M.T., 24, 31
Calfee, R.C., 23, 32, 98, 103
Calhoon, A., 95, 97, 106, 184, 199
Capute, A.J., 154
Cardoso-Martins, C., 89, 103
Carlson, G., 200
Carpenter, P.A., 45, 56
Carr, T.H., 26, 28, 33
Carroll, J.B., 182, 196
Carter, B., 23, 35, 51, 56
Cary, L., 51, 56, 144, 152, 178, 199
Castle, J.M., 14, 32
Castles, A., 135, 152
Catts, H.W., 31
Cazden, C.B., 208, 210
Chall, J.S., 12, 13, 26, 32, 79, 103, 213,
   224, 226

Chapman, J.W., 182, 198
Chapman, R., 23, 32
Chen, R., 227
Chew, J., 193, 196
Chiappe, P., 135, 155
Christian, C., 211
Chun, C., 86, 104
Clark, E.V., 202, 210
Clark, H.H., 203, 210
Clay, M.M., 208, 210
Cole, J.K., 10
Cole, M., 3, 11
Coleman, E.B., 16, 36
Coltheart, M., 33, 47, 55, 105, 110, 111,
   118, 121, 122, 128, 129, 130, 135,
   152, 153
Cooper, W.E., 33
Corman, L., 211
Cornoldi, C., 77
Cramer, B.B., 24, 25, 39, 51, 58, 122,
   130
Cress, C., 105
Crossland, J., 24, 32, 180, 196
Cunningham, A.E., 17, 18, 24, 25, 28, 32,
   39, 41, 51, 58, 67, 76, 103, 110, 122,
   128, 130, 196
Cunningham, P.M., 29, 33, 80, 105
Curry, C., 211
Curtis, B., 118, 128

Davies, P., 116, 128
Davies, P., 182, 196
Davis, C., 25, 40
De Abreu, M., 89, 103
de Barrera, F., 182, 198
DeFrancis, J., 49, 50, 55
DeFries, J.C., 141, 153
DeGroff, L., 18, 35
Delaney, S., 47, 57
Denckla, M., 227
Deneen-Bell, N., 60, 65, 68, 77
deSanchez, M., 218
Desberg, P., 106
Dewey, J., 223
Dewitz, P., 106
DiBenedetto, B., 18, 37
Diehl, R.L., 161, 171
Diringer, D., 221, 226
Dixon, M., xii, 109, 113, 116, 122, 130

Domgaard, R.M., 137, 154
Donnelly, K., 105
Dornic, S., 37, 77
Downer, M., 105, 182, 197
Downing, J., 104, 131, 152
Drake, C., 138, 156
Drake, D.A., 103
Dressman, M., 211
Drum, P.A., 22, 35, 85, 106
Duncan, L.G., 116, 128, 187, 189, 190, 196, 197
Durgunoglu, A.Y., 19, 33
Durrell, D.D., 182, 200
Dykstra, R., 224, 226

East, M., 184, 187, 189, 198
Edelsky, C., 5, 10
Ehri, L.C., xii, xv, xvi, 22, 23, 32, 33–5, 39, 53, 55, 79, 80, 81, 84–6, 88, 90, 92, 94, 95, 97, 98, 103–7, 118, 122, 128, 129, 158, 172, 184, 197, 204, 211
Ehrlich, S.F., 18, 33, 45, 55, 72, 76
Ekman, P., 7, 10
Elbro, C., xii, 133–8, 141, 143, 145, 147, 148, 150–2, 154
Elder, L., 22
Eliot, C.W., 223, 226
Elliott, B., 211
Elliott, C.D., 114, 117, 129
Ellis, A.W., 25, 28, 34, 180,185, 197
Evans, H.M., 135, 155, 187, 188, 200
Evans, M.A., 26, 28, 33

Fawcett, A.J., 138, 154
Fayol, M., 197
Feeman, D.J., 17, 18, 39, 41
Felman, L.B., 172
Felton, R.H., 14, 26, 28, 32, 33, 224, 226
Ferrand, L., 193, 198
Ferreiro, E., 110, 129, 167, 172
Fielding-Barnsley, R., 25, 32, 88, 89, 103, 110, 128, 145, 152
Fischer, F.W., 23, 35, 51, 56
Fischler, I., 73, 76
Fleming, J.T., 18, 30
Fletcher, J.M., 131, 137, 139, 153, 227
Flores d'Arcais, G., 36
Fodor, J., 18, 33

Foorman, B.R., 26, 33, 131, 139, 144, 151, 153, 202, 210, 224, 227
Forster, K.I., 18, 33
Foster, M.R., 17, 38
Fowler, A.E., 146, 153, 167, 172
Fox, B., 51
Fox, R., 7, 10
Francis, D.J., 26, 33, 131, 139, 153, 227
Francis, J., 110, 128
Freebody, P., 169, 171, 172
Freeman, D., 7, 10
Freidman, M., 106
Frensch, P., 39
Friere, P., 5, 10
Frith, U., 23, 33, 83, 103, 105, 135, 139, 153
Frost, J., 25, 35, 110, 129, 144, 172
Frost, R., 31, 35, 57, 154
Funnell, E., 119, 129

Gadow, K., 37
Gale, F.G., 2, 11
Gallagher, M., 139, 153
Gaskins, I., 80, 96, 105, 182, 197
Gaskins, R., 105, 182, 197
Gates, A., 169, 171
Gee, J.P., 4, 11
Gelb, I.J., 50, 56
Gentile, L., 103
Gentner, D., 175, 197
Gilger, J.W., 141, 153
Gjessing, H.-J., 136, 153
Glaser, R., 42, 56
Gleitman, L.R., 50, 56
Goldman, S.R., 16, 36, 45, 57
Gollasch, F.V., vii, viii, 67, 68, 69, 70, 76
Gombert, J., 174, 179, 182, 183, 187–90, 195, 197, 198
Goodman, K.S., vii, viii, 12, 15, 19, 20, 25, 27, 29, 33, 59–64, 67, 68, 71–3, 76, 81, 105, 170–2, 201, 202, 210
Goodman, Y.M., 85, 105, 210
Goody, J., 3, 11
Goswami, U., xiii, 6, 23, 24, 25, 33, 80, 91, 97, 105, 108, 118, 129, 139, 151, 158, 172, 174–80, 182–4, 187, 189–91, 193, 194, 197, 198, 200
Gottardo, A., 135, 155

Gough, P.B., ix, x, xii, xiv, xv, 1, 16, 19, 21–4, 29, 32, 34, 39, 53, 56, 59, 64, 65, 67, 68, 70, 71, 74, 76, 77, 84, 85, 103–5, 107, 108, 111, 128, 129, 158, 172, 202, 203, 210, 211
Goulandris, N., 119, 129
Grainger, J., 193, 198
Graves, M.F., 57
Greaney, K.T., 182, 198
Green, P.A., 133, 154
Greenbaum, S., xvi
Gregg, L., 32
Griffith, P.L., 21, 29, 34, 53, 56, 77, 84, 85, 105
Groff, P., 12, 34, 40
Grundin, H., 27, 34
Guszak, F.J., 208, 210
Guttentag, R., 79, 105

Haith, M.M., 79, 105, 133, 154
Haller, M., 118, 128
Halford, G.S., 175, 199
Hammond, K., 18, 35
Hansen, J., 95, 97, 98, 102, 178, 184, 190, 196, 198, 199
Harding, L.M., 18, 34
Harris, L.A., 105
Harris, M., 198
Harste, J., 85, 106
Hart, B., 74, 77
Hatcher, P., 25, 26, 28, 34
Hatano, G., 198
Haven, D., 134, 152
Head, M., 85, 106
Heath, S.B., 3, 11
Heinecke, S., 222
Henderson, E., 106
Henry, M., 98, 106
Herbart, J.F., 227
Herriman, M.L., 51, 53, 58, 110, 129
Herrnstein, R.J., 218, 227
Hiebert, E.H., 14, 30, 85, 106, 208, 211
Hill, D., 18, 36
Hill, S., 116, 128, 187, 196, 197
Hillinger, M.L., 19, 21–3, 34, 74, 77, 85, 105, 203, 210
Hoffman, J.V., 205, 206, 211
Hogoboam, T.W., 16, 36, 45, 57

Hoien, T., 182, 199
Holden, M., 86, 106
Holley-Wilcox, P., 64, 76
Hoover, W.A., 25, 40, 67, 70, 77, 111, 129
Houghton, G., 184, 200
Huggins, A., 94, 102
Hughes, C., 51, 57
Hulme, C., 23, 25, 28, 34, 37, 89, 107, 118, 129, 151, 182, 185, 186, 187, 199
Hummer, P., 91, 108
Humphreys, G.W., 18, 34
Hurford, J., 173

Impey, L., 136, 152
Iversen, S., 14, 27, 28, 34, 208, 211
Izard, C.E., 7, 11

Jacobson, C., 131, 153
Jandorf, B.D., 134, 152
Jiménez González, J.E., 166, 172
Job, R., 129
Johnson, D., 98, 108, 145, 154
Johnson, M.C., 145
Jorm, A., 21, 23, 24, 34, 87, 107
Joshi, R.M., 36, 152
Juel, C., xii, xiii, xiv, 18, 21, 22, 28, 34, 53, 56, 77, 84, 85, 97, 98, 105, 106, 138, 153, 201–5, 208, 211
Just, M.A., 45, 56

Kaestle, C.F., 222, 227
Kamhi, A.G., 31
Kamil, M.L., 29, 37, 39, 78, 103, 104, 106, 198, 211, 212
Karegianes, M., 28, 37
Katz, L., 31, 35, 57, 153, 172
Katz, R.B., 146, 153
Kavanagh, J., 34
Kay, P., 7, 10
Kessler, B., 193, 199
Kibby, M.W., 18, 35, 41
Kintgen, E.R., 2, 11
Kintsch, W., 53, 56
Kirtley, C., 199
Kluender, K.R., 161, 171
Knafle, J.D., 110, 129
Knight, C., 173

Knights, R.M., 153
Korat, O., 167, 172
Kramer, S.N., 2, 11
Kuhl, P.K., 161, 172
Küspert, P., 144, 154

LaBarre, W., 7, 11
LaBerge, D., 29, 35, 79, 106
Landerl, K., 149, 155, 182, 200
Langer, J., 106
Langer, P., 17, 38
Large, B., 180, 185, 197
Larson, K., 65, 77
Laughon, P., 24, 40
Laxon, V., 116, 129, 139, 153
Lee, C.H., 60, 68, 77
Leech, G., xvi
Lehr, F., 214, 227
Leong, C.K., 36, 131, 152
Lesgold, A., 18, 35–6, 57–8
Leslie, L., 95, 97, 106, 184, 199
Leu, D.J., 18, 35, 38
Levin, I., 167, 172
Levy, B.A., 76
Levy, C.T.H., 76
Lewkowitz, N., 23, 35
Liberman, A.M., xiii, 12, 20, 25, 35, 144, 157, 160, 161, 172, 203, 211
Liberman, D., 12, 26, 33
Liberman, I.Y., 12, 20, 23, 25, 35, 51, 56, 167, 172, 203, 211
Lie, A., 25, 28, 35
Lillas, C., 18, 36
Lindblom, B., 161, 172
Lomax, R., 85, 106
Lorsbach, T., 17, 38
Lovett, M.W., 18, 35
Lukatela, G., 47, 56
Lundberg, I., 25, 35, 51, 56, 110, 129, 131, 144, 151, 153, 154, 199
Lundberg, J., 182, 199
Lyon, G.R., 153

Macedo, D., 5, 10
McCarthey, S.J., 211
McClelland, J.L., 75, 77, 202, 211
McCormick, S., 79, 84, 98, 104
McCutchen, D., 18, 36

McGee, L., 85, 106
MacGinitie, W., 86, 106
McGuiness, D., 193, 194, 199
McKenna, M., 12–14, 36
MacKinnon, G.E., 31, 34, 35, 103, 106, 210
Maclean, M., 24, 26, 32, 35, 180, 185, 196, 199
Maclean, R., 87, 107
Mann, H., 222, 227
Mann, V.A., 51, 56
Marsh, G., 80, 106
Marshall, J., 33, 105, 153
Marx, H., 144, 154
Mason, J., 85, 90, 106
Masonheimer, P.E., 22, 35, 85, 106
Massaro, D.W., 97, 108
Masson, M.E.J., 45, 56
Masterton, J., xii, 109, 111, 113, 114, 116, 122, 129, 130
Mather, N., 12, 35
Matherne, D., 211
Mathews, M.M., 221–3, 227
Matthews, R., 87, 107
Mattingly, I.G., 34, 161, 172
Maybin, J., x, xvi
Mayringer, H., 138, 155
Mead, F., 179, 198
Mead, M., 7, 10, 11
Medlin, D.L., 57
Meek, M., 127, 129
Mehta, P., 227
Meyer, D.E., 72, 77
Michel, G.F., 138, 156
Miller, G.R., 16, 36
Miller, J., 12, 36
Monaghan, E.J., 5, 11
Monk, R., 65, 77
Morais, J., 51, 56, 178, 199
Morgan, S., 25, 40
Morris, D., 86, 88, 106, 107
Morris, R., 153
Morrow, L.M., 211
Moryadas, A., 67, 77
Mosenthal, P.B., 12, 36, 39, 78, 104, 106, 198, 211, 212
Moss, G., x, xvi
Moustafa, M., 184, 199

Mullennix, J., 181, 200
Murray, B., 24, 38
Murray, D.J., 114, 129
Murray, F.B., 103, 105
Muter, V., 81, 107, 184, 185, 199

Näslund, J.C., 149, 154
Nathan, R., 17, 39
Nation, K., 182, 185–7, 199
National Research Council, 52, 56
Nesdale, A.R., 25, 27, 28, 40, 51, 53, 58,
    110, 129
Nicholson, T., 14, 18, 32, 36, 77, 107,
    138
Nickerson, R.S., 218
Nicolson, R.I., 72, 81, 154
Nielsen, I., 13, 138, 152
Nikiforuk, A., 61, 62
Niles, J.A., 105
Noel, R.W., 47, 57
Norris, D., 18, 36
Novy, D.M., 26, 33
Nunes, T., 154

Oakhill, J.V., xiv, xvi, 6, 12, 30, 42, 44,
    58, 77
O'Hara, C., 105
Olofsson, A., 28, 36, 51, 56, 144, 154,
    199
Olson, M.W., 29, 34, 227
Olson, R.K., 25, 37, 67, 77, 133, 145,
    154, 224
Ortony, A., 196, 197
Osborn, J., 214, 227
Ovrut, M., 138, 156

Paap, K.R., 47, 57
Parker, F.W., 223, 227
Patterson, K., 33, 75, 77, 105, 119, 129
Pearson, L.S., 114, 129
Pearson, P.D., 37, 39, 78, 104, 106, 198,
    211, 212
Pennington, B.F., 47, 58, 133, 134, 141,
    153, 154, 173
Perfetti, C.A., x, xi, xii, 12, 14, 16–20,
    23, 27, 31, 34, 36, 42, 45–8, 51, 52,
    56–8, 73, 92, 107, 110, 129, 197, 202,
    211, 212
Perney, J., 88, 107

Petersen, D.K., 110, 133, 138, 141, 143,
    147, 152, 154
Petersen, O.P., 25, 35, 129, 144, 154
Peterson, C.L., 9, 11, 67, 71, 77
Pflaum, S., 28, 37
Pinker, S., 49, 57
Plaut, D.C., 75, 77
Pollatsek, A., 17, 31, 45, 57, 79, 107
Popper, K., 225, 227
Porpodas, C., 182, 198
Potter, M.C., 67, 77
Pratt, A., 227
Pressley, M., 12, 14, 37
Pring, L., 17, 37

Quinlan, P., 113, 130
Quirk, R., x, xvi

Rabbitt, P.M.A., 77
Raberger, T., 138, 155
Rack, J.P., 23, 25, 37, 67, 77, 89, 107,
    118, 129, 133, 154, 224, 227
Rankin, J., 12, 14, 37
Rasher, S., 28, 37
Rashotte, C.A., 23, 24, 40, 145, 155
Rayner, K., 36, 45, 55, 57, 72, 76, 79,
    107
Read, C., 88, 107
Reber, A.S., 56
Reese, H., 37, 198
Reinking, D., 12, 36
Reitsma, P., 82, 94, 107, 120, 129, 146,
    150, 154
Resnick, L.B., 18, 35, 108, 204, 211
Riach, J., 14, 32
Richardson, E., 18, 37
Richman, B., 182, 196
Richmond-Welty, E.D., 181, 200
Rieben, L., 34, 51, 56, 57, 58, 197, 212
Ring, J., 145, 154
Risley, T.R., 74, 77
Robbins, C., 81, 90, 97, 104, 184, 197
Robinson, R., 12, 36
Roper-Schneider, D., 85, 105, 205, 211
Rosenberg, S., 36
Roth, S.F., 18, 19, 36, 46, 57, 144, 154
Routh, D.K., 51, 55, 104
Routman, R., 59, 73, 77
Rozin, P.K., 50, 56, 57

Rubenstein, H., 16, 30, 37
Ruddell, M.R., 104, 211
Ruddell, R.B., 33, 104, 105, 210, 211
Ruddy, P., 72, 77
Rumelhart, D.E., 16, 37
Russell, B., 65
Ryan, E.B., 23, 25, 38
Ryan, S.M., 24, 31
Rzoska, M., 18, 36

Samuels, S.J., 29, 35, 37, 79, 106
Sanders, M., 17, 38
Sartori, G., 129
Savage, R., 180, 190–2, 199
Scanlon, D.M., 24, 40, 51, 58, 227
Scarborough, D.L., 56
Scarborough, H.S., 137, 139–43, 154
Scarpati, S., 17, 31
Schatschneider, C., 227
Scheffler, I., xiv, xvi
Schneider, W., 144, 149, 154, 155, 182, 200
Schommer, M., 105
Schvaneveldt, R.W., 17, 37, 72, 77
Schwantes, F.M., 17, 37
Schwartz, R.M., 18, 37
Scott, J., 14, 30
Scribner, S., 3, 11
Seidenberg, M.S., 17, 37, 38, 47, 57, 75, 77, 202, 211
Semlear, T., 17, 37
Seymour, P.H.K., 22, 38, 116, 128, 135, 155, 187, 188, 196, 197, 200
Shankweiler, D.P., 23, 35, 51, 55, 56, 77, 153, 157, 158, 171, 200
Shannon, P., 5, 11
Shapiro, B.K., 154
Share, D.L., 14, 21, 23, 24, 34, 38, 53, 57, 87, 95, 107, 121, 129, 158, 173
Shaywitz, B.A., 131, 139, 153
Shaywitz, S.E., 131, 139, 153
Shewell, C., 119, 129
Sidhu, R., 135, 155
Siegel, L.S., 23, 25, 38, 39, 135, 155
Simmons, K., 24, 40
Simons, H.D., 18, 35, 38
Simpson, G.B., 17, 38
Singer, H., 33, 76, 104, 105, 210, 211
Singleton, C., 132, 142, 143, 155

Sipay, E., 227
Small, S., 227
Smith, F., 15, 16, 20, 29, 38, 111, 129, 201, 211, 212, 222, 223
Smith, J.K., 211
Smith, N.B., 227
Smith, S.D., 133, 154
Smith-Burke, M., 106
Snowling, M.J., 17, 23–5, 37, 38, 67, 77, 81, 89, 107, 118, 119, 129, 133, 146, 151, 154, 155, 184, 185, 199, 224, 227
Söderbergh, R., 203, 212
Sommers, C.H., 2, 11
Spiegel, D.L., 29, 38
Stadler, B., 138, 155
Stafford, C., 146, 155
Stahl, S.A., 12, 24, 36, 38, 214, 227
Stahle, D., 211
Stammer, J., 85, 103
Stanback, M.L., 181, 200
Stanovich, K.E., x, xi, xv, 12, 14, 17, 18, 19, 23–5, 27, 29, 37, 38, 39, 40, 41, 45, 46, 51, 53, 57, 58, 67, 72, 76, 78, 95, 101, 107, 110, 111, 122, 130, 135, 138, 155, 182, 199, 201, 212, 224, 227
Stanovich, P.J., x, xi, xv, 12, 110, 130, 202
Sterling, T.D., 16, 30
Sternberg, S., 39
Stevens, K.N., 161, 173
Stiefbold, D., 67, 77
Stone, G.O., 47, 58, 173
Strange, M., 18, 30, 40
Street, B.V., ix, x, xiv, xv, xvi, 1, 2, 11
Stuart, M., xii, 109, 110, 111, 113, 114, 116, 118, 121, 122, 129, 130, 180, 184, 190–2, 199
Studdert-Kennedy, M., 157, 172, 173
Stuebing, K.K., 131, 153
Sulzby, E., 53, 58, 172
Svartvik, J., xvi
Sweet, J., 53, 55, 86, 104
Swets, J.A., 218

Taft, M., 50, 57
Tanenhaus, M.K., 37, 47, 57, 200
Tangel, D.M., 25, 31
Taylor, B.M., 57
Taylor, S., 81, 107, 184, 185, 199

Teale, W., 172
Teberovsky, A., 110, 129
Telushkin, J., 2, 11
Templeton, S., 88, 106, 107
Thimke, B., 97, 106
Torgesen, J.K., 23–5, 40, 145, 155
Torneus, M., 51, 56
Trabasso, T., 53, 58
Trachtenberg, P., 29, 40
Treiman, R., 24, 25, 32, 34, 39, 40, 51,
    58, 88, 97, 103–5, 107–8, 128, 158,
    172, 177, 178, 181, 184, 193, 196,
    199, 200, 211
Tunmer, W.E., 14, 25, 27, 28, 34, 40, 51,
    53, 58, 71, 77, 110, 129, 182, 198,
    208, 211
Turner, M., 132, 155
Turvey, M.T., 47, 56
Tzeng, O.J.L., 76

Underwood, G., 17, 31
Underwood, N., 184, 196

Vala-Rossi, M., 17, 39
Vallance, E., 2, 11
Valtin, R., 104
van den Broek, P., 53, 57, 58
van Orden, G.C., 47, 58, 133, 154, 166,
    173
Vaughan, L., 190, 196, 198
Vellutino, F.R., 14, 24, 27, 40, 51, 58, 90,
    108, 224, 227
Venezky, R.L., 23, 32, 80, 92, 97, 98,
    108, 111, 117, 130
Verhaeghe, A., 144, 152
Vincent, D., xvii, 42
Visé, M., 144, 154
Vosniadou, S., 196, 197

Wagner, E.B., 75, 76
Wagner, R.K., 23, 24, 40, 84, 108, 145,
    155
Wagstaff, J.M., 200
Wagtendonk, B., 146, 155

Walberg, H.J., 28, 37
Walker, E., 33
Wall, S., 51, 56, 199
Waller, T.G., 31, 34, 35, 103, 106, 210
Walsh, M.A., 74, 77
Walton, P.D., 184, 200
Warrick, N., 189, 197
Waters, G.S., 17, 37, 38, 57
Watts, J., 60, 65, 68, 77
Weaver, C., 12, 34, 40, 108, 211
Webster, N., 221, 227
Welch, V., 106
Wesseling, R., 146, 150, 154
West, R.F., 17, 23, 39, 40, 41, 45, 58
Whaley, J., 18, 41
Wheelwright, S., 182, 198
Whitehouse, D., 17, 38
Wightman, J., 23, 37, 89, 107, 118,
    129
Wilce, L., 85, 88, 89, 94, 95, 104
Wilkinson, I., 14, 30
Wilkinson, L.C., 211
Williams, J., 23, 25, 27, 41, 84, 105
Williams, P., 116, 128
Willinsky, J., xiv, xvi, 6, 11
Wilson, M.R., 67, 76
Wimmer, H., 91, 108, 138, 149, 155,
    182, 200
Wise, B.W., 25, 27, 41, 145, 154
Wixson, K.L., 18, 41
Wolf, M., 135, 155
Wolff, P.H., 138, 156
Wolraich, M., 104
Woodward, V., 85, 106
Wren, S., xii, xv, 59–60, 65, 68, 70, 77
Wylie, R.E., 182, 200

Yopp, H.K., 29, 41
Yuill, N., 44, 158

Zhang, S., 47, 48, 57
Zola, D., 72, 78
Zorzi, M., 184, 200
Zukowski, A., 178, 200

INDEX